What people are sa

MW00745648

Don Hutchinson's *Under Siege* is a remarkable accomplishment in its embrace of the legal, social, and practical concerns of the day. Don's appearances before the Supreme Court, and his own advocacy and research, make him pre-eminently qualified to engage and interpret the relationship between church and society, faith and culture. Hutchinson avoids the us vs. them syndrome that has been too much a part of orthodox faith. More importantly, Hutchinson gives courage and wisdom to the notion that Christians can engage with vigour and integrity a legal and political system that is for all of us.

—Jeremy Bell
Executive Minister, Canadian Baptists of Western Canada

In *Under Siege*, Don has written an outstanding resource-driven book which outlines not only our religious freedoms in Canada, and how our culture has arrived at this point, but how we might best engage today. *Under Siege* is recommended reading for all followers of Jesus, not just leaders.

—Jason Boucher
Lead Pastor, Lifecentre, Ottawa

Don Hutchinson shares his history with religion and religious freedom in *Under Siege*. The book is like a series of very informative coffee dates. By the end of the book, not only will you be well informed, but you will also feel like you have made a new friend.

—Janet Epp Buckingham
Director, Laurentian Leadership Centre
Professor, Trinity Western University

This book is historically informative, well-researched, and written with a compelling passion for religious freedom in our country. *Under Siege* needs to be read slowly and digested to grasp fully where we have come from, where we are today, and where we can go, with God's help, in the future. This book has deepened my resolve to not believe the myth of neutrality but to be a voice for the Church, for Christ, and for our life-giving message of hope and spiritual transformation. *Under Siege* is timely, needed, and must be read!

—Margaret Gibb
Founder and Executive Director, Women Together

This book is profoundly invigorating for readers from any Christian background—and perhaps especially for the spiritually inclined who are not presently active in a particular church. Hutchinson's own faith odyssey is something to move mountains. He weaves together his knowledge of human nature, Christianity, history, politics, the law, and Canadian society to produce something that will strike virtually any reader equally firmly in both head and heart.

—David Kilgour
former Member of Parliament
Secretary of State for Africa and Latin America (1997–2002), Asia-Pacific (2002–3)
Nobel Peace Prize nominee (2010)

Don Hutchinson has offered us a personal, historical, and legal perspective in these pages that both inform and persuade the reader of the importance of the current situation in Canada. It was especially interesting to learn about some of the lesser known but historically very significant contributors in the battle for freedom in our society. The author has been uniquely positioned throughout his career to understand the larger sweep of legal trends in our nation. Politicians, pastors, and lawyers need to read this book for the sake of Canada's future.

—Richard Long
Director, Love Ottawa
Executive Director, Together Canada

Who would have believed that Canada would move so far from its Judeo-Christian roots and that our religious freedoms, which we have so enjoyed as a first-world country, could be slowly taken from us? In *Under Siege*, Don Hutchinson clearly covers this important topic with elegance of text underpinned by meticulous research to present us with a clear picture of where we stand and what the future outcomes could be. *Under Siege* is a must-read for anyone who values their faith and loves our nation.

—David Macfarlane
Director of National Initiatives,
Billy Graham Evangelistic Association of Canada

The *Canadian Charter of Rights and Freedoms* professes to guarantee freedom of conscience and religion to all Canadians. But in practice, freedom of religion in Canada is "under siege." I wholeheartedly commend to concerned Canadians Don Hutchinson's analysis of the challenge and prescriptions for engagement.

—Preston Manning
Founder, Manning Centre for Building Democracy
former Leader of the Official Opposition in the Canadian House of Commons

In a day when the last acceptable expression of discrimination is against Christians, the Church needs knowledge and understanding to counter it—and my friend's writing is a good source. There are few people in the nation with as much experience as Don, who has been one of the frontline fighters for freedom of religion and freedom of expression.

—Charles McVety
President, Canada Christian College
& School of Graduate Theological Studies

Don Hutchinson asks the question, "Will we engage?" Will Canadians respond with passion to confront injustice, prejudice, and persecution while delivering a message of hope in the spirit of love? *Under Siege* is the heartbeat of a man I have known for many years. I have found him to be committed to his family and to his faith, a man of wisdom and courage while possessing the attributes of humility and quirky humour.

—Gerry Organ
Yield Ottawa Lead with One Way Ministries
former Executive Director of Christian Business Ministries Canada
two-time Grey Cup champion with the Ottawa Rough Riders

Don Hutchinson has that rare combination of gifts: a deep thinker, an excellent writer, and able to make complex subjects easily understood. *Under Siege* is a must-read for Christians who care about the mission Christ gave His church but feel hindered by the current Canadian legal and social environment. Hutchinson puts it all in perspective and gives suggestions for how we can continue to undertake the church's mission in Canada today.

—John Pellowe
Chief Executive Officer, Canadian Council of Christian Charities

As a lawyer whose practice is largely focussed on religious freedom litigation, I read about the issues and cases referred to in *Under Siege* on a regular basis. Don Hutchinson has been able to present a legal and political history of religious freedom in Canada in a manner that is not only easy to follow and understand, but also personal and engaging. It is written for lawyer or layperson and is equally accessible. Having been involved in a number of the cases addressed in *Under Siege*, I can assure the reader that the book they hold in their hands is unique: it is accurate and educational, while being engaging and personal.

—Albertos Polizogopoulos
Constitutional Law Lawyer
Partner, Vincent Dagenais Gibson

Religious freedom is not only the first fundamental freedom in the *Charter*; it is the first of all freedoms. If a person is not free in his relationship with God, where else can he be free? Religious freedom has returned to the global agenda in the twenty-first century, as it is "under siege" from both religious and secular extremists. Don Hutchinson is uniquely situated to tell the story, and it's a story that urgently needs to be told.

—Father Raymond J. de Souza
Editor-in-Chief of Convivium.ca, Canada's site for faith in our common life

Under Siege is a wonderful contribution to the ongoing discussion about the place of religion in Canada. And I love that I can heartily recommend it to every pew-sitter in the nation. This is not a book for stuffy academics or nerdy policy wonks. Hutchinson's work is uniquely written for the average Canadian Joe to understand where we've come from, where things are at now, and where we can go from here on questions of religion and the law.

—André Schutten
General Legal Counsel & Director of Law and Policy,
Association for Reformed Political Action (ARPA)

Don Hutchinson in *Under Siege* walks us through the critical issues of freedom of religion in a country where one might naively assume its record is stellar. His message is that there is always the need for vigilance. In a time when the secular assumption that faith will soon ebb away carries with it a belief that there is no need to protect its freedom, this book advises the opposite. A timely and wise warning.

—Brian C. Stiller
Global Ambassador, World Evangelical Alliance

Hutchinson does what few have done: make religious freedom human, personal, and Canadian. At the same time, I feel I am caught up in a brilliant lecture that I don't want to end.

—Michael Van Pelt
President and CEO, Cardus

My colleague Don Hutchinson, from his years of experience, study, and wisdom, provides in *Under Siege* a crucial read for those who seriously desire to be salt, light, and grace in our country today. Integrating constitutional and legal history with personal anecdotes, biblical perspective, and strategic guidance, Don has provided followers of Jesus with a valuable resource as they respectfully engage the contexts and relationships they are called to.

—David Wells
General Superintendent, The Pentecostal Assemblies of Canada

UNDER SIEGE

RELIGIOUS FREEDOM AND THE
CHURCH IN CANADA AT 150 (1867-2017)

DON HUTCHINSON

1 Thess 5:11

Printed in Canada

ISBN: 978-1-4866-1452-3

Word Alive Press
131 Cordite Road, Winnipeg, MB R3W 1S1
www.wordalivepress.ca

Library and Archives Canada Cataloguing in Publication

Hutchinson, Don (Donald), author
        Under siege : religious freedom and the church in Canada at 150 (1867-2017) / Don Hutchinson, B.A, J.D.

Issued in print and electronic formats.
ISBN 978-1-4866-1452-3 (softcover).--ISBN 978-1-4866-1453-0 (ebook)

        1. Freedom of religion--Canada--History. 2. Canada--Church history. I. Title.

BR575.H88 2017   261.7'20971   C2017-900354-2
                                             C2017-900355-0

This book is dedicated to my parents:
Lionel Noel Hutchinson (1924–2015)
and Thelma Elaine Wallace (née Greenidge) (1926–present).

Thank you for choosing Canada.

CONTENTS

PART III: FAITHFUL CHRIST-FOLLOWERS ASK "HOW SHOULD WE THEN ENGAGE?"

The light shines in the darkness, and the darkness has not overcome it.

—John 1:5

ACKNOWLEDGEMENTS

Expressing thank yous is a dangerous thing. Someone will inevitably be, or feel, left off the list, their name either coming to mind too late or simply being excluded for reasons of space. Still, here's a shot at it.

I am grateful for the encouragement and assistance of a number of people who have particularly influenced the writing of this book. I suspect when Jeremy Bell asked me to speak on this topic at the October 2016 pastors and spouses conference for the Canadian Baptists of Western Canada, he did not imagine a one-hour talk becoming this book. Neither did I when I said yes. But Someone had a plan. I trust it has unfolded in the way He intended, knowing that over time life's experiences adjust the context and content of whatever we have to share. From the idea to the research and writing, I had much prayer support.

Klaus Richter was the teacher who gave me *the* detention in Grade Seven that helped change the direction of my life. He convinced me that I had more to offer than continually seeking attention as the class clown.

Tom Axworthy took a politics-obsessed university student, settled him down a bit, and encouraged him to go to law school as a precursor to more serious political engagement. That advice met with my dad's desire for me and my Heavenly Father's plan for my life.

Ed Bryant, Willie Alexcee, Ray and Nora Morrison, and Rita Hayward treated this *k'amksiwah* (white man) "like an Indian"[1] when my wife Gloria and I needed friends and counsel in an unfamiliar culture. This was the beginning of my often interrupted interest in understanding the hidden history that merged into my life as a result of being born in Canada.

---

1   My Indigenous friends will understand this historic reference, which was how it was stated to me in the 1980s.

My faithful and longsuffering friend Trevor Owen has supported me in life, challenging and informing my theological and political positions in robust conversation. Barry Boucher helped me refocus on my identity in Christ when I was recovering from having lost something of myself in losing my work.

Brian Stiller, Bruce Clemenger, Janet Epp Buckingham, and Doug Cryer provided me the privilege of building upon a sound foundation of work and accomplishments at The Evangelical Fellowship of Canada's Centre for Faith and Public Life. There, God provided me with an excellent team in Julia Beazley, Jocelyn Durston, Anita Levesque, and Faye Sonier, who built on that foundation with me. You did good work that made my contribution better.

Jason Boucher, David Kilgour, Richard Long, Gordon Mamen, Gerry Organ, John Pellowe, Albertos Polizogopoulos, André Schutten, and Ron Suter reviewed portions or all of a draft, offered their encouragement, and proposed constructive suggestions that made the book more readable. Rick Hiemstra commented on, and improved, Chapter Twenty-Three ("Lies, Damned Lies, and Statistics").

Much appreciation to the team at Word Alive Press who made a manuscript into a book. Warren Benson presented a generous opportunity. Tia Scarborough challenged me and laughed with me as we worked through tight deadlines to arrive at the final product. Evan Braun made this a far more readable work than the original manuscript submitted on January 3, 2017. Nikki and Konrad made sure this book was attractive enough to catch your attention and keep reading. Any errors are my own.

In addition to my Mum and Dad, my parental cheerleaders in life have included Lew, Elba, and Mary, along with my siblings. Thank you.

Finally, and most significantly, I acknowledge Gloria, Grace, and John, without whom my life would be incomplete and I would not be who I am today. You make me a better person.

PREFACE

History can seem like dry facts on which any reader might choke. And from experience, we know the facts are not always necessarily factual. It has been said that to the victor go the spoils, including the writing of history. To later victors, the rewriting of history.

For me, the most compelling records of history have been those written by their authors while in the midst of it or as personal memory, witnesses sharing their recollections, reflections, and perspectives on experienced reality. I find myself engrossed reading history written by those who lived it. The writings of Elie Wiesel, Aleksandr Solzhenitsyn, Richard Wurmbrand, and others stand as strong testimony precisely because they lived to tell the tale. This may contribute to why I find the history of the world as experienced by God's chosen people, and the written record of the life of Jesus and the early Church, to be both compelling and convincing. Like Wiesel, Solzhenitsyn, and Wurmbrand, the Bible offers a combination of history with timeless and sound advice for living, learned from experience.

The New Testament is filled with epistles, letters to churches and individuals, providing insight into the history of both authors and recipients. Even the Revelation of John contains records of letters from Jesus to seven churches.

Early in congregational ministry, I took a course on the letters of Paul. One of the concluding exercises was to write a letter in Paul's style to a fictitious church. I originally considered subtitling this book *A (Long) Letter to Christians about Religious Freedom and the Church in Canada in the 21st Century* because it is written in the spirit of encouraging, admonishing, and informing the Canadian Church, but it's a little longer than a long letter and I'm not Paul. Neither do my experiences compare to Wiesel, Solzhenitsyn, or Wurmbrand.

In this reflection on the Church and the recent history of religious freedom in the comparatively young nation of Canada, celebrating its sesquicentennial in 2017, anyone born or educated here in the 1960s or earlier will see glimpses of shared memory. This is, however, a recent history with profound implications for our immediate future, the future of the Church in Canada. Christians in Canada have been relatively complacent while this history has unfolded, leaving the battle for our continued freedom to practise our faith to trusted leaders and loud, not always trustworthy voices. Will we remain complacent? Or will we engage our culture the way Jesus and the early Church did? That account will be written at a later date.

INTRODUCTION

Finally, be strong in the Lord and in the strength of his might. Put on the whole armor of God, that you may be able to stand against the schemes of the devil. For we do not wrestle against flesh and blood, but against the rulers, against the authorities, against the cosmic powers over this present darkness, against the spiritual forces of evil in the heavenly places.

—Ephesians 6:10–12

Waxed. Waned. Balanced.

Those three words describe my interaction and relationship with religious freedom over the course of several decades serving in Christian leadership. Waxing, waning, and balance have to some degree been the consequence of my Christian life and experience intertwining with two significant dates in Canada's constitutional history, both of which have impacted religious freedom.

On April 17, 1982, Canada's constitution was amended, adding the *Canadian Charter of Rights and Freedoms* (see Appendix III). Three years later, the equality rights provision of the *Charter* became operational.

At spring convocation in 1981, I received my B.A. from Queen's University in Kingston, rounding the corner toward law school and a planned career in politics. My dad used to jokingly say, with a definite hint of seriousness, "Man appoints. But God dis-appoints." This was his paraphrase of Solomon's words, *"The heart of man plans his way, but the Lord establishes his steps"* (Proverbs 16:9). We don't always understand what God is up to in the process. Sometimes, in fact, it baffles us to imagine that God could be present at all in some of the circumstances of life. But He is.

In September 1981, I arrived on the Point Grey campus of the University of British Columbia ready to start law school. However, there had been a change in my life during the summer. I'd met a girl, and she had invited me to church. Three Sundays in a row I went to her little Salvation Army church, so after a flight across the country, I figured I should find a Salvation Army church in Vancouver and keep going.

The Kitsilano Corps (The Salvation Army term for a small church is "corps") was about a twenty-minute bicycle ride from where I was living. That's where I settled in. Not being wise to the ways of the Church, and too proud to say I didn't know better, when I saw the push-in-the-plastic-letters notice board that said services were on Sundays at 11:00 a.m. and 6:30 p.m. and Bible study on Wednesdays at 7:00 p.m., I assumed going to church meant attending all three. So I did.

Being a little slow on the uptake—which figures into why my interest in religious freedom waxed and waned before becoming balanced—it wasn't until late November that I realized I wasn't actually a Christian. I had not been raised in a church-going family but had somehow concluded that I was a Christian because I was a Canadian, a conclusion I now refer to as the same definitional mistake made by terrorists in regard to North Americans and westerners in general.

Having read the Bible from cover to cover and with nearly four months of church attendance (Bible study and twice on Sundays) under my belt, I asked my pastor if she had something I could read that would give me a better understanding of what it meant to be a Christian. She loaned me a copy of a book written by the German pastor and Bible school teacher Dietrich Bonhoeffer. In the foreword to *The Cost of Discipleship*, George Bell—the Anglican Bishop of Chichester, not the former slugger for the Toronto Blue Jays—opens with these words:

"When Christ calls a man," says Dietrich Bonhoeffer, "he bids him come and die."[1]

That book is one of only two books of substance that I have felt compelled to read in one sitting, interspersed with food and bathroom breaks. I started reading shortly after breakfast on Saturday morning, December 5, 1981, and finished its 350 pages at about 10:30 that night.

Bonhoeffer's words made it abundantly clear that I needed to make a decision about my past, present, and future. At the time, I didn't know any other way to accept that Jesus was who He said He was in the Bible, the Son of the living God, than to go to the prayer bench (called "the mercy seat" in The Salvation Army) at the front of our little church after the speaker finished.

---

1   Dietrich Bonhoeffer, *The Cost of Discipleship* (London, UK: SCM Press Ltd., 1949), 7.

I purposed in my heart that night to go forward the next morning and declare my acceptance of Jesus as the Christ.[2] In making that decision, as Bonhoeffer so clearly explained, I was accepting two things: that Jesus was my personal Saviour from the sin that so easily entangles (Hebrews 12:1) and that as God He was the Lord of my life. For me, this meant that I had to set aside my plan for my life in favour of His plan.

With experience, I now realize that I made the decision to become a Christ-follower, a disciple of Jesus, at 10:30 p.m. that Saturday night rather than the next morning when kneeling at the mercy seat in the Kitsilano Corps. At the time, I didn't know any better. I did know that I didn't need to have my life in order, understand Church, or fully grasp everything about God to receive His generous gift of a fresh start.

It wasn't as if I hadn't had any warning about what was about to happen. In addition to attending church three times a week for several months, I'd had an unexplained private prompting as a teenager that God wanted me in His ministry. I hadn't gone to church since I was four, except to attend my sister's wedding. I hadn't known what the prompting meant. It's a story for another day how I explored that prompting while in high school. Suffice to say, it wasn't long before my December decision led me to leave law school to become a pastor.

The day after writing the final exam of my first year of law school was April 17, 1982. That morning, I got on my bicycle and rode a fair distance to my friend Mitch's house. He was one of the few people I knew who owned a colour television—a twenty-six-inch screen at that! It was a beautiful, sunny day in Vancouver—and pouring rain in Ottawa. Mitch had invited a bunch of fellow law students to his place for an unusual kind of party, one that has not been repeated in my lifetime. We watched the live broadcast as Prime Minister Pierre Elliott Trudeau and Queen Elizabeth II, on the front steps of Parliament Hill, signed the official documentation to transition Canada's constitution from an act of the British Parliament (the *British North America Act*, now referred to as the *Constitution Act, 1867*) to the Canadian-held and Canadian-amendable *Constitution Act, 1982*. While often referred to as the repatriation of our constitution, it was actually the patriation of our constitution, as this was the occasion when it became the property of Canada and Canadians for the first time.

Canada, established July 1, 1867, did not actually become a sovereign nation until April 17, 1982. Also on that day, Canadian law was forever changed by the

---

2   "Christ" is the Greek word for "Messiah," which is the Hebrew word for "Anointed One," the Son of God.

inclusion of thirty-four sections in Part I of the *Constitution Act, 1982*. These sections are known as the *Canadian Charter of Rights and Freedoms*.

A few days later, I left Vancouver to prepare for and then enter Christian ministry as a pastor. None of us in that living room on a sunny west coast morning had any idea how dramatically the amendment to our constitution would change the practice of law, the practices of Canadians, or the very nature of our nation.

Precisely three years later, as provided in the *Constitution Act, 1982*, on April 17, 1985, the equality rights provision of the *Charter* came into effect. As a result of the time required for legal cases to make their way through the court system, exactly seven days later the Supreme Court of Canada issued its first decision on the *Charter*'s guarantee of freedom of religion in *R v Big M Drug Mart*.[3] But already the seeds planted in 1982 were producing fresh growth that would in short order revise Canada's legal landscape.

Not long afterward, I was asked by the Canadian leader of my church denomination, The Salvation Army, to return to law school to prepare myself to establish a national legal department.

At the time, my wife Gloria and I were co-pastoring a church in the Lax Kw'alaams ("place of the wild roses") village, commonly called Port Simpson, part of the Port Simpson No. 1 Reserve of the Tsimshian First Nation in northern British Columbia. We had an early brush with religious freedom when our comments about heaven were taken out of context and we were confronted with potential expulsion from the reserve. The Lax Kw'alaams band members, recognized members of the local Indigenous community, voted in our favour and we stayed.

One of the things I learned in Port Simpson, a fishing village, was about the increase and decrease in the tide that accompanied the waxing and the waning of the moon. One would think that the son of parents from Barbados would have understood the tides, but I was raised a city boy in a suburb of Toronto where ocean tides were of little concern to me.

Before leaving, Gloria and I were both adopted into the nation and given Tsimshian names in the Sm'algyax language. Gloria received the name *'Yaal*, meaning "high princess," as a member of the Wolf crest—a fitting name for a daughter of the King, who has evidenced a serving heart for as long as I have known her.

When I received my name, I had to force myself to hold the smile on my face in an effort to hide my initial disappointment. *Tu'utsgm Sah* is in the Eagle crest. It means "the dark cloud on the horizon that signals a change in weather."

---

3   [1985] 1 SCR 295.

Spotting that cloud told the fishermen of the coastal village it was time to seek safe harbour. I held that smile, but my eyes might have given away my feelings. Only then was I told that the name had been chosen for me in reference to the story in 1 Kings 18 in which Elijah sent his servant to look for a sign that Elijah's prayer for rain had been heard by God and answered, signalling an end to three years of drought. Seven times the servant was sent to look to the sea before he returned with the answer: *"Behold, a little cloud like a man's hand is rising from the sea"* (1 Kings 18:44). It's easy to smile when you're told that you're an answer to prayer. Perhaps, however, the name was also a prophetic message signifying that the times, like the weather, were changing.

After a transitional pastorate in Williams Lake, Gloria and I co-pastored a church in Vancouver while I completed two more years of law school. Gloria had been the senior pastor at the Kitsilano Corps before we married, and she resumed that responsibility at the North Burnaby Corps while I attended to my studies.

At North Burnaby, I had a second encounter with a matter of religious freedom. The city had passed a bylaw requiring that a permit be obtained in order to "perform," including preaching, on a public sidewalk or in a public park. We had a little brass band at the corps and decided to play a few tunes outside the Pacific National Exhibition. We advised The Salvation Army's Vancouver headquarters that we would not apply for a permit, instead relying on the historic precedent that Salvation Army brass bands had engaged in street ministry across the nation for over a century. I was forbidden from playing as a precaution against earning a criminal record that could derail the intent of my education. The band was prepared to play on without me, and I prepared to argue their case. Alas, it poured rain. No one was arrested that day.

Upon graduation from law school, our little family moved to Toronto where I completed the requirements to become a member of the Law Society of Upper Canada. While completing those requirements, I also became the Chairman of the Board of Directors for the Christian Legal Fellowship (CLF) and a member of the Canadian Christian Corporate Lawyers Association (CCCLA). Both organizations drew me into the world of religious freedom as it was being litigated in Canadian courts. Who knew Christians and pastors could get into so much trouble just for being Christians and pastors? The only Supreme Court of Canada cases I had encountered in law school had concerned either Jehovah's Witnesses or business owners who wanted to open their stores on Sundays to be free from laws inspired by religion.

Shortly after moving to office space at The Salvation Army's national headquarters in Toronto, I experienced my first clash between freedom of religion and
gay and lesbian rights, those rights being acknowledged in the Ontario *Human
Rights Code* and soon thereafter by the Supreme Court of Canada under the equality rights provisions of the *Charter*. The Salvation Army had conducted outdoor
Sunday night meetings in Nathan Philips Square, at Toronto's city hall, since it
opened in 1965. Before that, The Salvation Army band had played on the street
corner where the square had been built since some time in the 1880s. However,
in 1990 a city councillor insisted that The Salvation Army sign a contract requiring their agreement with non-discrimination on the basis of sexual orientation
in all its operations, including withdrawal of its biblical position statement on
homosexuality (as it was referenced at the time). The position statement upheld
the dignity of all persons as being made in the image of God (*imago Dei*) and affirmed the biblical position that chastity was the standard outside marriage, with
sexual relations confined to marriage between one woman and one man. Following a public hearing before the full city council, agreement was reached that
acknowledged The Salvation Army's right as a religious institution to adhere to
its religious beliefs and practices. The Sunday evening services outside city hall
continued.

My involvement with The Salvation Army, CLF, and the CCCLA increasingly meant living with legal battles, big and small, that resulted from efforts to
redefine religion and its place in Canada's public square in the closing decade of
the twentieth century. This was a time when my interest and involvement in religious freedom waxed. But after nearly a decade, I grew tired of the seemingly
endless and increasing skirmishes and battles. I retreated to the relative calm of
pastoral ministry. My interest remained but my involvement waned.

After little more than a handful of years, I found myself again in the throes
of what had by then been dubbed "the culture wars." During the national debate
on same-sex marriage, a church where I was working hosted a "Defend Marriage"
seminar. Early in the morning, someone put "Adam and Eve NOT Adam and
Steve" lawn signs along the boulevard in front of our church building. It didn't
take long for them to be removed as that church held a similar position to the one
promoted by The Salvation Army: treat all people with dignity, and engage in
discourse on matters of principle with *imago Dei* in mind and practice.

I did not then anticipate that it would be only a short time before I would be
participating in media interviews on the topic of religion and same-sex marriage
after passage of the *Civil Marriage Act* by Parliament in 2005. I briefed churches

on how to make previously unnecessary preparations to hold fast to their biblical beliefs and practices in regard to marriage and other matters of religious freedom. For seven and a half years I served with The Evangelical Fellowship of Canada, including as vice-president, general legal counsel, and director of its Centre for Faith and Public Life.

During that time, I also became more extensively aware and engaged in the fight for religious freedom that is occurring in almost every nation around the globe.

While the battle waxed, my engagement became more balanced. The Supreme Court of Canada had established strong guidelines for religious freedom and I had become more settled in the biblical principle that *"we do not wrestle against flesh and blood, but against the rulers, against the authorities, against the cosmic powers over this present darkness, against the spiritual forces of evil in the heavenly places"* (Ephesians 6:12).

Nor was I alone in the battle. Compatriots had taken different, but biblically supported, positions. All were under fire. Some were drawing fire for their incendiary behaviour. Others were under fire as they continued respectful, strategic engagement. Still others were under siege, hiding themselves away in hopes that they could withstand the attacks of the present age by hiding in what I refer to as "stained-glass closets."

This book is for all three of these. For the incendiaries, it will hopefully inspire balance. For the respectful, it will hopefully inform strategy. For the hiding, it will hopefully encourage them to come out of the closet.

For I am not ashamed of the gospel, for it is the power of God for salvation to everyone who believes...

—Romans 1:16

Preston Manning, former politician and leader of Her Majesty's Loyal Opposition, has admonished that when we carry the message of the gospel into the world around us we should heed the words of Jesus to *"be wise as serpents and harmless as doves"* (Matthew 10:16, KJV), and not be "vicious as snakes and stupid as pigeons."[4]

I'm hoping this book will be of benefit both in wisdom and in doing no harm in publicly living out our Christian faith in Canada today.

Soli Deo gloria.

---

4   Preston Manning, "Lessons from the Life and Teachings of Jesus," Navigating the Faith-Political Interface (seminar), Toronto. May 11, 2007.

PART I:
THE FOUNDATION

He shall have dominion also from sea to sea, and from the river unto the ends of the earth.

—Psalm 72:8 (KJV)

Et dominabitur a mari usque ad mare, et a flumine usque ad terminos terrae.

—Psalm 72:8 (Latin)

A Mari usque ad Mare

—Canada's official motto

CHAPTER ONE

UNDER SIEGE

A wise man scales the city of the mighty and brings down the stronghold in which they trust.

—Proverbs 21:22

IT'S SAID THAT CONFESSION IS GOOD FOR THE SOUL. I CONFESS THAT I AM NOT A MILITARY strategist. But I am a student of the Bible, have studied a little more than the mandatory elementary and high school courses in Canadian history, enjoyed J.R.R. Tolkien's *Lord of the Rings* and C.S. Lewis' *Chronicles of Narnia*, and have long been intrigued by the story of Masada.

Putting oneself in the position to be under siege is a dangerous option. Withdrawing into a fortified and inescapable structure should be the result of serious strategic consideration. But that isn't always the case.

It seems there are only two good reasons to engage a siege mentality. Being outmatched, one can decide to withdraw from the field of battle in the hope that the enemy will give up the fight for one reason or another—lack of will, lack of supplies, or some other lack. The other is a strategic retreat with the intention of resuming the battle. Perhaps such a retreat provides the opportunity to rest before reengaging, to adjust one's strategy or await reinforcements.

Whether Cair Paravel, Gondor, or the Plains of Abraham, one must understand certain rules of war before retreating behind a wall to be besieged by the enemy. Of course, one must first calculate the relative strength of one's own forces. Next, those of one's opponents. That may determine whether it is wise to engage the enemy or retreat. Also to be factored into the equation is one's preparedness to suffer in order to succeed, or literally die trying.

This basic understanding of common rules is also the foundation of team sports. One team lines up on one side of the field or ice surface and another team on the other side. Then they engage in battle.

Commentator and former NHL coach Don Cherry has said that the most dangerous lead in hockey is 2–0. Each game begins 0–0. At that point in time, each team has a game plan that includes offensive and defensive strategies for each twenty-minute period. In ice hockey, no one starts the game playing for a tie.

The 2–0 lead is dangerous because it shifts the mindset of players and alters the game plan. The team with the lead starts protecting the two-goal margin and thinks about the potential for their goaltender to get a shutout. The result is the development of a siege mentality; the team that's up 2–0 settles in to defend their own end while the team behind mounts a stronger offensive effort. It is difficult to transition from that siege mentality back to goal-scoring when, almost inevitably, the need arises.

I was twelve years old when the eight-game 1972 Summit Series took place between Canada and the Soviet Union. I watched every minute of every game as it unfolded. Game one saw Canada score two quick goals to secure the most dangerous lead in hockey. At the end of a 7–3 trouncing by the Soviet team, Canada's finest looked shell-shocked.

Canada dramatically altered its lineup for game two and stormed back for a 4–1 victory. Everything was going to be okay. Or so we all thought. Two games later, after a tie and another loss, Canadians were booing their fellow Canadians as Team Canada left the ice.

What was about to unfold is worthy of *Ripley's Believe it or Not* consideration. Toronto Maple Leaf Paul Henderson had a breakout thirty-eight-goal season in 1971–72, but a lot of Leafs fans, myself included, wondered about his selection to Team Canada. Until Henderson scored early in game one to give Canada the 2–0 lead. He scored again in game three to give Canada a 4–2 lead. That game ended in a 4–4 tie.

After game four, the series turned to four games in Moscow. The few hundred Canadian fans in the bleachers learned some limited Russian to chant the loudest sound heard on Canadian television sets over the next four games: "Da, da, Canada! Nyet, nyet, Soviet!" ("Yes, yes, Canada! No, no, Soviets!") Those who made the journey had gone to great expense to demonstrate their national pride. The booing was over. (The Russian fans didn't boo. They hissed.)

In game five, the first game on Russian ice, Henderson again hit the twine, lifting Canada to a 4–1 lead—before the team surrendered 5–4 to the Soviets.

All the Soviet team needed was one more win and they would claim world domination on the ice. If the remaining games tied, under European rules the Soviets would claim victory based on the goal differential. And home ice advantage was theirs for the next three games.

But with the series lead and home ice advantage came pressure to close the deal. The siege mentality set in for Team Soviet Union. They started to play not to lose.

What happened in the next three games would make Paul Henderson a Canadian hockey legend.

Game six started off as the most tenuous of the series. The first goal wasn't scored until the second period. With the Soviet Union up 1–0, Team Canada stormed the net and scored three goals in ninety seconds. Henderson scored the third, which held up to be the game winner with a final score of 3–2.

In game seven, Henderson scored to break a 3–3 tie with just two minutes left in the game. Canada won 4–3.

Canadians proudly refer to "the goal," also called "the sports moment of the century,"[1] scored on September 28, 1972 in game eight. With a minute left in a game tied 5–5, the faceoff was in the Canadian end of the ice; all Team Soviet Union needed to do was hold on. As the Canadian team rushed down the ice, Paul Henderson felt a prompting and called Peter Mahovlich to the bench. As Mahovlich arrived, Henderson leapt onto the ice. With thirty-four seconds left in the game, Henderson scored his improbable third game-winning goal in a row to secure Team Canada's victory in the series 4–3–1. I still have the commemorative Summit Series picture book!

The letdown after the series left Paul Henderson searching for something more in life. He had the family, fortune, and fame many dream about, but something was missing. In 1975, Henderson surrendered his life to Jesus Christ. In 1984, he founded what is now LeaderImpact as a means of helping others who had found success in life to secure their foundation in Christ.[2]

In battle, whether on the ice or in the theatre of war, it is essential to know that engaging the enemy will necessitate taking fire. Succeeding will also require a strategy of offense and the knowledge that barricading oneself in with the hope of outlasting the other side is a poor technique. It is the last line of defence, not driven by faith or hope, but by fear.

---

1   Randy Pascal, "Paul Henderson in Sudbury May 21," *Sudbury Sports*, May 15, 2015.

2   Paul Henderson with Roger Lajoie, *The Goal of My Life: A Memoir* (Toronto, ON: Fenn/McClelland & Stewart, 2012).

[Jesus] said to them, "But who do you say that I am?"

Simon Peter replied, "You are the Christ, the Son of the living God."

And Jesus answered him, "Blessed are you, Simon Bar-Jonah! For flesh and blood has not revealed this to you, but my Father who is in heaven. And I tell you, you are Peter, and on this rock I will build my church, and the gates of hell shall not prevail against it."

—Matthew 16:15–18

Too many Christians have developed the mistaken idea that the gates of hell are attacking the Church. Gates are not offensive weapons. Gates are closed for defence, most often as the last alternative to engaging on the field of battle.

In Revelation 12, we read the apostle John's recorded vision of a great war in heaven between the forces of the enemy of God and heaven's militia. In verses 10–11 a loud voice proclaims,

Now the salvation and the power and the kingdom of our God and the authority of his Christ have come, for the accuser of our brothers has been thrown down, who accuses them day and night before our God. And they have conquered him by the blood of the Lamb and by the word of their testimony, for they loved not their lives even unto death.

—Revelation 12:10–11

The "blood of the Lamb" is a reference to the sacrifice of Jesus the Christ through His death on the cross. The reference to conquering "by the word of their testimony" pertains to the similar good confession made by Simon Peter. When the enemy forces are compelled to move into siege, their gates will not hold against those who conquer through their belief in Jesus of Nazareth as the Christ, the Son of the living God, and through their life in Him.

In January 2014, I made my first trip to Israel. Apart from my treasured interaction with the people, two things made a significant impression on me.

First, I was struck by how close everything was. Israel is 424 kilometres (263 miles) from north to south (the distance from Ottawa to Toronto) and ranges between 114 kilometres (seventy-one miles, half the distance from Ottawa to Montreal) and fifteen kilometres (nine miles) wide. The total area is a little under twenty-one thousand square kilometres (eight thousand square miles, about two-thirds the size of Vancouver Island). The Old City of Jerusalem is less than one square kilometre in size (one-third of a square mile, or one hundred hectares).

The walk from Capernaum, on the shore of the Sea of Galilee, to Nazareth is about forty-five kilometres, and from Capernaum or Nazareth to Jerusalem is about 150 kilometres.

The second thing that struck me is how large the fortress at Masada is. Built on a mountain plateau with cliff sides, the climb on the high side is four hundred meters (1,300 feet) and ninety meters (three hundred feet) on the low side. The plateau is nearly 150,000 square meters (1.6 million square feet, or fifteen hectares) with a four-meter wall (thirteen feet) of 1,300 meters (4,300 feet in length). By comparison, the wall around Jerusalem is four thousand meters long and twelve meters high. Jerusalem was a bustling city and Masada a fortified palace. Comparatively speaking, Masada was enormous!

Three decades before the birth of Christ, Herod the Great had fortified Masada as a place of escape in the event of revolt against his rule. The feared revolt would not come until long after Herod's death, three decades after the crucifixion and resurrection of Jesus.

In 66 A.D., a small army of Jewish zealots overwhelmed the Roman garrison at Masada, which was no small feat. Masada had been set up by Herod with cisterns to catch and hold rainwater, vast supplies of grain, and other food. It even had baths and a synagogue. From Masada, the zealots, known as the Sicarri, raided nearby villages. When Flavius Silva, the Roman governor of Judea, had enough of their taunting he took an entire Roman legion and thousands of Jewish prisoners to lay siege to the fortress.

The Romans constructed a 114-meter high (375 feet) assault ramp and a giant battering ram. Nearly fifteen thousand troops camped around the base of the mountain for months. When the walls were finally breached, the Romans found all the food on fire; the nearly one thousand occupants had committed a form of mass suicide. The few survivors found hiding in the fortress noted the words of the zealot leader Eleazar ben Yair:

> Since we long ago resolved never to be servants to the Romans, nor to any other than to God Himself, who alone is the true and just Lord of mankind, the time is now come that obliges us to make that resolution true in practice… We were the very first that revolted, and we are the last to fight against them; and I cannot but esteem it as a favor that God

has granted us, that it is still in our power to die bravely, and in a state of freedom.[3]

The Romans were robbed of their victory. But neither was there victory in battle for the zealots. Some regard the stand at Masada as a symbol of Jewish heroism. Others consider it the death place of radical extremists. When taking the battle to the enemy, the Sicarii captured the fortress. When under siege, they lost it. And their lives.

When we withdraw temporarily to study, perhaps to fast and pray, to prepare to face those who are unaware that the battle is spiritual or that the victory ultimately belongs to Christ, then we may be besieged but we have not developed a siege mentality. If we move to a siege mentality, it's most often because we have given in. Perhaps we have given in to a sense of inevitable cultural defeat. More likely, we have given in to a sense of fear.

The apostle Paul wrote that *"we are more than conquerors through him [God] who loved us"* (Romans 8:37). Giving in to siege, we become less than conquerors. We may look to Jesus as Saviour, but we don't trust Him as Lord. We may stand fast, but we attempt to stand unseen. Locking ourselves in stained-glass closets, we diminish our true selves and inhibit the gospel from advancing in the world.

The Church must not confine itself to a building, for the Church is not a building. The Church is a global collection of people and communities, congregational and para-congregational, who follow Jesus as Saviour and as Lord. When we step out of our stained-glass closets and onto the field of battle, we will take fire—we will take fire even when we try to live a private, closeted faith—but we know the end has been revealed and the gates of hell will ultimately be the enemy's last line of defence. And they will not prevail against us (Matthew 16:18).

Before we step out, let's consider the strategic realities of engaging the battle for our faith that's being contested on Canadian soil.

---

3   "Excerpts from the Eleazar Ben-Yair Speech" (Josephus Flavius, *The Wars of the Jews, VII*, 320-336), Masada National Park (brochure), Israel Nature and Parks Authority.

CHAPTER TWO

A LITTLE CANADIAN HISTORY AND A MINOR LESSON IN CANADIAN CIVICS

These are the numbers of the divisions of the armed troops who came to David in Hebron to turn the kingdom of Saul over to him, according to the word of the Lord... Of Issachar, men who had understanding of the times, to know what Israel ought to do, 200 chiefs, and all their kinsmen under their command.

—1 Chronicles 12:23, 32

Now the acts of King David, from first to last, are written in the Chronicles of Samuel the seer, and in the Chronicles of Nathan the prophet, and in the Chronicles of Gad the seer, with accounts of all his rule and his might and of the circumstances that came upon him and upon Israel and upon all the kingdoms of the countries.

—1 Chronicles 29:29–30

BRITISH MEMBER OF PARLIAMENT AND PHILOSOPHER EDMUND BURKE IS ATTRIBUTED AS having said, "Those who do not know history are destined to repeat it." Atheist philosopher George Santayana wrote it this way: "Those who cannot remember the past are condemned to repeat it."[1] *New Yorker* cartoonist Tom Toro presents another version of this quote that is both humorous and, perhaps, representative of how too many feel in twenty-first-century Canada:

Those who don't study history are doomed to repeat it. Yet those who *do* study history are doomed to stand by helplessly while everybody else repeats it.[2]

---

1   George Santayana, *The Life of Reason: Reason in Common Sense* (New York, NY: C. Scribner's Sons, 1905), 284.

2   Tom Toro, *Toro*, "Cartoons." Date of access: January 17, 2017 (http://tomtoro.com/cartoons/).

There are many who don't know Canadian history. Either they cannot remember what they learned in school, they have chosen to ignore its lessons, or they were educated in another country.

To understand our times—the circumstances which have come upon Canada and the world—and gain guidance in what we ought to do, it is beneficial to have an awareness of Canadian history. It is particularly important to have at least a cursory understanding that pertains to freedom of religion and religion's relationship to the way Canadians govern themselves. Just as 1 Chronicles 29 ends with the notation that there are several other books about the life of David, so there are many and more extensive books about Canadian history and civics. For a fuller exploration of the importance of religion in that context, I recommend *Fighting Over God: A Legal and Political History of Religious Freedom in Canada*, by Janet Epp Buckingham, which is extensively footnoted with additional sources for study.[3]

Canadian history as I learned it through elementary, secondary, and postsecondary education focused principally on the relationship between the French and the British. Unfortunately, although improving, even today history instruction tends to offer only glimpses into the cultures of Canada's Indigenous peoples, and then usually from the perspective of their relationship with the French or the British. Thus, the question of religion was largely a matter of mediating between predominantly French Roman Catholicism and English Protestantism.[4]

So, what then of our understanding of Canadian history? How might it inform us in today's "free and democratic" society?

First, it is vital to acknowledge the Indigenous peoples of Canada, to listen to and hear their voices and engage the effort required to restore their considerable role in Canada's past, present, and future. This will be neither a short nor easy process.

Second, we must set aside the current idea that those who immigrated to Canada generations ago or in the present-day generation have another home to which they may return. It's true that there are a small number of Canadians who feel a greater sense of kinship and belonging in a distant land, but for the vast majority of us Canada is our only home, in our hearts and lives as much as it is for Canada's Indigenous peoples.

---

3   Janet Epp Buckingham, *Fighting Over God: A Legal and Political History of Religious Freedom in Canada* (Montreal, QC: McGill-Queen's University Press, 2014).

4   Much of the history relayed in this book comes from memory. The Canadian history is supplemented by: J.H. Marsh, ed., *The Canadian Encyclopedia, Second Edition* (Edmonton, AB: Hurtig Publishers, 1988) and www.thecanadianencyclopedia.ca.

Third, we need to be cognizant of the important place religion has had in the development of our society, constitution, laws, and culture.

While there is clear evidence of European contact prior to the renowned voyage to the Americas of Christopher Columbus in 1492, serious European settlement efforts in what is now Canada didn't begin until the mid-1500s. Jacques Cartier claimed the "new" land for France in 1534, but it was Samuel de Champlain who would be the architect and builder of New France, establishing its capital, Quebec City, in 1608. From there, Champlain and other French explorers launched journeys into the interior.

The European rivalry between France and England was exported to North America. The English focused initially on St. John's, Newfoundland—where John Cabot had landed in 1497—and the Atlantic coast before leapfrogging the French to build settlements in what is now Ontario.

On the religion front, the French brought with them a zeal for missions in the name of the Roman Catholic Church, with a strong Jesuit presence. The English brought with them a similar zeal for the Anglican Church, a Protestant breakaway from Roman Catholicism established in 1534 by an act of the English Parliament.

New France (Quebec) became a British colony by conquest in 1759. In 1763, the Treaty of Paris formally transferred the French colony to the control of Great Britain, and also established the first signs of constitutional religious freedom in Canada. Article IV of the Treaty includes the following:

His Britannick Majesty, on his side, agrees to grant the liberty of the Catholick religion to the inhabitants of Canada: he will, in consequence, give the most precise and most effectual orders, that his new Roman Catholic subjects may profess the worship of their religion according to the rites of the Romish church, as far as the laws of Great Britain permit.

French military and political leaders returned to France. The French Roman Catholic clergy remained in Canada.

Both Francophone and Anglophone churches had a goal of converting to their respective expressions of Christianity the aboriginal peoples of Canada.

The *Quebec Act* of 1774 further affirmed the rights of Roman Catholics in Quebec. In 1851, the *Freedom of Worship Act* was passed, guaranteeing "the free exercise and enjoyment of Religious Profession and Worship, without discrimination or preference, so as the same be not made an excuse for acts of licentiousness, or a justification of the practices inconsistent with the peace and safety" of the British colonies, including Quebec.

Further immigration saw the expansion of national Anglophone churches in Canada—Scottish Presbyterian, German Lutheran, English Methodist, and others—along with Anglophone Roman Catholics, but Francophones and Roman Catholicism were generally regarded as synonymous with one another.

Education was delivered by the Church, so denominational education guarantees were constitutionally put in place. When government began to assume responsibility for education, it was still delivered on a denominational basis, with guarantees of the same nature subsequently enshrined in the *British North America Act* (*BNA Act*, now *Constitution Act, 1867*). Beginning in 1888, the federal government financially supported church-run residential schools for aboriginal children. These schools had the twin goals of converting the children to Christianity and assimilating them into the European Canadian culture.

At the same time, minority Christian religious communities fleeing persecution elsewhere in Europe began making their way to Canada, a land of relative religious freedom (apart from the legislated prohibition against practising aboriginal religious rituals). Mennonites, Hutterites, and Doukhobors made their way from Europe to the new nation. Soon after, quasi-Christian immigrants began to filter in from the United States: Mormons and Jehovah's Witnesses. All would end up figuring prominently in disputes concerning religious practices.[5]

With Confederation under the *BNA Act*, four strong provinces—Upper Canada (Ontario), Lower Canada (Quebec), New Brunswick, and Nova Scotia—held on to significant governing authority. Federally, in addition to a representative-elected House of Commons, there would be an appointed Senate to look out for the interests of the provinces and the Crown, whether King or Queen, who retained executive power over the legislatures.

The federal government was given broad powers over matters that crossed provincial boundaries—to "make Laws for the Peace, Order, and good Government of Canada." This included criminal law, a postal service, navigation and shipping, banking, legal tender, the definition of marriage, and other matters, including "Indians, and Lands reserved for the Indians."[6]

As a side note, Lesslie Newbigin shares an interesting comment that may also have been on the minds of those who framed the *BNA Act* when they decided to

---

5   On this broad Church history, see: John Webster Grant, *The Church in the Canadian Era* (Vancouver, BC: Regent College Publishing, 1998).

6   *Constitution Act, 1867*, Section 91.

use the terminology "Peace, Order and good Government" in regard to the public service of governance. Commenting on similar concepts from Augustine's *The City of God*, Newbigin summarizes Augustine's thoughts on this point of reference:

> But peace is only possible when there is order, and order depends on proper government; but government in which one is sub-ordinated to another is only right if the one who is called to govern does so for the sake of those he governs—as their servant. The motive power of order is therefore love.[7]

Among the powers retained by the provinces were hospitals (healthcare), education, natural resources, the administration of justice, the solemnization of marriage, charities, and property and civil rights. Civil rights are better known in Canada as human rights, and provincial jurisdiction led to the rise of variant human rights acts and codes across the country in the latter half of the twentieth century. It is significant to note that education, hospitals, care for widows and orphans, and other charitable work, as well as the solemnization of marriage, were all matters largely carried out by the Church at the time of Confederation.[8]

Confederation is also the term applied to the subsequent joining of the provinces of Manitoba (1870), British Columbia (1871), Prince Edward Island (1873), Alberta and Saskatchewan (1905), and Newfoundland (1949, renamed Newfoundland and Labrador in 2001). The three territories of Canada are often included in the term Confederation: the Northwest Territories (NWT, purchased from the Hudson's Bay Company in 1870, and out of which the provinces of Manitoba, Saskatchewan, and Alberta were established), the Yukon Territory (1898, renamed Yukon in 2003, also established out of the NWT), and Nunavut (1999, also established out of the NWT).

There is no specific provision in regard to religion or religious freedom being assigned to federal or provincial jurisdiction in our constitution. The development of law as it impacted religion and religious freedom would be determined by the courts and cut across the constitutional powers of both federal and provincial levels of government.

---

7   Lesslie Newbigin, *Foolishness to the Greeks: The Gospel and Western Culture* (London, UK: Wm. B. Eerdmans Publishing, 1986), 103. *The City of God Against the Pagans* was written by Augustine, Bishop of Hippo Regius in North Africa, in the fifth century A.D.

8   Note that charities are still subject to provincial regulation. Those that are registered for issuance of donation receipt benefits are federally regulated only for purposes of the *Income Tax Act*.

For the majority of Canada's history, the dominant disputes in regard to religious freedom were between Roman Catholics and Protestants, or other quasi-Christian religious communities. The decision-makers charged with resolving these disputes shared a Christian education, background, and faith, even if only nominally. It was generally accepted that a "Christian" interpretation would be given to application of the laws in resolving such matters. Not until the latter part of the twentieth century would contests of religious freedom in Canada begin to be addressed or adjudicated by elected representatives who were not at least churchgoers, and judges who claimed no affiliation with a Christian church congregation. At the same time, immigration patterns changed, bringing non-Christian (or quasi-Christian) religions into the public square for resolution of conflict resulting from new differences in belief and practice. Culture and religious demographics were both shifting.

CHAPTER THREE

CANADA'S CULTURAL REVOLUTION COMES TO CHURCH

But understand this, that in the last days there will come times of difficulty. For people will be lovers of self, lovers of money, proud, arrogant, abusive, disobedient to their parents, ungrateful, unholy, heartless, unappeasable, slanderous, without self-control, brutal, not loving good, treacherous, reckless, swollen with conceit, lovers of pleasure rather than lovers of God, having the appearance of godliness, but denying its power.

—2 Timothy 3:1–5

Born in Canada, my history of North America was learned from a Canadian perspective. Perhaps, even more narrowly, an English Canadian perspective. Born in 1960, I learned it while growing up during the unfolding of the Western world's own "cultural revolution," which was more than simply a sexual revolution, as it is often described. This was a post-World War II societal shift, resulting in a reduced commitment to religious beliefs and constraints even while people maintained certain religious practices. Individual and societal morals and ethics were also revisited, which manifested in the public life of the nation.

At the conclusion of the American Revolutionary War, as summer drew to a close in 1783, another Treaty of Paris was signed. This treaty established boundaries on the North American continent that awarded states south of the forty-ninth parallel to the fledgling United States of America and the Great White North to Great Britain. A brief incursion by the United States, an early expression of American continentalism, was repelled in the War of 1812.[1]

The emerging nineteenth-century notion of "manifest destiny" propelled Americans to pursue a nation from Atlantic to Pacific, capturing people's imagination with the idea of a transcontinental railway. In that environment, British

---

1   We won. That's how I learned about it in school.

colonies to the north sought a stronger union as protection against American interests, and a railway of their own. The *British North America Act* mandated the federal government to develop an interprovincial railroad from Halifax to the St. Lawrence River (keeping in mind that the four founding provinces were Nova Scotia, New Brunswick, Quebec, and Ontario). As part of the commitment to British Columbia when it joined Canada in 1870, the Canadian Pacific Railway, started in 1881 and completed in 1885, created a transnational rail link from the west coast that connected with the interprovincial railroad at Montreal. It was a full 1,600 kilometres longer than the American transcontinental rail that had been completed in 1869. There would be more rail lines to come, with Canada eventually struggling to support three transcontinental railways by the beginning of the Great War (WWI).

Canada's churches engaged their membership in the formation and growth of the nation. Church historian John Webster Grant notes,

> Canada grew up under the tutelage of its churches. The pulpit, the school and the press were the leading forces in moulding the Canadian character... By preaching, editorializing, and founding universities, they sought on the one hand to lay the moral and spiritual foundations of nationhood, and on the other, to act as a conscience to the state.[2]

The spirit of Canadian expansionism was also present in the Church. Denominations sought ways to transition from colonial and regional activity to having a presence throughout the growing nation. In 1925, there was a uniquely Canadian merger of the Methodist Church, Congregational Church, and two-thirds of Canada's Presbyterian Churches to form the United Church of Canada. At its union, the United Church became the largest Protestant denomination in the country and quickly emerged as the primary Protestant public and political voice to counter that of the Roman Catholic Church. Other potential mergers, including between the United and Anglican churches, would be discussed among Protestant church leaders for another half-century.

However, general awareness of the Bible and confidence in the Church would begin to wane, for a variety of reasons that started to become obvious in the second half of the twentieth century.[3]

---

2   John Webster Grant, *The Canadian Experience of Church Union* (London, UK: Lutterworth Press, 1967), 23.

3   John Webster Grant, *The Church in the Canadian Era* (Vancouver, BC: Regent College Publishing, 1998).

For a decade and a half following WWII, Quebec was led by Premier Maurice Duplessis and his Union Nationale party. Duplessis had, or was perceived to have, strong support from and connection with Quebec's Catholic Church. He was a strong-arm political leader. His death in September 1959 created a vacuum in Quebec's political leadership just as some of his government's less favourable attributes were becoming public knowledge. The resulting backlash against the Union Nationale entangled the Catholic Church in what is referred to as *La Révolution tranquille*, the Quiet Revolution. The push toward a Quebec society free from influence of the Church—previously venerated as the intermediary institution offering the only way for right relationship between God and people—was led by the Liberal government of Premier Jean Lesage, elected in 1960 using the slogan *Maîtres chez nous* ("Masters of our own house"). Among other things, the government moved quickly to take control of education and healthcare from the Church.

People recall different things about 1963. Musically, Bob Dylan recorded "The Times They Are A-Changin'", a prescient song for the U.S., Canada, and the world, and not just because the era of sex, drugs, and rock 'n' roll was beginning to unfold. Politically, whether south or north of the border, when Friday, November 22, 1963 is mentioned, most think of where they were when they first heard the news that U.S. President John Fitzgerald Kennedy was assassinated. People remain largely unaware of the deaths of two other significant figures on the same day: renowned Christian author C.S. Lewis and dystopian philosopher, pantheist, and psychedelic drug user Aldous Huxley, author of 1931's *Brave New World*, a religionless "negative utopia."[4] Fewer still consider it the year when the course of Canadian politics, society, culture, and Church were extraordinarily— some say irreparably—changed. The times, they were indeed a-changin'.

Lester Pearson had been instrumental in establishing the United Nations and would have been its first Secretary-General but for a Security Council veto by the Soviet Union. As Canada's foreign affairs minister, he won the Nobel Peace Prize in 1957 for his role in establishing the United Nations Emergency Force, forerunner to U.N. peacekeeping forces. Six years later, as leader of the Liberal Party, Pearson became Prime Minister. A key part of his leadership was a plan to revitalize the relationship between Quebec and the rest of Canada by recruiting high-profile Quebeckers to the federal party.

---

4   "Huxley himself called his world a 'negative utopia,' the opposite of the traditional utopia." See: *Cliffs Notes*, "About *Brave New World*." Date of access: January 5, 2017 (https://www. cliffsnotes.com/literature/b/brave-new-world/about-brave-new-world).

Three of Pearson's invitations were accepted and one declined. Jean Marchand, Gerard Pelletier, and Pierre Trudeau were all elected to Parliament in 1965. The French media nicknamed them "the three doves." The English media went with "the three wise men." The recruit who declined was popular media personality René Lévesque, who at the time was a provincial Liberal cabinet minister and would go on to establish the Parti Quebecois, become premier of Quebec, and lead Canada into a near constitutional crisis with the 1980 referendum on Quebec independence.[5]

Five seats shy of a majority, from 1963 to 1965 Pearson led a minority Liberal government that was dependent on support from the New Democratic Party to survive. The NDP was led by Baptist minister and social democrat Tommy Douglas. Douglas had brought universal healthcare to Saskatchewan as its premier from 1944 to 1961, along with government ownership of hydroelectricity and auto insurance, unionization of the public service, and the Saskatchewan *Bill of Rights* which was passed in 1947, a year before the United Nations' *Universal Declaration of Human Rights*.

Douglas had observed that the needs of people during the Great Depression and two World Wars outstripped the Church's capacity to respond. He carried those concerns from church to government. This was part of a developing trend of the Church turning to government with Bible-based compassionate solutions that required government-sized funding. Douglas brought these "social gospel" policies to Ottawa and pushed the governing Liberals to implement national healthcare and pension plans, as well as the Canada Student Loan Program.

Pearson won a second minority, short by two seats, in 1965 and remained Prime Minister until 1968, when he relinquished the reigns of leadership to Pierre Trudeau. As Minister of Justice and then Prime Minister, Trudeau introduced legislation that decriminalized homosexual sexual activity between adults and provided for no-fault divorce and qualified surgical abortion.

Paralleling the political reordering were adjustments in the Canadian Protestant Church. In 1963, the Anglican Church of Canada retained a former Anglican, Pierre Berton, to conduct an assessment of them and write a general

---

5 Pierre Elliott Trudeau, *Memoirs* (Toronto, ON: McClelland and Stewart, 1993), 75–77; Pierre Elliott Trudeau, *The Essential Trudeau*, ed. R. Graham (Toronto, ON: McClelland and Stewart, 1998), 106, 139; and René Levesque, *Memoirs*, trans. Philip Stratford (Toronto, ON: McClelland and Stewart, 1986), 149–154, 194–195. In Chapter Twenty-Three of Levesque's memoirs, he tells the story of the initial attempt by Premier Jean Lesage to recruit all four of them to provincial politics in 1960, with the first three declining the opportunity. Trudeau shares his version of the story in his own memoirs (71).

critique. After publication, Berton was invited to share his thoughts on them by other traditional Protestant churches, the United Church of Canada, and the Presbyterian Church in Canada, leaving aside Roman Catholics, evangelicals, and several smaller denominations as different genres of Christianity.

The Comfortable Pew: A Critical Look at the Church in the New Age was published in 1965.[6] This 145-page pocket-sized book was a Canadian bestseller with record sales. In the introduction, Berton notes that "if the Christian Church is ailing, it is certainly worth reviving."[7] However, he also notes that his recommendations for reviving it come from his perspective as someone who had left the very same Anglican Church. He quickly zeroed in on what he thought was ailing the large, mainline denominations of his day.

> Large numbers of nominal Christians are no longer either very hot or very cold, for the virus that has weakened the Church is apathy.[8]

The picture painted was of a church that was wealthy and insular, endorsed a private, unchallenged faith, was filled with people primarily there for social and business reasons, and failed to offer guidance on issues of morality or public engagement—from business ethics to political matters. In the instances of the Church's disconnect with culture, rather than a return to the Scriptures which he himself had abandoned, Berton proposed a solution that involved looking at the Church's need to engage with culture at the point of changes in culture. This necessarily involved reconsidering or setting aside historic (i.e. no longer in touch with the contemporary culture) principles of Scripture.

Church historian Phyllis Airhart tells us that while leaders of the United Church "may have taken exception to some of the particulars of Berton's book, they agreed with the central thesis."[9] Berton's strategy was broadly discussed, then overwhelmingly embraced in Anglican, United, and Presbyterian denominations.

The heftiest part of the Protestant Church in Canada drifted from its focused connection with the Bible and principles that would have facilitated alignment with the social gospel as expressed in Douglas' policies, a biblically based public

---

6   Pierre Berton, *The Comfortable Pew: A Critical Look at the Church in the New Age* (Toronto, ON: McLelland and Stewart, 1965).

7   Ibid., 13.

8   Ibid., 29.

9   Phyllis Airhart, *A Church with the Soul of a Nation: Making and Remaking the United Church of Canada* (Montreal, QC: McGill-Queen's University Press, 2014), 233.

activism. Its leadership challenged its congregants to stop being an influential social club that had gradually set aside the gospel and to reengage the culture as social activists, without reembracing the primacy of the gospel itself.

Government, in the meantime, was busy embracing much work previously done by the Church. The Church passively abdicated responsibility—with Catholics, The Salvation Army, and a few others negotiating a continued presence—protesting only when the government made decisions with which the Church disagreed based on the social paradigms it had embraced. Significant parts of the Canadian Church began to look less like the Christianity C.S. Lewis envisioned and more like the religionless society Aldous Huxley had imagined.

For the most part, the evangelical part of the Protestant Church was wary of social activism and certain elements of the social gospel until a quarter of a century later. As U.S. evangelical leaders embraced the "moral majority" political movement, Canadian evangelicals became more openly and politically active, either to distinguish themselves from their American evangelical cousins, as the great majority cautiously did, or to align themselves with American-style expression.

It should be no surprise that political activity did not draw people to the Church, or keep them there. Jesus cannot be reduced from being the Son of God to simply an activist figure, no matter the cause.

As biblically and doctrinally based membership in the Church waned, attendance became more a matter of social practice, or simple socialization. By welcoming Canada's cultural revolution into the Church, societal pressure to have an identifiable church of origin, as distinct from actual attendance, also dissipated. Birth records once maintained by the Church became the purview of government. The collective result has been a departure from both attendance and affiliation. Statistically, the result in Canada has been an increase in the number of religiously unaffiliated, increasingly referred to by the box they tick on the census—"None." The rapid rise of the Nones is not surprising, given that their or their parents' presence in church was often driven by reasons other than commitment to Christ.

New immigration policies established under Pearson in the 1960s heralded a redirection of immigration trends. The policies facilitated the growth of the Orthodox Church in Canada—particularly Greek, Ukrainian, and Egyptian (Coptic)—along with an upsurge in other non-Christian religious communities.

One of the difficulties encountered by the Canadian Church in the twenty-first century is an inability to overcome long shadows cast by the Church of prior centuries, whether because of its influence on government and the population, its presence as a place of social gathering, or its role in the abuses that occurred during the operation of residential schools for Indigenous and orphaned children. A more recent shadow is that of the division between a culturally oriented Church and a biblically oriented Church, both claiming to follow Christ.

Some of these long shadows reveal the fallen nature of all humanity, including those in the Church. Others create the misperception of a nation that was Christian and is now backsliding, when in fact it was never Christian, at least constitutionally, and is now lost.

Canada's cultural elite—academics, politicians, bureaucrats, media, judges, etc.—seem to be leading in a direction that is fixated on removing our societal anchor from the Rock, Jesus Christ, and instead instituting an illiberal libertarian socialist shell of an expression of that Christian heritage. Human rights have been separated from *imago Dei* and replaced by human precepts. A rights-obsessed society focuses increasingly on personal autonomy that demands the state's interests be set aside and, at the same time, the state foot the bill for individual preference. Non-conformists are ostracised and marginalized.

In this setting, the Church is struggling to break out of its own shadows and be marketable, or at least not marginalized. The shadows cast by a fading light are being manipulated by those who oppose the Church in an attempt to suggest that the light was actually darkness. The new secularists argue there is a new light, a light *from* the world, which necessitates at best dimming and at worst extinguishing the Light *of* the world. In this brave new world, voices of restraint are disregarded and religious voices of restraint are often ignored, if not entirely unwelcome.

For the Church to engage society in twenty-first-century Canada, it must approach society as an outsider to the lost rather than an insider who has come to restore those who once were found. It's important to see the lost as lost, not as wrong. God's Word is not considered authoritative by those who do not embrace it, whether within or outside church buildings, and certainly not before government or the courts. The principles of Scripture must be translated into the language of listeners who reject or are unaware of its Author. And Christians must be sufficiently knowledgeable of the Bible, culture, and law to do so wisely.

CHAPTER FOUR

THE CONSTITUTION, THE COURTS, AND THE CHEESE

Whereas Canada is founded upon principles that recognize the supremacy of God and the rule of law...

—preamble to the *Canadian Charter of Rights and Freedoms*

May he have dominion from sea to sea, and from the River to the ends of the earth!
—Psalm 72:8

As the century and millennium were about to roll over all four numbers on the dial, an interesting little book started a five-year run on the *New York Times* bestsellers list. 1998's *Who Moved My Cheese? An Amazing Way to Deal with Change in Your Work and in Your Life*, by Dr. Spencer Johnson, was a business fable that used the characters of two mice and two miniature people seeking cheese in a maze to describe four typical reactions to inevitable change.[1]

Before Jim Collins' *Good to Great*[2] and the separate *Good to Great and the Social Sectors*[3] addendum introduced us to Big Hairy Audacious Goals (BHAGs), business leaders, government leaders, and yes, church leaders in North America were all about chasing cheese. Another confession: I chased the cheese.

At one point in the book, following a period of personal reflection, one of the tiny people writes on a wall the following lessons he learned from his quest for cheese:

---

1   Spencer Johnson, *Who Moved My Cheese? An Amazing Way to Deal with Change in Your Work and in Your Life* (New York, NY: G.P. Putnam's Sons, 1998).

2   Jim Collins, *Good to Great: Why Some Companies Make the Leap... and Others Don't* (New York, NY: HarperCollins Publishers Inc., 2001).

3   Jim Collins, *Good to Great and the Social Sectors: A Monograph to Accompany Good to Great—Why Business Thinking Is Not the Answer* (Boulder, CO: Jim Collins, 2005).

Change Happens
They Keep Moving The Cheese.
Anticipate Change
Get Ready For The Cheese To Move.
Monitor Change
Smell The Cheese Often So You Know When It Is Getting Old.
Adapt To Change Quickly
The Quicker You Let Go Of Old Cheese, The Sooner You Can Enjoy New Cheese.
Change
Move With The Cheese.
Enjoy Change!
Savor The Adventure And Enjoy The Taste Of New Cheese!
Be Ready To Change Quickly And Enjoy It Again
They Keep Moving The Cheese.[4]

This list might just as easily have been written by someone reviewing the life and development of Canada's constitution and courts, and the interpretation of the constitution by those courts.

Let's begin with the constitution.

The provinces of Canada (Upper Canada, Lower Canada, Nova Scotia, and New Brunswick), the original petitioners to the Parliament of Great Britain, "expressed their Desire to be federally united into One Dominion"[5] under the name of Canada. While John A. MacDonald favoured Canada being a kingdom, New Brunswick Premier Sir Samuel Leonard Tilley suggested the term Dominion, inspired by Psalm 72:8. This is also echoed in Canada's motto: *A Mari Usque Ad Mare* (Latin for "from sea to sea"). The request was granted on March 29, 1867, with the date of implementation to be determined within six months.

There's a reason July 1, 1867 is referred to as Confederation. Canada is not a federation of independent states; it was established as a federation of previously independent colonies. Representatives of those colonies negotiated the *British North America Act*, which established a federal Parliament with a provincially represented balance in the upper chamber, the Senate, and ensured the provinces would retain independent legislatures with significant constitutional powers.

---

4   Johnson, *Cheese*, 74.

5   *Constitution Act, 1867*, Preamble.

Since that date, there have been more than two dozen constitutional documents added to the mix, with the last being the *Constitution Act, 1982*. The *Constitution Act, 1982* renamed the *British North America Act* as the *Constitution Act, 1867*, repealed six of the other enactments, and brought authority over the constitution to Canada. This is often referred to as the patriation (or repatriation) of the constitution. The 1982 act's formula for amending the document again recognized the unique status and strength of the provinces.

In addition to the collection of written constitutional documents, the *Constitution Act, 1867* sets out in the preamble that the uniting provinces desired Canada do so "with a Constitution similar in Principle to that of the United Kingdom,"[6] much of which is not written down and is the result of, and subject to, interpretation by Parliament and the courts. It is worth noting that the United Kingdom's Parliament has an elected House of Commons and an upper chamber appointed by the monarch, the House of Lords.

Because there was a lack of agreement at the Confederation conferences about establishing a national court of appeal, there wasn't one. The *Constitution Act, 1867*, Section 101, provided Parliament with the authority to establish such a court. Initially, however, the provinces retained the highest court in each of their own jurisdictions. French-style civil law prevailed in Quebec and the British common law in the other provinces, as it does to this day.

It was nearly a decade before the *Supreme Court Act, 1875* established the Supreme Court of Canada as the young nation's senior court of appeal. However, Supreme Court decisions could be further appealed to the Judicial Committee of the Privy Council in London, England. Initially, cases could also be appealed directly to the Privy Council by the provinces, bypassing the Supreme Court altogether.

A pattern soon developed in judicial decision-making. The Judicial Committee of the Privy Council answered questions in a way that inclined toward the provinces. The Supreme Court of Canada interpreted constitutional questions to favour a strong federal government.

The Supreme Court of Canada became the final court of appeal in criminal matters in 1933, criminal law being a matter of federal jurisdiction under the *Constitution Act, 1867*. It was not until 1949 that appeals to the Privy Council were discontinued in regard to all other matters.

The Supreme Court continued in its strong federalist ways until 1973.

---

6   Ibid.

In 1970, Bora Laskin became the first Jewish justice on the Supreme Court, appointed by Prime Minister Pierre Trudeau. Trudeau had expressed a vision for Canada as a "just society" and had a personal goal of establishing constitutional protection for individual rights. With the retirement of Chief Justice Gerald Fauteux in December 1973, Trudeau elevated Laskin to Chief Justice. This was a controversial appointment because tradition held that the Prime Minister appointed the senior-most member of the Court to the position of Chief Justice, and Laskin was the second most junior of the eight remaining justices when Fauteux stepped down.

With a background in labour law and constitutional law, Laskin also had a reputation as a strong supporter of civil liberties, particularly individual human rights. In addition to federal and provincial powers being disputed before the Supreme Court, the rights of the individual began to hold a more significant place under Laskin's direction. Chief Justice Bora Laskin served long enough to preside over the constitutional patriation case and the early days of the *Canadian Charter of Rights and Freedoms*.[7]

In my first month of law school, on September 28, 1981, the Supreme Court of Canada issued a provocative decision in the constitutional patriating case, *Re Resolution to amend the Constitution*.[8] The Court held that Canada's constitutional conventions—unwritten procedural requirements resulting from having "a Constitution similar in Principle to that of the United Kingdom"—obliged Parliament to secure a substantial degree of provincial consent to amend the constitution, and, at the same time, that Parliament could, as a matter of law, unilaterally seek constitutional amendment from the Parliament of the United Kingdom without provincial consent.

Prime Minister Trudeau chose to engage a new and aggressive round of constitutional negotiations that culminated in the *Constitution Act, 1982*, which was formalized in a signing ceremony in Ottawa with Queen Elizabeth II on April 17, 1982.

Included in the *Constitution Act, 1982* is the *Canadian Charter of Rights and Freedoms*, a declaration of human rights as applicable between government and its citizens. Remember, under Section 92 of the *Constitution Act, 1867*, civil rights are the jurisdiction of provinces. Accordingly, human rights disputes between individuals, individuals and corporations, or individuals and provincial governments

---

7   James G. Snell and Frederick Vaughan, *The Supreme Court of Canada: History of the Institution* (Toronto, ON: The Osgoode Society, 1985), 217–225.

8   [1981] 1 SCR 753.

are the subject of provincial human rights legislation. Similarly, the *Canadian Bill of Rights* and *Canadian Human Rights Act* apply in matters of federal jurisdiction only under the *Constitution Act, 1867*. However, the *Charter* has an overarching applicability between Canadians and our federal and provincial governments, as well as organizations and other levels of government established by those governments. Note: territorial governments and municipal governments in the territories are established under the constitutional jurisdiction of the federal government, and municipal governments in the provinces are established under the constitutional jurisdiction of provincial governments. But the *Charter* only applies to the relationship with and responsibilities of government.

Politically, Canada's constitutional cheese had been continually moving, with thirty adjustments to the *British North America Act* in a little over a hundred years.

The Supreme Court of Canada was invigorated with the new challenge of interpreting the *Constitution Act, 1982*, particularly the *Charter*. It wasn't long before the Court anchored judicial doctrine in a way that would keep the constitutional cheese moving to this day. The Court both secured the constitution in the Westminster parliamentary tradition of the United Kingdom and unfettered it from its historic estate to be a "living tree," adaptable to changes in Canadian opinion, values, and culture.[9] The one doctrine bound the Court to precedent. The other set it free from such bonds. These opposing conservative and liberal methods of judicial interpretation would, over time, be applied by the Court as it determined best, constrained only by the *Constitution Act, 1982*'s "notwithstanding clause," found in Section 33, which was designed to protect the authority of Canada's Parliament and the provincial legislatures in accordance with the Westminster tradition of parliamentary supremacy. Future chapters will examine the use of the *Charter* by the courts without attachment to absolutes such as the stabilizing principles of "the supremacy of God" as found in the Bible and referenced in the *Charter*'s preamble.

The mixture and development of courts and tribunals in Canada has required a similar "move with the cheese" mentality.

The previously mentioned historical process of identifying the highest court of the land continued until 1949. The Supreme Court of Canada is now the undisputed final court of appeal in Canada—except for exercise of the

---

9   Chief Justice Antonio Lamer stated in *Re B.C. Motor Vehicle Act*, [1985] 2 SCR 486, paragraph 53: "If the newly planted 'living tree' which is the Charter is to have the possibility of growth and adjustment over time, care must be taken to ensure that historical materials, such as the Minutes of Proceedings and Evidence of the Special Joint Committee, do not stunt its growth."

"notwithstanding clause" by a federal or provincial parliament in regard to fundamental freedoms (Section 2), legal rights (Sections 7 to 15), or equality rights (Section 15) under the *Charter*.

From there, the basic court structures revolve primarily around the division of powers between the federal and provincial governments outlined in Sections 91 and 92 of the *Constitution Act, 1867*.

Each province had its own judicial structure at Confederation, and still does. A province's court system is responsible for civil matters (disputes between individuals) and criminal matters, even though criminal law is the jurisdiction of the federal government. Specialty tribunals were added based on legislation in the areas of provincial jurisdiction: labour law, landlord and tenant disputes, child and family concerns, among others. Of significance, civil rights (human rights) are the jurisdiction of the provinces, except in constitutionally identified areas of federal jurisdiction. Human rights tribunals feature prominently in the consideration of religious freedom. The tribunal structures provide different methods of appeal to the judicial system, where appeals are heard variously by one or three judges. Like cases heard at the initial level of the courts, such decisions are then appealed to the province's court of appeal, and then to the Supreme Court of Canada.

Courts of appeal are usually presided over by three judges, to avoid ties if there is disagreement on a decision. The Supreme Court of Canada is usually presided over by a group of seven or nine for the same reason.

Similar to provincial courts, there are federal specialty tribunals, a federal lower court, and a federal court of appeal. The federal court system has jurisdiction over federal matters, except criminal matters.

The Canadian legal system is structured on the concept of precedent. The decisions of higher courts are generally considered to be determinative of similar matters when heard by the lower courts.

Even though there has been almost constant restructuring of significant elements of the tribunal and court systems across the country, there are some key elements of the structure that are pretty much consistent. The chart below outlines the basic concept:

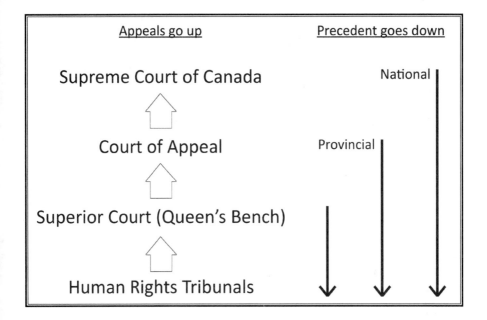

CHAPTER FIVE

UNLIKELY HEROES

And Jesse said to David his son, "Take for your brothers an ephah of this parched grain, and these ten loaves, and carry them quickly to the camp to your brothers. Also take these ten cheeses to the commander of their thousand. See if your brothers are well, and bring some token from them."...

Then Saul clothed David with his armor. He put a helmet of bronze on his head and clothed him with a coat of mail, and David strapped his sword over his armor. And he tried in vain to go, for he had not tested them. Then David said to Saul, "I cannot go with these, for I have not tested them." So David put them off. Then he took his staff in his hand and chose five smooth stones from the brook and put them in his shepherd's pouch. His sling was in his hand, and he approached the Philistine.

—1 Samuel 17:17–18, 38–40

RIGHTS AND FREEDOMS ARE ASPIRATIONAL, PERHAPS EVEN STRONGLY ARTICULATED, during times of relative tranquillity and societal agreement. But the truth of their acceptance is challenged by, and they are most defined by, conflict.

During the 2014 Israel-Gaza conflict, a rabbi friend of mine and several people from his synagogue went to Israel where they picked up pizza and delivered it hot to Israel Defense Forces personnel on the front lines. As I shared earlier, Israel is geographically small. Can you imagine if one of the pizza delivery guys had offered to singlehandedly put an end to the encounter? Would the leaders of Israel have agreed?

Of course not. But something like it did happen once before.

David, a shepherd boy, was asked by his father, Jesse, to deliver lunch to his brothers, who were in the army of Israel that was led by King Saul. The Israelites and Philistines were at war. Following the rules of war, each side lined up its warriors across from one another and prepared to engage in battle. But there was no fighting. The opposing generals had come to an agreement that the winner would be determined by one army's champion fighting the other army's champion. There was only one problem: nobody wanted to fight the Philistine champion, a giant of a man named Goliath.

David showed up with lunch just as the two sides were forming up against each other. When Goliath walked to the middle of the battlefield and challenged *"the army of the living God"* (1 Samuel 17:26) to send out a champion, no one responded. David didn't understand why. He offered to fight when no one else would, so the king Rambo-ed him up with the king's own armour. The armour was outside the shepherd's comfort zone, so instead… well, here are the words to a little song we used to sing with our kids in Sunday school:

Only a boy named David, only a little sling,
only a boy named David, but he could pray and sing.
Only a boy named David, only a rippling brook,
only a boy named David, but five little stones he took.
And one little stone went in the sling,
and the sling went round and round.
And one little stone went in the sling,
and the sling went round and round,
and round and round and round and round,
and round and round and round.
And one little stone went up in the air,
and the giant came tumbling down.[1]

The delivery boy defeated the warrior. Thus inspired, the army of Israel attacked the more numerous Philistine army and trounced them. David used the weapons with which he had been well-prepared: his faith in God, prayer, and that little sling he carried around to protect his father's sheep.

In retrospect, with the benefit of knowing history, David's win is not a surprise. Although not known by those standing on the front lines before the menacing giant, David had been anointed by the prophet Samuel to replace Saul as

---

1   Arthur Arnott, "Only a Boy Named David," 1931. See: *Hymnary.org*, "Only a Boy Named David." Date of access: January 6, 2017 (http://www.hymnary.org/text/only_a_boy_named_david).

king, and Goliath's downfall was just one step along the way for the sheepherder, an outsider who seemed the unlikely hero.

Over the span of Canada's history, many unlikely heroes have arisen to champion the defining of religious freedom by Canadian courts in unanticipated conflicts.

I had the pleasure of meeting one such person, one of my personal heroes, at a gathering in Toronto. Forty-one years my senior, Glen How was in his seventies when we met. Mr. How was not an imposing figure by any stretch of the imagination. Short and slim, Glen, as he suggested I call him, had aged gracefully into his wispy white hair. Glen's stature, however, had not prevented him from casting his own long shadow across Canadian law, including credit from many in the legal and political communities for having a strong influence on implementation of the *Canadian Charter of Rights and Freedoms*.

Barely called to the Bar—"called to the Bar" being the term used in Canada when a lawyer is officially licensed to practice law—of the Law Society of Upper Canada in 1943, it was as a twenty-four-year-old novice lawyer that Glen How found himself embroiled in litigation that, over the course of decades, would compel Canadian courts to define religious freedom in a way that would restrain government imposition on religion, both before and after the *Charter*.

Born in Montreal to an accountant father and homemaker mother, the family moved while How was still a small child and he was raised in Toronto. Glen might have been the prototypical Canadian of the mid-twentieth century except for two things. One, he was a lawyer—subsequently also called to the Bars of Quebec, Alberta, and Saskatchewan. Two, as a teenager he had become a devout member of the Watch Tower Society, better known as Jehovah's Witnesses.

Jehovah's Witnesses are generally regarded as a quasi-Christian sect. Some consider them a cult. The Witnesses have their own translation of the Bible, which has some variances in wording from the book that is more broadly accepted. Founded on a difference of belief about the Second Coming of Christ—establishing a date and the number of the elect who would accompany Christ to heaven—the Witnesses are an exclusionist group that reject all other expressions of Christianity, publicly denouncing Roman Catholicism and Protestants in their publications, most searingly Catholicism. Additionally, Jehovah's Witnesses deny expressions of nationalist loyalty, refusing to sing national anthems, salute flags, or serve in the military.

The anti-nationalist expression was the cause for Glen How's introduction to the conflict for religious freedom. Canada's 1940 *War Measures Act* declared membership in the Jehovah's Witnesses to be illegal. The legislation was an initiative by the Roman Catholic federal Minister of Justice, Ernest Lapointe from Quebec, a province that would feature prominently in How's several appearances before the Supreme Court of Canada. The Witnesses were not supportive of the nation at war and were openly critical of Catholicism. They were also advocates for an American-style bill of rights, repeatedly (annoyingly?) lobbying the federal government to have such an amendment passed by the U.K. Parliament at Westminster. In Canada, civil rights were constitutionally a matter of provincial jurisdiction. The Witnesses' efforts to effectively move civil rights to federal jurisdiction created a particular tension with Quebec. This would not stop How from personally continuing to advocate for such a constitutional bill of rights until 1982 when the task, to a degree, was accomplished.[2]

The Jehovah's Witnesses had a legal department in the U.S., but Glen How and Associates became the Canadian legal department, relieving the Witnesses of the effort to find lawyers willing to represent their group of Canadian outsiders, and preparing them to take on the battle to define freedom of religion in the courts, from a perspective other than the historic Protestant and Catholic differences.

Lapointe, who had served as Justice Minister for an astounding seventeen years, died shortly after passing the regulations banning the Witnesses. Appointed in his stead was another Quebecer, Louis St. Laurent. One of Glen How's first acts as a lawyer was to submit a brief to Prime Minister William Lyon Mackenzie King, going over the head of the Justice Minister because St. Laurent had refused to remove the ban implemented by his predecessor. King denied the request as well. King remained Prime Minister until 1948, succeeded by St. Laurent, who held office until 1957. This was an intense era of bringing the Jehovah's Witnesses claims for religious freedoms before the courts, largely due to the government turning a deaf ear to their claims.[3]

As How's January 2009 obituary in the *Globe and Mail* stated,

> He relentlessly argued that Jehovah's Witness ministers, many of whom had been interned in labour camps (during WWII), were entitled to conscientious-objector status, like other clergy. He also defended the

---

2   William Kaplan, *State and Salvation: The Jehovah's Witnesses and Their Fight for Civil Rights* (Toronto, ON: University of Toronto Press, 1989), 15.

3   Ibid., 118.

rights of the children of Jehovah's Witnesses to refuse to sing the national anthem in school ceremonies.[4]

The ban drew to a close with the end of WWII, but one Canadian jurisdiction refused to give any ground to the Jehovah's Witnesses: the historically Roman Catholic province of Quebec. The government of Maurice Duplessis legislated to suppress them. Duplessis, both Premier and Attorney General, "considered the Witnesses a serious threat to the dominance of the Roman Catholic Church." There were at the time about ten thousand Jehovah's Witnesses in Canada, fewer than five hundred of whom lived in Quebec. This was to be a crucial battleground for How.[5]

How's obituary continues,

> Between 1946 and 1953, Witnesses were involved in more than 1,500 criminal prosecutions, ranging from disturbing the peace to sedition. Mr. How spent so much time commuting to and from Quebec that he moved there in the late 1940s to set up a legal practice. Every morning, his first job was to find out how many Witnesses had been arrested the day before and then try to arrange bail for them.[6]

Quebec City's council had passed a bylaw forbidding distribution of "any book, pamphlet, booklet, circular, or tract whatever without a permit from the chief of police."[7] The Witnesses refused to acknowledge or comply with a regulation clearly intended to restrict their freedom of speech and expression. They could regularly be found on street corners or going door to door distributing literature about the "false" teachings of the Roman Catholic Church. The Witnesses also developed a four-page tract called "Quebec's Burning Hate for God and Christ and Freedom is the Shame of All Canada," in which was listed names, dates, and places of violence against Jehovah's Witnesses. They printed five hundred thousand

---

4   Sandra Martin, *The Globe and Mail,* "He Helped Win Freedom for All Canadians." January 21, 2009 (http://v1.theglobeandmail.com/servlet/story/LAC.20090121.OBHOW21/BDAStory/BDA/deaths).

5   Kaplan, *State,* 232.

6   Martin, "He Helped Win Freedom for All Canadians."

7   Kaplan, *State,* 241.

copies and started distributing them across Canada in 1946, which elicited Duplessis' response of "a war without mercy against the Witnesses of Jehovah."[8]

Aimé Boucher, and over one hundred others, was charged with sedition for acts criticizing the government and distributing the "Quebec's Burning Hate" pamphlet. Laurier Saumur was arrested over one hundred times for violation of the Quebec City distribution bylaw. Premier Duplessis personally revoked the liquor licence of Montreal restaurant owner Frank Roncarelli, a Jehovah's Witness who was a prime source of bail money. All three cases ended up before the Supreme Court of Canada.[9]

The defence in the *Boucher* case[10] was truth. The case has the distinction of being heard twice by the Supreme Court. The first time, three of five judges found that a new trial was in order. The unusual appeal for the Supreme Court to reconsider its own decision, on the question of whether Boucher could be convicted of seditious libel, resulted in all nine judges hearing the case and deciding 5–4 on a dismissal of the charges, establishing a definition of "sedition" that was much narrower than the concept of opposition to government through exercise of free expression (speech), particularly free expression based in religious belief. All of the Witnesses who had been charged under the law had their cases dismissed.

The *Saumur* case[11] determined that it was beyond the authority of a municipal or provincial government to take actions that restricted a person's right to practise their religion, including distribution of religious literature. More than a thousand charges under the bylaw were dismissed.

The *Roncarelli* case,[12] in which Roncarelli sued Duplessis in his personal capacity, established that the discretionary authority of public officials is to be used in good faith, not arbitrarily against individuals for personal reasons.

In Ontario, Glen How also took up the cause of Jehovah's Witness children who were expelled from school for refusing to sing the national anthem ("God Save the Queen") or salute the flag. At the time, Ontario had no human rights code and there was no constitutional bill of rights. Without a constitutional basis to claim freedom of religion, How used judicial and legislative precedent to establish a case for conscientious objection, based largely on cases where Jehovah's Witnesses had been exempted from military service, while drawing parallels

---

8   Ibid., 233.

9   Buckingham, *Fighting Over God*, 109.

10   *Boucher v. The King*, [1951] SCR 265.

11   *Saumur v. City of Quebec*, [1953] 2 SCR.

12   *Roncarelli v. Duplessis*, [1959] SCR 121.

to the accommodations made for students of other religions in regard to other school experiences (for example, Jewish children were not required to eat pork and Roman Catholic children were not required to eat meat on Fridays). The conscientious religious objection of the Witness children was not causing harm to others, and they could easily be excluded from the exercises. In the end, both the Ontario Court of Appeal and Supreme Court of Canada affirmed that there was a right to say "no" when doing so was founded in sincerely held beliefs—in this instance, religious.

More controversially, How also fought for the right of Witnesses and their children to refuse blood transfusions, based on their belief that the Bible prohibits the eating or consumption of blood in any manner.

This is just a sampling of the work of Glen How and Associates, including bringing before the Supreme Court the matter of defining what is or is not recognized as a religious denomination, breaking free from the traditional understanding of clergy in the Catholic and Protestant contexts for a broader legal recognition of religion and religious operational structure.[13]

Glen How ultimately accepted the designation as Queen's Counsel, but only after being assured that he would not have to swear allegiance to the Queen to do so. Similarly, he accepted admission to the Order of Canada and other awards, including the Law Society Medal from the Law Society of Upper Canada.

There are a number of lessons I take from the life of Glen How.

First, if you believe in your cause and engage it, you are likely to have an impact in its favour regardless of the resources you do or do not have behind you. Sticking with it in the long run will likely bring even more favourable results.

Second, the way religious freedom is defined for the Jehovah's Witnesses, or any other religious community, is determinative of the way religious freedom is defined for me and my community of faith.

Third, religious communities tend to keep to themselves, intending their engagement with others to be inoffensive. But they will engage in a civil version of Augustine's and Aquinas' just war theory when attacked—battling fiercely for recognition of rights equal to those of other Canadians and perhaps, like Frank Roncarelli, even taking the offensive to the battlefield of the courtroom if necessary to prevent further harm, the aim being to obtain peace.

Fourth, it's valuable to be intentional about thinking creatively. Inside-the-box thinking results, at best, in inside-the-box results. Outside-the-box application of principles might instead establish a new or bigger box. For

---

13   *Greenless v. Attorney General for Canada*, [1946] SCR 462.

example, Glen How identified and applied a parallel experience (conscientious objection to military service) to the one confronting him (seeking to have Witness children attend school despite not singing the anthem). Thinking outside the box on freedom of religion may include consideration of matters of freedom of conscience (individual) or freedom of assembly (group), which turn out to be closely related to one another and freedom of religion in practicalities of both life and law.

Finally, never underestimate the underdog, particularly one who is well-prepared.

CHAPTER SIX

THE LAW IS A JEALOUS MISTRESS

You shall have no other gods before me. You shall not make for yourself a carved image, or any likeness of anything that is in heaven above, or that is in the earth beneath, or that is in the water under the earth. You shall not bow down to them or serve them, for I the Lord your God am a jealous God, visiting the iniquity of the fathers on the children to the third and the fourth generation of those who hate me, but showing steadfast love to thousands of those who love me and keep my commandments.

—Exodus 20:3–6

And one of them, a lawyer, asked him [Jesus] a question to test him. "Teacher, which is the great commandment in the Law?"

And he said to him, "You shall love the Lord your God with all your heart and with all your soul and with all your mind. This is the great and first commandment. And a second is like it: You shall love your neighbor as yourself. On these two commandments depend all the Law and the Prophets."

—Matthew 22:35–40

AT HIS AUGUST 1829 INAUGURATION AS A PROFESSOR OF LAW AT HARVARD UNIVERSITY, U.S. Supreme Court Justice Joseph Story remarked,

I will not say with Lord Hale, that "the law will admit of no rival, and nothing to go even with it;" but I will say, that it is a jealous mistress, and requires a long and constant courtship. It is not to be won by tri-fling favours, but by a lavish homage.[1]

Justice Story was referring to Sir Matthew Hale (1609–1676), who had served as a Member of the English Parliament, Chief Justice of the King's Bench[2] in England, and in the House of Lords. Hale's point as lawyer, judge, and lawmaker was not lost on Story, and Story's point was little different. Lawyers, judges, and lawmakers often see the law as all-absorbing, if not all-encompassing.

Beverly McLachlin became Chief Justice of the Supreme Court of Canada in January 2000. On October 9, 2002, speaking at the Pluralism, Religion, and Public Policy conference held at McGill University, she stated her opinion that it is the responsibility of the courts to find somewhere "in the comprehensive claims of the rule of law, a space in which individual and community adherence to religious authority can flourish."[3] The Chief Justice recognized that in the claims of law and religion, "two comprehensive worldviews collide. It is at this point that the treatment of religion becomes truly exigent... both lay some claim to the whole of human experience."[4] It was the Chief Justice's conclusion that the courts must meet this challenge in society and that they have been charged with the responsibility for creating this space, "a space within the rule of law in which religious beliefs can manifest."[5]

The assertion that supreme authority resides with the state—even, more narrowly, with the law—is not unique to one judge, one court, one politician, or even one government. It is a worldview, a perspective on all of life, which is formed by the law.

The Canadian Church's response to such an assertion has fallen along a broad spectrum.

---

1   Joseph Story, "Value and Importance of Legal Studies: A Discourse Pronounced at the Inauguration of the Author, as Dane Professor of Law in Harvard University, August 25, 1829" in William W. Story, ed., *The Miscellaneous Writings of Joseph Story, Associate Justice of the Supreme Court of the United States and Dane Professor of Law at Harvard University, Vol. 3* (Boston, MA: Charles C. Little and James Brown, 1852), 523.

2   The courts in England are referred to in reference to the ruling monarch.

3   Beverly McLachlin, "Freedom of Religion and the Rule of Law: A Canadian Perspective" in Douglas Farrow, ed., *Recognizing Religion in a Secular Society: Essays in Pluralism, Religion, and Public Policy* (Montreal, QC: McGill-Queen's University Press, 2004), 20. Her thoughts from that conference were published in full in this essay.

4   Ibid., 21.

5   Ibid., 33.

At one end of the spectrum are those Christians who, quite frankly, don't care. Their only real concern with Christianity is that church buildings be available when they have need of them. Christmas. Easter. Mother's Day. Weddings. Funerals. Baby dedications. Church is an invitation-only activity for those who hold roughly the same definition of Christianity as I once did: "I am Canadian and therefore must be Christian because Canada is a Christian country." (Which it is not.)

Progressing along the spectrum, we arrive at those who would be concerned *if* they thought it affected them. Not generally engaged with the Church or the world around them, their concern is that church buildings be available for the kinds of events noted above plus the annual picnic, church bazaars, bake sales, and other such events. They also wish that their names not be removed from the church records.

The next group is slightly more concerned. In addition to previous groups' concerns, this group's church congregation, building, and denomination are the focal point of their participation in social justice causes. If the legal accommodation provided impacts their ability to get a charitable donation receipt for their financial contributions or their ability to march in select parades and processions behind a church banner or comment to the media as a "church member," then they declare that "the law is an ass."[6] This phrase will likely be attributed to either Shakespeare or the Bible, as they've heard it before, perhaps said it before, but have not read *Oliver Twist* by Charles Dickens to understand its source, context, or meaning.

As the spectral progression continues, we arrive at those who would object to the Chief Justice's words and are willing to find a way to declare their right to religious freedom as contained in the constitution. In doing so, they may even reference the *Canadian Charter of Rights and Freedoms*. These regular churchgoers, at least more regular than the special event people and bake-salers, have a firm commitment to church attendance, at least on Sundays after Thanksgiving, when the cottage is closed for the winter, and before sometime mid-April, when the cottage opens again, except for conflicts with a round of golf, family events, children's sports activities, or their favourite football team's early game. Armed with the knowledge gained from grandparents, parents, and their pastor quoting the Bible (they're pretty sure it was the Bible), as well as whatever Christian ardour they have picked up from social media, they will seriously consider engaging in complaints to their spouse or "click slacktivism" (i.e. liking and potentially sharing or retweeting

---

6   Charles Dickens, *Oliver Twist, Second Edition, Volume III* (London, UK: Richard Bentlet, 1839), 279. The quote arises when Mr. Bumble is told in court, "[T]he law supposes that your wife acts under your direction." In response, we get the actual quote as written by Dickens: "'If the law supposes that,' said Mr. Bumble, squeezing his hat emphatically in both hands, 'the law is a ass—a idiot. If that is the eye of the law, the law's a bachelor...'"

on social media posts about religious freedom in Canada being compromised). They may even add their name to an online petition.

Are you getting the picture? In his July 2016 article "The State of the American Church: When Numbers Point to a New Reality,"[7] American researcher and church missiologist Ed Stetzer refers to the end of the spectrum I've described thus far as cultural Christianity and casual Christianity. Cultural Christians believe themselves to be Christian "simply because their culture tells them they are. They are Christians by heritage."[8] That's the belief I held until December 1981. Casual Christians (or congregational Christians, another term Stetzer uses) "at least have some connection to congregational life. They have a home church they grew up in and perhaps where they were married. They might even visit occasionally."[9] Stetzer calls his third category convictional Christians because "they are actually living according to their faith."[10] I call this third group Christ-followers. Like the others, Christ-followers occupy several segments along the spectrum.

I suppose it depends on how wide a swath each group has on the spectrum, but I think there are more nuanced steps to consider before one gets to the group of Christians who are committedly engaged to following Christ, those who regard faith in Christ, with its beliefs and practices, as all-encompassing while recognizing the place for individual and community adherence to the law of the state as a reasonable part of citizenship.

When Jesus said the now-famous words found in John 3:16—*"For God so loved the world, that he gave his only Son, that whoever believes in him should not perish but have eternal life"*—He wasn't suggesting that believing in His existence was sufficient without believing in the truth of His message, and practising it. The truth of His message both enables a fresh start in life and requires it, so that we might follow Him. Have you ever played Simon Says? To stay in the game, you have to follow Simon's direction to the very word and demonstrate the actions of a Simon follower. To follow Jesus, He not only gives us a fresh start but also His Spirit to live with us for the one purpose of helping us follow our commitment to live as children of God (Romans 8:14–17).

---

7   Ed Stetzer, "The State of the American Church: When Numbers Point to a New Reality," *Evangelical Missions Quarterly*, Vol. 52, No. 3, July 2016, 230–237. Also available at https://emqonline.com/node/3520.

8   Ibid.

9   Ibid.

10   Ibid.

The claim made on my life by Jesus Christ is to my whole life, not just a part. My pastor, Jason Boucher, has expressed the following, based on a message spoken by Bruxy Cavey, Teaching Pastor at The Meeting House.[11] The gospel in one word is "Jesus." The gospel is the entire story of Jesus. When asked to consider the gospel in three words, the culture chooses "Jesus is love." This is true, but an incomplete and inadequate definition of the gospel. It only tells part of the story. The Bible tells the Church that the three-word answer is "Jesus is Lord." As Lord, He is the one who has the right to tell us how to live.

Those who think God desires only a few hours of our time on Sunday morning, when it's convenient for us, may need a rethink. The Christian worldview begins from relationship with Christ and sees all of life from His perspective, anchored in His Word, the Bible. To be in right and real relationship with Jesus Christ is to respond to His challenge of *us* loving *Him*, with *all* of who we are: our hearts, our souls, our minds, and our strength.[12]

"When Christ calls a man, he bids him come and die," wrote Dietrich Bonhoeffer.[13] To think of Jesus as Saviour—the ticket-to-heaven guy or simply the inherited God of Canadians—without acknowledging that He is Lord, the God who demands our all, is to accept a myth. Yes, Jesus paid the price for our sins, but not *only* for our sins. The true exchange to be made for accepting His grace—His all—is giving our lives, our all, to be lived for Him. Bonhoeffer explains further,

> Cheap grace is the grace we bestow on ourselves. Cheap grace is the preaching of forgiveness without requiring repentance, baptism without church discipline, Communion without confession... Cheap grace is grace without discipleship, grace without the cross, grace without Jesus Christ, living and incarnate.[14]

Jesus said, *"If anyone would come after me, let him deny himself and take up his cross daily and follow me. For whoever would save his life will lose it, but whoever loses his life for my sake will save it"* (Luke 9:23–24). This is what it means to follow Christ 24/7/365, not one morning a week. In Jesus' day, His challenge for people to take up their cross meant asking them to be willing to suffer public humiliation

---

11 Bruxy Cavey, *Bruxy.com*, "The Gospel in 1, 3 and 30 Words." August 23, 2012 (https://bruxy.com/2012/08/23/the-gospel-in-1-3-and-30-words/).

12 This is added to Matthew 22:37 in the parallel passage in Luke 10:27.

13 Bonhoeffer, *Cost of Discipleship*, 99.

14 Ibid., 47.

for their beliefs and be willing to die as an outcast from the culture in which they lived. That's what it meant to face the penalty of crucifixion, to be a cross carrier.

This stands in stark contrast to the claims made by the state that its laws hold full control over all of one's life—heart, soul, mind, and strength. A state that is willing to allocate space for our religious beliefs and practices, placing limits on that space based on its own interests, acts as if it is supreme. Likewise, a court that is supreme in the judicial system, interpreting and applying law, cannot hold the place of ultimate supremacy in the life of a Christ-follower.

When we are serious about our relationship with God, which requires our involvement in seeking the best for the world we live in, i.e. our neighbours, then the idea that the law would be permitted to set boundaries on our beliefs or practices will attract our attention and our effort to ensure that freedom is free, not just doublespeak for "you can have what we give you."

As Moses recorded, our God is a jealous God (Exodus 20:5, 34:14; Deuteronomy 4:24, 5:9, 6:15). Or as Story shared, the law is a jealous mistress. Or as Hale put it, "the law will admit of no rival."[15] There is bound to be tension between these two assertions of absolute comprehensive claim on human life.

People of the law—lawyers, judges, lawmakers, and fellow citizens—will seek to break religion, forcing its submission rather than accommodating its presence.

This is the experience of those in dozens of nations around the world where the law is not as generous toward religion as ours currently is. And we are trending in that less generous direction in Canada. Increasingly, government and social pressures reveal the creeping approach of non-inclusive secularism that regards religious beliefs and practices as inconvenient, or offensive. Some believe what they are doing is the right thing to do, that religion is dangerous and needs to be controlled, reshaped to fit our nation's shifting cultural values, or eliminated altogether. Others have less wholesome reasons for the same pursuit.

Are we, you and I, the Church in Canada, far enough along the spectrum of Christian commitment to be Christ-followers, cross-carriers, that we're prepared to stand firm in our faith? Are we prepared to perhaps one day be imprisoned for our faith, to die for our faith or risk living out our faith even if it is illegal to do so? These scenarios are the reality in dozens, leaning toward scores, of nations around the world.

On February 2015, twenty-one men in orange jumpsuits peacefully preferred beheading on a Mediterranean beach to compromising their belief in Jesus

---

15 Story, *The Miscellaneous Writings of Joseph Story,* 523.

Christ.[16] If you or I were accused of being a Christian, would there be enough evidence for a conviction?

It has not reached that point in Canada, and I pray it never does. Still, we need to be prepared in our relationship with Christ, and the nation in which we live, to stand publicly in our faith as witnesses to Him whom we live for. One key to that preparation is engaging fully our commitment to Christ, His Church, and His Word (the Bible). Another is being accurately aware of how Canadian courts are defining what the *Canadian Charter of Rights and Freedoms* refers to as the "fundamental freedom" of freedom of religion.

The next part of this book will summarize vital and relevant implications for the Canadian Church, and freedom of religion generally, resulting from a selection of significant decisions of Canadian courts following the enactment of the *Canadian Charter of Rights and Freedoms*. The third part of the book will consider how we should then engage our neighbours and our nation as Christ-followers in twenty-first-century Canada.

---

16 Jared Maslin, "Christians Mourn Their Relatives Beheaded by ISIS," *TIME Magazine* . February 23, 2015 (http://time.com/3718470/isis-copts-egypt/).

PART II:
RELIGIOUS FREEDOM AS INTERPRETED BY THE COURTS

You shall appoint judges and officers in all your towns that the Lord your God is giving you, according to your tribes, and they shall judge the people with righteous judgment. You shall not pervert justice. You shall not show partiality, and you shall not accept a bribe, for a bribe blinds the eyes of the wise and subverts the cause of the righteous. Justice, and only justice, you shall follow, that you may live and inherit the land that the Lord your God is giving you.
—Deuteronomy 16:18–20

Two tall statues stand next to the steps of the Supreme Court of Canada building: *Veritas* (Truth) to the west and *Ivstitia* (Justice) to the east. Misericordia (Mercy) does not stand outside, but remains part of the equitable jurisdiction of the Court, to make a decision that is fair even though it may not strictly conform with the law. The Minister of Justice has a similar "mercy power" under the Criminal Code in regard to applications alleging a miscarriage of justice.

The following commentary on the law is not intended as legal advice.

CHAPTER SEVEN

A FEW WORDS ABOUT THE *CHARTER*

But they shall sit every man under his vine and under his fig tree, and no one shall make them afraid, for the mouth of the Lord of hosts has spoken. For all the peoples walk each in the name of its god, but we will walk in the name of the Lord our God forever and ever.

—Micah 4:4–5

I am a Canadian, free to speak without fear, free to worship in my own way, free to stand for what I think right, free to oppose what I believe wrong, or free to choose those who shall govern my country. This heritage of freedom I pledge to uphold for myself and all mankind.

—John Diefenbaker
House of Commons Debate on
the Canadian Bill of Rights, July 1, 1960.

We now have a Charter which defines the kind of country in which we wish to live, and guarantees the basic rights and freedoms which each of us shall enjoy as a citizen of Canada.

—Pierre Elliott Trudeau
Remarks by the Prime Minister
at the Proclamation Ceremony on April 17, 1982.
Ottawa: Office of the Prime Minister, 1982.

THERE WAS A FRENZY AMONG CANADIANS TO GET THEIR HANDS ON A COPY OF THE *Canadian Charter of Rights and Freedoms* shortly after patriation of the constitution in 1982. In the early 1960s, when he was the chief engineer at the King Edward

Sheraton Hotel in Toronto, my dad received a copy of the *Canadian Bill of Rights*[1] from the hand of then Prime Minister John Diefenbaker. He safeguarded it until together we laminated it to a wooden frame when I was around twelve years old. Dad had been exploring the opening of a laminating business. We flew to Denver to check out the equipment and he brought the scroll with him. We laminated it together. He gave it to me. Nine years later, I entered law school. When I received a copy of the *Charter*, I kept it safely stored until I could laminate it in similar fashion.

Diefenbaker was justifiably proud of the *Canadian Bill of Rights*—often referred to as "Diefenbaker's bill of rights"—and he was also disappointed. As mentioned in Chapter Three, the first bill of rights in Canada had been passed by Tommy Douglas' government in Saskatchewan in 1947. Diefenbaker grew up in Saskatchewan. He was well aware of Douglas' efforts and the *Universal Declaration of Human Rights* proclaimed by the United Nations General Assembly in 1948. A champion of human rights himself, Diefenbaker campaigned for a constitutional bill of rights for over a decade. He expressed his campaign in the appointment of Canada's first female cabinet minister, Ellen Fairclough; in the appointment of Canada's first aboriginal senator, James Gladstone; and extending the vote to Canada's First Nations and Inuit peoples. Diefenbaker tried to establish a bill of rights as part of a package that would have brought Canada's constitution home. Negotiations with the provinces were unsuccessful, but his desire for a national bill of rights was not quieted.[2]

Passed by Parliament in 1960, the *Canadian Bill of Rights* was considered a quasi-constitutional document. As a federal statute, it had application only to areas of federal jurisdiction under the *Constitution Act, 1867*, in similar fashion to provincial human rights acts and codes being both quasi-constitutional and only applicable in the provincial jurisdiction in which they were passed.

It is in the preamble to the *Canadian Bill of Rights* that we find a precursor to the *Charter* preamble's recognition of "the supremacy of God" and "the rule of law":

> The Parliament of Canada, affirming that the Canadian Nation is *found-ed upon principles that acknowledge the supremacy of God*, the dignity and

---

1   *The Statutes of Canada*, 1960, Chapter 44.

2   John G. Diefenbaker, *One Canada: The Years of Achievement 1957–62* (Toronto, ON: MacMillan of Canada, 1976), 250–265.

worth of the human person and the position of the family in a society of free men and free institutions;

Affirming also that men and institutions remain free only when freedom is *founded upon* respect for moral and spiritual values and *the rule of law*;

And being desirous of enshrining these principles and the human rights and fundamental freedoms derived from them, in a Bill of Rights which shall reflect the respect of Parliament for its constitutional authority and which shall ensure the protection of these rights and freedoms in Canada...[3]

In Section 2 of the *Canadian Bill of Rights,* we find provision for Parliament to maintain ultimate responsibility for the law by declaration that a law may be operational "notwithstanding" the provisions of the *Canadian Bill of Rights*, another concept imported into the *Charter*:

2. Every law of Canada shall, unless it is expressly declared by an Act of the Parliament of Canada that it shall operate notwithstanding the *Canadian Bill of Rights*...

The "notwithstanding" authority was used only once prior to the *Charter* coming into force. Prime Minister Pierre Trudeau used it to declare operation of the *War Measures Act* in October 1970 to address the crisis resulting from the violent actions of the Front de libération du Québec (FLQ).

In Section 5 of the *Canadian Bill of Rights* is found the first hint of what in the *Charter* would become a more expansive equality rights provision, as well as recognition of any non-enumerated rights:

5. (1) Nothing in Part I shall be construed to abrogate or abridge any human right or fundamental freedom not enumerated therein that may have existed in Canada at the commencement of this Act...

Diefenbaker was ahead of Canada's time in this effort. However, his bill of rights would inform the efforts of future Prime Minister Pierre Trudeau. Trudeau would also find inspiration in the work of Canadian John Peters Humphrey, U.N. Director of the Division of Human Rights, who was called upon by U.N.

3   Emphasis added.

Secretary-General Tryve Lie to lead the project of drafting the *Universal Declaration of Human Rights*, acting as its principal drafter.[4] Trudeau had received his secondary school education at Collège Jean-de-Brébeuf, a Jesuit school, where he was introduced to the work of Catholic philosopher Jacques Maritain in regard to natural law and rights. Maritain was another of the drafters of the 1948 *Universal Declaration*, whose writings also influenced Trudeau's *Charter* efforts.[5]

Trudeau's first effort at patriating the constitution, including a bill of political rights, was the 1971 *Victoria Charter*, which failed when Quebec Premier Robert Bourassa ultimately objected to the proposal. The document had provided a veto on constitutional amendments for the federal government and Canada's two largest provinces, Ontario and Quebec. Bourassa exercised his province's veto.

The Quebec referendum of 1980 introduced a surge of nationalism that Trudeau would ride to constitutional patriation, including an enhanced bill of rights. In *Reference Re Resolution to amend the Constitution*,[6] the Supreme Court of Canada held that the federal government could seek patriation without provincial approval. However, the Court also held that there was an unwritten constitutional convention that required provincial consent to seek amendment of the constitution on matters that would affect the provinces. This triggered another round of constitutional negotiations, this time with two advantages: the participation of key figures who had been involved in the 1971 negotiations and the impetus of the national mood following the barely averted crisis occasioned by the Quebec referendum on independence. The new negotiations sought consensus but offered no veto privileges. In the end, all provinces except Quebec agreed to the text of the *Constitution Act, 1982*, including the *Canadian Charter of Rights and Freedoms*.[7] Quebec has its own *Charter of human rights and freedoms*, which the Supreme Court of Canada has interpreted in a manner consistent with the Canadian *Charter*.[8]

The *Canadian Charter of Rights and Freedoms* is comprised of a series of brief statements, negotiated with the intention of summarizing the recognized rights and freedoms of Canadians after 115 years of Canada's existence. There are a few

---

4 Johannes Morsink, *The Universal Declaration of Human Rights: Origins, Drafting and Intent* (Philadelphia, PA: University of Pennsylvania Press, 1999), 5–9.

5 Pierre Elliott Trudeau, *The Essential Trudeau*, ed. Ron Graham ed. (Toronto, ON: McClelland and Stewart, 1998), 5.

6 [1981] 1 SCR 753.

7 Appendix III contains the full text of the *Canadian Charter of Rights and Freedoms*.

8 Jean Chretien, "Bringing the Constitution Home" in Thomas S. Axworthy and Pierre Elliott Trudeau, eds., *Towards a Just Society: The Trudeau Years* (Markham, ON: Viking, Penguin Group, 1990).

details about the *Charter* that are important to note before considering decisions of the courts in regard to freedom of religion.

First, it is vital to note that the *Charter* applies between government—federal, provincial, municipal, school boards, and other agencies of government—and Canadians. The *Charter* does not guarantee rights or apply in regard to disputes between citizen and citizen, whether individual citizens or corporate citizens. A number of Canadians assert *Charter* rights in regard to their relationships with other Canadians or their treatment by corporate entities, situations where no such *Charter* rights exist. Civil rights—rights between citizens—remain the jurisdiction of the provinces under the *Constitution Act, 1867*. Section 32 of the *Charter* states the extent of its application:

> **32.** (1) This Charter applies
> (*a*) to the Parliament and government of Canada in respect of all
> matters within the authority of Parliament including all matters
> relating to the Yukon Territory and Northwest Territories; and
> (*b*) to the legislature and government of each province in respect of
> all matters within the authority of the legislature of each province.

Section 32 has been found by the Supreme Court of Canada to require human rights codes and acts, federal and provincial, to be interpreted in a manner that is consistent with the *Charter*.

Section 1 of the *Charter* establishes that no *Charter* right or freedom is absolute:

> 1. The *Canadian Charter of Rights and Freedoms* guarantees the
> rights and freedoms set out in it subject only to such reasonable
> limits prescribed by law as can be demonstrably justified in a free and
> democratic society.

The Supreme Court of Canada has settled on a theoretically objective test for assessing whether or not laws and regulations established by various levels of government and government authorized bodies are constitutionally acceptable "reasonable limits." To be reasonable, the initiative violating a right must be:

i   Prescribed by law
ii   Have a pressing and substantial purpose
iii   Be reasonable and demonstrably justified, i.e.

    i Rationally connected to the law's purpose, and

    ii Resulting in minimal impairment of the right

  iv And, finally, proportionate to attaining the intended effect.[9]

The first freedoms mentioned in the *Charter* are stated to be "fundamental." One would think this to be a reference to the essential, primary, and underlying freedoms of the nation as a free and democratic society. However, the Supreme Court of Canada has determined that there is, at least theoretically, no hierarchy of rights.

The first fundamental freedom listed is "freedom of conscience and religion"; however, the other fundamental freedoms listed in Section 2 of the *Charter* are relevant to religious practice, particularly expression, assembly, and association:

> **2.** Everyone has the following fundamental freedoms:
>
> (*a*) freedom of conscience and religion;
>
> (*b*) freedom of thought, belief, opinion and expression, including freedom of the press and other media of communication;
>
> (*c*) freedom of peaceful assembly; and
>
> (*d*) freedom of association.

In addition, the equality rights provisions of Section 15 explicitly include application in regard to discrimination based on religion:

> **15.** (1) Every individual is equal before and under the law and has the right to the equal protection and equal benefit of the law without discrimination and, in particular, without discrimination based on race, national or ethnic origin, colour, religion, sex, age or mental or physical disability.
>
> (2) Subsection (1) does not preclude any law, program or activity that has as its object the amelioration of conditions of disadvantaged individuals or groups including those that are disadvantaged because of race, national or ethnic origin, colour, religion, sex, age or mental or physical disability.

The Supreme Court of Canada has interpreted Section 15 of the *Charter*, which provides for equal protection and equal benefit of the law, as providing

---

9   *R. v. Oakes*, [1986] 1 SCR 103. A summary of the "Oakes test."

rights for analogous categories of rights to those specifically listed in the *Charter*. The interpretation of Section 15 in this way arises from the drafters' use of the words "in particular," which the Court determined to refer to examples of an open list rather than the statement of a closed list. Perhaps the most legally contentious recognition has been to grant an analogous right of equal treatment under the law without discrimination on the basis of sexual orientation, which has produced a competing right with certain religious beliefs and practices and has been the subject of many court cases.

The Court has determined this approach to be consistent with Section 26:

> **26.** The guarantee in this Charter of certain rights and freedoms shall not be construed as denying the existence of any other rights or freedoms that exist in Canada.

As noted earlier, in Chapter Four, the Supreme Court has described the constitution as a "living tree" that changes with the times and shifting Canadian values, rejecting the concept that the *Charter* was designed to capture and hold the existing record of foundational democratic freedoms established in the first 115 years of the Canadian legal system, anchored in the prior constitutional principles on which those freedoms were established.

Another note of *Charter* interpretation is found in Section 27:

> **27.** This Charter shall be interpreted in a manner consistent with the preservation and enhancement of the multicultural heritage of Canadians.

I mention Section 27 in the context of religious freedom because Canada's multicultural heritage and continuing immigration results in a multi-religious heritage.

Section 33 is the "notwithstanding clause" that was included at the insistence of provincial negotiators in order to retain the governmental supremacy of legislative bodies over the courts:

> **33.** (1) Parliament or the legislature of a province may expressly declare in an Act of Parliament or of the legislature, as the case may be, that the Act or a provision thereof shall operate notwithstanding a provision included in section 2 or sections 7 to 15 of this Charter.

(2) An Act or a provision of an Act in respect of which a declaration made under this section is in effect shall have such operation as it would have but for the provision of this Charter referred to in the declaration.

(3) A declaration made under subsection (1) shall cease to have effect five years after it comes into force or on such earlier date as may be specified in the declaration.

(4) Parliament or the legislature of a province may re-enact a declaration made under subsection (1).

(5) Subsection (3) applies in respect of a re-enactment made under subsection (4).

Constitutionally, Canada remains a parliamentary democracy; however, since 1982 increasing deference has been paid to the courts, particularly the Supreme Court of Canada. As a result, Canada is often referred to as a constitutional democracy, i.e. the constitution is supreme over Parliament and the legislatures. On one level, even noting parliamentary supremacy as a constitutional provision makes the reference to a constitutional democracy appropriate. Also, Section 52 of the *Constitution Act, 1982* notes:

52. (1) The Constitution of Canada is the supreme law of Canada, and any law that is inconsistent with the provisions of the Constitution is, to the extent of the inconsistency, of no force or effect...

That brings us to the *Charter*'s preamble:

Whereas Canada is founded upon principles that recognize the supremacy of God and the rule of law...

The preamble to legislation establishes the framework in which the provisions of a statute or constitutional provision, such as the *Charter*, was developed. It establishes the narrative for the legal or constitutional provisions, but it is not in itself part of the legal or constitutional consideration that follows. A preamble may be helpful in identifying the context for consideration of the provisions that follow, including any issues intended to be addressed by the legislation.

The *Charter*'s preamble could easily have been interpreted as respecting the biblical equality of all people made in the image of God, *imago Dei*, the natural law provision of human rights and the rule of law provision of human rights, both judicial and legislative. However, the context of interpretation in contemporary courts is an environment that prefers the "rule of law" alone. The Court has avoided reference to the principles that would be occasioned by considering contemporary recognition of the supremacy of God *and* the rule of law, preferring to reflect on Canadian values. Principles are unchanging. Values shift with culture.

The preamble to the *Charter*, particularly the reference to the supremacy of God, was largely buried by the courts until the 2002 decision of the Supreme Court in *Chamberlain v. Surrey School District No. 36*.[10] In *Chamberlain*, the Court defined the concept of a secular society as one that embraces the non-religious and the religious people in its midst in all aspects of life, including the public square, concluding that "everyone has 'belief' or 'faith' in something, be it atheistic, agnostic or religious."

Some object to any influence being given to this concept (a secular society being inclusive of both non-religious and religious aspects), which was expounded upon in the dissent written by Justice Charles Gonthier. However, Chief Justice Beverly McLachlin, in her decision on behalf of the majority, noted agreement with him on this and other points:

Chamberlain v. Surrey School District, SCC 2002—A kindergarten teacher wanted to use children's books about same-sex parents. To avoid controversy with religious parents, the school board refused. The Court sent the decision back to the school board with instruction to reconsider based on tolerance and non-religious assessment.

> My colleague, Gonthier J., and I, while differing in the result, agree on many points in this appeal:
> ...that the requirement of secularism laid out in s.76 does not prevent religious concerns from being among those matters of local and parental concern that influence educational policy...[11]

Let me then give the final words of this chapter to Justice Gonthier. These words from his decision in *Chamberlain* are among my favourite:

> ...nothing in the *Charter*, political or democratic theory, or a proper understanding of pluralism demands that atheistically based moral

---

10   2002 SCC 86, [2002] 4 SCR 710.

11   Ibid., Paragraph 3.

positions trump religiously based moral positions on matters of public policy. I note that the preamble to the Charter itself establishes that "… Canada is founded upon principles that recognize the supremacy of God and the rule of law." According to Saunders J. [of the British Columbia Supreme Court where the case was heard at trial], if one's moral view manifests from a religiously grounded faith, it is not to be heard in the public square, but if it does not, then it is publicly acceptable. The problem with this approach is that everyone has "belief" or "faith" in something, be it atheistic, agnostic or religious. To construe "secular" as the realm of the 'unbelief' is therefore erroneous. Given this, why, then, should the religiously informed conscience be placed at public disadvantage or disqualification? To do so would be to distort liberal principles in an illiberal fashion and would provide only a feeble notion of pluralism. The key is that people will disagree about important issues, and such disagreement, where it does not imperil community living, must be capable of being accommodated at the core of modern pluralism.[12]

---

12 Ibid., Paragraph 137.

CHAPTER EIGHT

THE GOVERNMENT CAN SERVE MONEY, BUT NOT GOD

*Do not lay up for yourselves treasures on earth, where moth and rust destroy and
where thieves break in and steal, but lay up for yourselves treasures in heaven,
where neither moth nor rust destroys and where thieves do not break in and steal.
For where your treasure is, there your heart will be also... No one can serve two
masters, for either he will hate the one and love the other, or he will be devoted to
the one and despise the other. You cannot serve God and money.*

—Matthew 6:19–21, 24

I arrived back at UBC in September 1986 for my second year of law school.
The four-year break in my attendance meant I was required to take a course on the
Canadian Charter of Rights and Freedoms, which had become part of our constitution
the day following my final exam of first year law. UBC's first year Constitutional
Law course had been radically overhauled in light of the *Charter*, even though
there wasn't much to work with in terms of Supreme Court of Canada decisions
interpreting its various provisions. I consider myself fortunate to have studied
constitutional law in the pre-*Charter* era; the policy and governance components
of our constitution have been eclipsed in the minds of too many lawyers by the
focus on *Charter* rights. Canada is not a nation of individuals in silos, asserting
their rights. Like the Church, the state exists through the engagement of individuals making contributions to the life of the nation. Even with individual rights
enshrined in the constitution, there are national interests of greater importance
than individual happiness.

Full credit must be given to law professor Lynn Smith, who was soon to
become Dean and is best known today as the B.C. trial court judge in the *Carter*

v. Canada[1] case on physician-assisted suicide. Smith assembled a binder of trial court and appeal court decisions from across the country, along with the few Supreme Court of Canada decisions then available. That resource would become the framework in which we would study the courts' interpretation of the rights which, in legal time, had only recently been enshrined in the constitution. It can take years for a case to reach the courtroom, another year or more to get to the court of appeal, and then a similarly long wait to be heard by the Supreme Court, all of which have intervals of six to eighteen months for a decision to be researched, written, and released.

I distinctly remember receiving three-hole-punched mimeographed pages as the course progressed. These were then inserted into the binder as the Supreme Court issued decisions on cases for which we had only appeal court decisions at the beginning of the course. And likewise, appeal court decisions were clicked into the binder behind trial court rulings. This was the era of dial-up modems for location-to-location computer connection. There was no internet. There were no search engines or databases. Notebooks contained lined paper, and pens were required if one was going to take notes. Professor Smith did a terrific job of staying on top of decisions as they were released and getting copies faxed or couriered into her hands, then mimeographed (a now seemingly ancient substitute for photocopying) for her students.

One of the cases for which the class had both court of appeal and Supreme Court of Canada decisions for our analysis was the 1985 decision in *R. v. Big M Drug Mart Ltd.*,[2] a case dealing with Section 2(a) of the *Charter*: freedom of religion. Unexpectedly, after we had discussed *Big M*, a second freedom of religion decision arrived from the Supreme Court just before Christmas. The decision in *R. v. Edwards Books and Arts Ltd.*[3] was issued on Thursday, December 18, 1986. The next day we would click it into our binders (there was no computer mouse clicking in that classroom, although UBC and Queen's were the only two law schools in the country to have computer labs at the time), able to take it home to read over Christmas break. This was a unique opportunity to consider the Court's reasoning on the same *Charter* provision after twenty months of feedback from outside the Court. The second case was argued nearly a year after

---

1   Trial decision from Smith J of the Supreme Court of British Columbia (2012 BCSC 886), overturned on appeal at the British Columbia Court of Appeal (2013 BCCA 435), and then appealed to the Supreme Court of Canada (2015 SCC 5, [2015] 1 SCR 331).

2   [1985] 1 SCR 295.

3   [1986] 2 SCR 713.

the first decision had been issued, and just days after the Court had released the decision in *R. v. Oakes*[4] that established the four-part test for the constitutional legitimacy of a law under Section 1 of the *Charter* (see Chapter Seven). For a second-year law student, this was pretty exciting stuff!

One of the first things I noticed in *Big M* and *Edwards Books* was the intervention at the Supreme Court by the Seventh Day Adventist Church. Adventists around the world have encountered many challenges to their own religious freedom and developed a strong foundation for the pursuit of religious liberty for all, not just for themselves. At first, their presence as interveners seemed natural since both cases dealt with Sunday closing laws and the Adventists are Saturday sabbath practitioners. But as I read the cases and realized how influential the decisions were for religious practice in Canada, I was curious as to why no other religious organizations had intervened before the Court. The Church had left the guardianship of our beliefs and practices in the hands of government—the federal government and three provinces in *Big M*; the federal government and all provinces but Prince Edward Island in *Edwards Books*—and a small nonconforming denomination that practised a Saturday sabbath. This would change in later cases as the broader Canadian Church became alert to the importance and impact of Supreme Court decisions on both Canadian life and religious practice. I would have the privilege of participating several times before the Court as a result.

Seven justices heard each case at the Supreme Court; five of them heard both.

At the start of each hearing before the Supreme Court, everyone in the courtroom is required to rise. A set of double doors are opened behind the bench and the court attendant announces, "The Court." This is the remnant of a tradition from a period when the Queen (or King) was the highest court and all would stand in reverence as she entered the room where she was "holding court," now simply the courtroom. After the justices enter, the court attendant closes the doors behind them without entering.

Canadians, whether they have read it or not, increasingly place their faith in the *Charter*. To do so is to also place one's hope in the institution that interprets it, just as the priests of old used to interpret the Bible for the people, the Book not being available in the common language of the day.

---

4   [1986] 1 SCR 103.

We will now begin to look at a contemporary understanding of Canada's freedom of religion, as interpreted by the most venerated judges in the land.[5]

R. v. Big M Drug Mart Ltd.

Between the hearing at the Court and the written decision in *Big M* being released, Chief Justice Bora Laskin died. The appointment of Brian Dickson as Chief Justice would signal the transition from a Court with a federalist outlook, deferent to Parliament, to a Court interpreting the *Charter* with its eye toward supremacy of the constitution and rights over legislatures.

Big M established the foundation and legal themes for freedom of religion in Canada that continue to underlie every decision on the subject to this day. In its decision, the Supreme Court would also establish the framework for the comments made by Chief Justice McLachlin found in Chapter Six.

The *Lord's Day Act* was federal legislation that established a nationwide Sunday sabbath. It had previously been unsuccessfully challenged on jurisdictional grounds under the separation of powers between Canada and the provinces under the *Constitution Act, 1867*, and was upheld as a valid exercise of the federal authority to enact criminal law.

R. v. Big M Drug Mart, SCC 1985—A Calgary drug store wanted to open on Sundays, in violation of the federal *Lord's Day Act*. The Court ruled the *Act* was unconstitutional because it had a religious purpose.

In *Big M*, the Alberta Court of Appeal split 3–2, striking down the legislation as being in violation of the *Charter*. The majority considered Canadian law and texts almost exclusively, noting two U.S. decisions in support of striking down the law. Writing in dissent, Justice Belzil referenced European and United Nations documents' freedom of religion provisions before stating, with insight into the minds of the *Charter*'s framers and foresight concerning future consequences of the court's proposed actions:

---

5   As we begin to look at some court decisions, please note that over the decades the style of reporting has changed from pages-only to numbered paragraphs. Some of the decisions that were released in pages-only format have been numbered in their electronic form. Decisions of the Supreme Court of Canada may be found in hard copy using the citations footnoted or by searching the Judgements of the Supreme Court of Canada website (http://scc-csc. lexum.com).

113. I do not believe that the political sponsors of the *Charter* intended to confer upon the courts the task of stripping away all vestiges of those values and traditions [the Christian influences on Western democracy he had referenced in paragraph 112], and the courts should be most loathe to assume that role. With the *Lord's Day Act* eliminated, will not all reference in the statutes to Christmas, Easter, or Thanksgiving be next? What of the use of the Gregorian Calendar? Such interpretation would make of the *Charter* an instrument for the repression of the majority at the instance of every dissident and result in an amorphous, rootless and Godless nation contrary to the recognition of the Supremacy of God declared in the preamble. The "living tree" will wither if planted in sterilized soil.[6]

On to the Supreme Court of Canada and the majority decision written by (Chief) Justice Dickson.

First, the Court noted that in challenging the constitutionality of a law, rights under the *Charter* could be asserted by both individual persons and corporate persons, i.e. Big M Drug Mart Ltd. could legitimately claim a constitutional freedom.[7] The Court was not required to decide, and did not decide in this case, whether a corporate person could exercise religious belief or practice.

Second, the Court stated that Section 52 of the *Constitution Act, 1982* set out "the fundamental principle of constitutional law that the Constitution is supreme."[8]

In striking down the law for being an enactment with a religious purpose, the court offered a robust consideration of freedom of religion under the *Charter*:

94. A truly free society is one which can accommodate a wide variety of beliefs, diversity of tastes and pursuits, customs and codes of conduct. A free society is one which aims at equality with respect to the enjoyment of fundamental freedoms and I say this without any reliance upon s. 15 of the *Charter*. Freedom must surely be founded in respect for the inherent dignity and the inviolable rights of the human person. **The essence of the concept of freedom of religion is the right to entertain such religious beliefs as a person chooses, the right to**

---

6   R. v. Big M. Drug Mart Ltd., 1983 ABCA 268 (CanLII), Paragraph 113.

7   *Big M*, SCC, Paragraph 37.

8   Ibid., Paragraph 38.

declare religious beliefs openly and without fear of hindrance or reprisal, and the right to manifest religious belief by worship and practice or by teaching and dissemination. But the concept means more than that.

95. Freedom can primarily be characterized by the absence of coercion or constraint. If a person is compelled by the state or the will of another to a course of action or inaction which he would not otherwise have chosen, he is not acting of his own volition and he cannot be said to be truly free. One of the major purposes of the *Charter* is to protect, within reason, from compulsion or restraint. Coercion includes not only such blatant forms of compulsion as direct commands to act or refrain from acting on pain of sanction, coercion includes indirect forms of control which determine or limit alternative courses of conduct available to others. Freedom in a broad sense embraces both the absence of coercion and constraint, and the right to manifest beliefs and practices. Freedom means that, subject to such limitations as are necessary to protect public safety, order, health, or morals or the fundamental rights and freedoms of others, no one is to be forced to act in a way contrary to his beliefs or his conscience.

96. What may appear good and true to a majoritarian religious group, or to the state acting at their behest, may not, for religious reasons, be imposed upon citizens who take a contrary view. The *Charter* safeguards religious minorities from the threat of "the tyranny of the majority".[9]

This robust definition of religious freedom is balanced with the conclusion found later:

123. ...The values that underlie our political and philosophic traditions demand that every individual be free to hold and to manifest whatever beliefs and opinions his or her conscience dictates, **provided *inter alia* only that such manifestations do not injure his or her neighbours or their parallel rights to hold and manifest beliefs and opinions of their own...**[10]

---

9   Ibid., Paragraphs 94–96. Emphasis added.

10   Ibid., Paragraph 123. Emphasis added.

I have emphasized in **bold** the crucial summary of religious freedom that has held in Canada going forward from this decision: the right to religious belief, practice, instruction, and sharing with others provided there is no "injury" to the parallel rights of one's neighbours. The concept of "injury" or "harm" is a legally fluid one that still features prominently in efforts of the courts to arrive at a definition.

The initial part of the Court's definition is similar to the wording of Article 18 of the United Nations' *Universal Declaration of Human Rights*, which has invited much international law conversation into the continuing Canadian courtroom dialogue on freedom of religion:

> Everyone has the right to freedom of thought, conscience and religion; this right includes freedom to change his religion or belief, and freedom, either alone or in community with others and in public or private, to manifest his religion or belief in teaching, practice, worship and observance.

R. v. Edwards Books and Arts Ltd.

Edwards Books presented a similar scenario with a variation on the facts. Several retailers had been charged under Ontario's *Retail Business Holidays Act*, which noted the observance of several specific holidays—some traditionally recognized as Christian holy days—and Sundays.

In making its analysis, the Court summarized and referenced parts of the decision in *Big M*, and gave more space to the consideration of American case law on a similar point.

The Supreme Court of Canada agreed with the Ontario Court of Appeal (where the case was referred to by the name of one of the other businesses, *R. v. Videoflicks Ltd.*[11]) that the legislation did not have a religious purpose, "providing uniform holidays to retail employees,"[12] although the dates selected had religious origins. The Court then proceeded to consider the effect of the legislation as distinct from its purpose. In that regard, particular attention was paid to the sentence in *Big M*, in regard to coercion, which

> *R. v. Edwards Books*, SCC 1986— Several Toronto stores wanted to open on Sundays, in violation of Ontario's *Retail Business Holidays Act*. The Court ruled the *Act* had a legitimate secular purpose in providing a uniform holiday for retail workers.

---

11 1984 CanLII 44 (ON CA).

12 *Edwards Books*, Paragraph 62.

I have underlined above at Paragraph 95 of the *Big M* decision. This led to the conclusion that the *Retail Business Holidays Act* occasioned unintentional or indirect coercion on the retailers before the court. The Supreme Court then stated:

> 97. This does not mean, however, that every burden on religious practices is offensive to the constitutional guarantee of freedom of religion. It means only that indirect or unintentional burdens will not be held to be outside the scope of *Charter* protection on that account alone. Section 2 (*a*) does not require the legislatures to eliminate every miniscule stateimposed cost associated with the practice of religion... The purpose of s. 2 (*a*) is to ensure that society does not interfere with profoundly personal beliefs that govern one's perception of oneself, humankind, nature, and, in some cases, a higher or different order of being. These beliefs, in turn, govern one's conduct and practices. The Constitution shelters individuals and groups only to the extent that religious beliefs or conduct might reasonably or actually be threatened. In short, legislative or administrative action which increases the cost of practising or otherwise manifesting religious beliefs is not prohibited if the burden is trivial or insubstantial...[13]

And further:

> 99. In *Big M Drug Mart Ltd.* this Court acknowledged that freedom of conscience and religion included the freedom to express and manifest religious nonbelief and the freedom to refuse to participate in religious practice. These freedoms, which may compendiously be referred to as the freedom from conformity to religious dogma, are governed by somewhat different considerations than the freedom to manifest one's own religious beliefs. Religious freedom is inevitably abridged by legislation which has the effect of impeding conduct integral to the practice of a person's religion. But it is not necessarily impaired by legislation which requires conduct consistent with the religious beliefs of another person. One is not being compelled to engage in religious practices merely because a statutory obligation coincides with the dictates of a particular religion. I cannot accept, for example, that a legislative prohibition of criminal conduct such as theft and murder is a stateenforced

---

13 Ibid., Paragraph 97.

compulsion to conform to religious practices, merely because some religions enjoin their members not to steal or kill. Reasonable citizens do not perceive the legislation as requiring them to pay homage to religious doctrine.[14]

In what might easily be passed over in the context of the decision is this statement, affirmed by the majority, which is critical to religious belief and practice:

145. In this context, I note that freedom of religion, perhaps unlike freedom of conscience, has both individual and collective aspects.[15]

Also:

153. (3) I have no hesitation in remarking that a business corporation cannot possess religious beliefs... A more difficult question is whether a corporate entity ought to be deemed in certain circumstances to possess the religious values of specified natural persons. If so, should the religion of the directors or shareholders or even employees be adopted as the appropriate test? What if there is a divergence of religious beliefs within the corporation?

The remedy granted to Nortown Foods Ltd. by the Ontario Court of Appeal implies answers to the above questions upon which I wish to express no further opinion in the present appeals.[16]

The remedy granted by the Ontario Court of Appeal to Nortown Foods, a small business owned and operated by a Jewish family that was closed on Saturdays and a party in this same case, was:

Nortown Foods Ltd.—appeal allowed and conviction quashed on the basis that, with respect to this appellant, s. 2 of the *Act* is of no force and effect because of inconsistency with s. 2(a) of the *Charter*.[17]

---

14   Ibid., Paragraph 99.
15   Ibid., Paragraph 145.
16   Ibid., Paragraph 153.
17   *Videoflicks*, decision of Tarnopolsky JA, "Summary of Dispositions of Appeals." Date of access: January 23, 2017 (https://www.canlii.org/en/on/onca/doc/1984/1984canlii44/1984canlii44.html).

While the legislation was found to infringe the freedom of religion of Saturday sabbath-observing retailers (reference was made to Wednesday-observing Hindus and Friday-observing Muslims, but their interests were not before the Court so were not ruled upon), the infringement was found to be justifiable under Section 1 of the *Charter*. The Sunday-closing requirement was removed from the *Act* by the Legislative Assembly of Ontario in 1992 by the NDP government of Premier Bob Rae.

In summary,

1. The government may not legislate for a religious purpose.
2. The right to religious belief, worship, practice, instruction, and dissemination is robust, but is limited at the point of "injury" to another's parallel right or where infringement by state action is minimal.
3. Freedom of religion has both individual and collective aspects.
4. A properly constituted and operated corporate entity may be identified with the religious values of specified, key natural persons.
5. Canada is a Christian-influenced country but not a Christian country.

CHAPTER NINE

WHEN STATE NEUTRALITY ISN'T NEUTRAL

So Pilate, wishing to satisfy the crowd, released for them Barabbas, and having scourged Jesus, he delivered him to be crucified.

—Mark 15:15

What shall we do with these men? For that a notable sign has been performed through them is evident to all the inhabitants of Jerusalem, and we cannot deny it. But in order that it may spread no further among the people, let us warn them to speak no more to anyone in this [Jesus'] name.

—Acts 4:16–17

For we did not follow cleverly devised myths when we made known to you the power and coming of our Lord Jesus Christ, but we were eyewitnesses of his majesty.

—2 Peter 1:16

ONE OF THE THOUGHTS PROVOKED BY THE DECISIONS IN *BIG M* AND *EDWARDS BOOKS* was that the *Charter* right to freedom *of* religion was being interpreted in a way that spoke more to freedom *from* religion. This concern was set in the context of a Western society in which Bonhoeffer well summarized, "God is being increasingly edged out of the world now that it has come of age. Knowledge and life are thought to be perfectly possible without him."[1] Canada's traditional church denominations were beginning to resemble an expression of Christianity that was unmooring itself from biblical foundations in search of the social relevance architecture recommended by Berton, someone who had himself rejected and left the Church.

---

1   Dietrich Bonhoeffer, *Letters and Papers from Prison* (London, UK: SCM Press Ltd, 1953). From a letter written on June 30, 1944.

Parallel in time, the "moral majority" movement in the United States came of age politically in the 1980s. The movement was led by a brand of evangelical Christians who shared a theology with their Canadian cousins but had become politically aggressive.

Those Canadian evangelical cousins were also transitioning in their attitude toward politics, where the traditional or mainline denominations had long been active. However, as Marci McDonald concluded after her research into evangelical political influence for her 2010 book *The Armageddon Factor*, "the Canadian evangelical community defies every attempt to stereotype it."[2] Influence there was, but it was not monolithic or supportive of a single party. Nor was it anything more than influence.

Brian Stiller, in his book *Jesus and Caesar: Christians in the Public Square*, briefly describes some key factors in the political conversion of Canadian evangelicals. Across evangelical denominations, conversing together in The Evangelical Fellowship of Canada (EFC) which was founded in 1964, notice was taken of the political adjustments occurring in Canada. The evangelical community had contributed significantly to the political life of several countries, including Canada, in the nineteenth century. In the early part of the twentieth century it had withdrawn, shifting focus almost single-mindedly to evangelism. This, Stiller notes, was occasioned by their rejection of an increasingly accepted liberal theology in Protestantism generally that emerged in the early twentieth century. This liberal theology led to church expression that no longer saw the Bible as inerrant, pursuing biblically based solutions to social ills through government more than through Church.[3]

By the 1960s, the sheer numbers of evangelical Christians in Canada—today still statistically in the neighbourhood of twelve percent of the Canadian population, over four million in number (see Chapter Twenty-Three)—and globally had created a situation where the question of societal engagement in addition to evangelism again became an important consideration, particularly as government "more and more viewed itself as an instrument not only to protect its people but to manage society."[4] We will discuss this phenomenon more in Chapter Fifteen.

---

2   Marci McDonald, *The Armageddon Factor: The Rise of Christian Nationalism in Canada* (Toronto, ON: Random House Canada, 2010), 9.

3   Brian Stiller, *Jesus and Caesar: Christians in the Public Square* (Oakville, ON: Castle Quay Books Canada, 2003), 29–30. See also: Debra Fieguth, *The Evangelical Fellowship of Canada*, "The EFC Holds True to Its Roots." Date of access: January 9, 2017 (http://www.evangelicalfellowship.ca/page.aspx?pid=286).

4   Ibid., 31.

Stiller stated, "There is a danger, for those living in a country with a strong Christian heritage, to sit back and let others lead."[5]

In 1983, around the same time Gloria and I moved to Port Simpson to pastor our first congregation as a married couple, Brian Stiller also shifted from leading Youth for Christ Canada to take on new responsibilities as president of the EFC, a position he held until 1997. In the midst of building a relational organization to serve the multidenominational evangelical Christian community, Stiller found necessity laid upon him (1 Corinthians 9:16) to find new ways to get Canadian evangelicals to engage the political world because of the impact of *Charter* decisions by the courts and the increasing role of government. Stiller was particularly concerned that the Church needed to counter the influence of advancing secularization, "a powerful and absorbing current,"[6] which he saw pushing faith out of public life, and in some cases even pushing it out of the hearts of citizens.

Noting the combined failure of the Supreme Court to uphold the standard of protecting all human life in striking Canada's abortion law and the subsequent failure of *Charter*-aligned abortion legislation on a final reading tie-vote in the Senate in 1991, among other compelling events, Stiller encouraged evangelicals to engage with government. He also noted the decisions of senior Canadian courts in cases dealing with the question of state neutrality in regard to religion, which seemed to follow in the freedom *from* religion disposition.

As did many Canadians of my vintage, I first recall learning the Lord's Prayer in public school:

> *Our Father which art in heaven, Hallowed be thy name. Thy kingdom come,*
> *Thy will be done in earth, as it is in heaven. Give us this day our daily bread.*
> *And forgive us our debts, as we forgive our debtors. And lead us not into tempta-*
> *tion, but deliver us from evil: For thine is the kingdom, and the power, and the*
> *glory, for ever. Amen.*
>
> —Matthew 6:9–13, KJV

Each morning we sang "God Save the Queen"[7] and recited the Lord's Prayer. This was a vestige from the days when the public schools were Protestant,

---

5   Ibid., 35.

6   Ibid., 27.

7   "God Save the Queen" was Canada's national anthem until the *National Anthem Act* was passed in 1980, making "O Canada" the daily song for opening exercises in schools across the land.

established and operated by the Church. I didn't attend church, and still didn't find anything disconcerting about this rote exercise. Neither did my mother.

Because of the recognition of freedoms secured by Jehovah's Witnesses, students who did not either sing the anthem or say the prayer left the classroom and stood in the hallway. No one at my school really thought anything of it, but some parents in Sudbury, Ontario did. Their children either uncomfortably remained in class, because their parents didn't want them to be singled out, or they stood in the hallway, apparently suspecting that their peers were talking behind their backs. These parents challenged the daily Christian religious practice of reciting the Lord's Prayer in state-funded non-religious public schools.

In *Zylberberg v. Sudbury Board of Education*,[8] Ontario's Court of Appeal concluded in 1988 that this requirement under Ontario's *Education Act* had a religious purpose, imposing Christian observance on non-believers and those of other faiths. The court struck down the relevant regulations. The practice of saying the Lord's Prayer was discontinued in Ontario's public schools, a discontinuance that rippled across the country. The decision in *Zylberberg* was followed the next year in a decision of the British Columbia Supreme Court, *Russow v. British Columbia*,[9] and a few years later by the Court of Queen's Bench in Manitoba in *Manitoba Association for Rights and Liberties v. Manitoba*.[10]

> *Zylberberg v. Sudbury Board of Ed.*, ON CA 1988—Parents challenged mandatory Christian religious exercises at the start of each school day in public schools. Ontario's Court of Appeal ruled that mandatory exercises in secular schools violated religious freedom.

In 1990, in *Canadian Civil Liberties Association v. Ontario Minister of Education* (often referred to as the *Elgin County* case),[11] Ontario's Court of Appeal struck down as indoctrination into the Christian faith the requirement for instruction in religious studies that contained only Christian content. Again, students could be excused from the classes at parents' request, but some parents considered that such excusal might or did stigmatize their children.

While many parents were upset by these decisions, the courts were right. Under Canada's constitution, the state has an obligation to remain neutral in regard to religion. The exceptions to that neutrality, particularly in regard to education,

---

8   (1988), 52 DLR (4th) 577.

9   (1989), 35 B.C.L.R. (2d) 29.

10   (1992), 82 M.R. (2d) 39.

11   (1990) 71 O.R. (2d) 341.

were specifically stated in the Canadian constitution (with some of those exceptions amended out of the constitution over time).

In the *Elgin County* case, Ontario's Court of Appeal set out guidelines for non-indoctrinational instruction on religion and moral values, but these were largely ignored by government. Instead, the Ontario Ministry of Education issued *Policy Memorandum 112/1991*, which ordered public schools to remove from the classroom all religious education and instruction that promoted one religious faith.

A significant and unfortunate side effect has been a misinterpretation of the courts' decisions, resulting in Christian groups that met for Bible study and prayer being denied use of classroom space, teacher sponsors, or

> *Elgin County*, ON CA 1990—Parents objected to mandatory Christian religious studies classes. Ontario's Court of Appeal ruled indoctrination in one religion in secular schools violated religious freedom.

official club status in Ontario schools. This is not what the courts decided. But there was (and remains) a "litigation chill" that causes many principals to fear the possibility of being sued if they allow religious behaviour, particularly Christian, on school campuses. We will look at the classroom in Chapter Sixteen, but for now let's grasp the point that in Canada it is not the place of the state to favour one religion over another or to engage in indoctrination on behalf of one religion.

The trends evidenced in these decisions contributed to the EFC's motivation to establish an office in Ottawa, which was done in 1996. Stiller states, "We realized that if we wanted to have a voice at the table, we had to be there early in the conversation."[12] The EFC established a variety of partnerships, both within the evangelical community (with taskforces and commissions to identify a denominational consensus on social issues for the EFC's engagement) and outside the evangelical community (with like-minded organizations from the Canadian Council of Churches and Canadian Conference of Catholic Bishops to multi-faith conversations and coalitions), to assert afresh influence in the Canadian public square. Partnership with Catholics was particularly important for three reasons. First, there is much alignment between Catholic and evangelical theological perspectives on a number of social issues. Second, Roman Catholics comprise the largest Christian denomination in the country, and when combined with evangelical numbers a majority of Canadians. Third, the defeat of the abortion bill was partially attributable to its opposition by the lay Catholic organization Campaign Life Coalition (CLC), whose leaders objected that the

---

12 McDonald, *Armageddon Factor*, 50.

legislation proposed inadequate protection for children in the womb. The CLC continues its principled and uncompromising public policy campaigns to this day. The political environment is not always welcoming of positions that don't allow for incremental movement on policy. Canada remains without any law limiting abortion prior to the moment of complete birth when the child fully emerges from the mother's body.

Evangelicals, other Christians, and other people of faith were entering a new public-square style of expression, being encouraged to again become citizen participants, without checking their faith at the door on their way into the public dialogue.

The principles of state neutrality were more recently addressed by the Supreme Court in its decisions in *S.L. v. Commission scolaire des Chênes*[13] and *Loyola High School v. Quebec (Attorney General)*.[14] In both of these cases, the EFC brought its arguments to bear as an intervener and I was privileged to participate. Interveners in court cases are participants who have relevant legal concerns to present to assist the court in making its decision and who are not actually parties to the case before the court. Interveners apply to the court in advance with an outline of their presentation, and the court assesses whether their contribution might be helpful.

Both cases concern themselves with the Quebec Ministry of Education's decision to promote "the development of attitudes of tolerance, respect and openness" in students, thus "preparing them to live in pluralist and democratic society"[15] through mandatory instruction on religion, culture, and ethics (referred to as the ERC course). Starting in 2008, all schools would be required to teach the ERC course, which was theoretically neutral instruction, although the nature of that neutrality was determined by the Quebec Ministry of Education.

S.L. v. Commission scolaire des Chênes

In *S.L.*, parents (who were required to use initials to protect the identities of their children) requested that their children be exempt from participation in the ERC course in accordance with Ministry of Education guidelines. The parents were concerned because the outline for the course indicated that instruction on

---

13 [2012] 1 SCR 235

14 [2015] 1 SCR 613.

15 Quebec Education Program, Secondary Education, "Ethics and Religious Culture Program," May 2008, Loisir et Sport Québec, Preamble.

their religious beliefs would be put on par with instruction of other religions, including the mythologies of the ancient Greeks and Romans. In essence, all religion and mythology would be presented as equal. They asserted that this would be confusing for their children. The request for exemption was turned down by the school, as was every similar request made in the province of Quebec.

You may recall from Chapter Eight that the robust definition of freedom of religion is limited by concern for "injury" or "harm" to one's neighbour's rights, a concept which the Supreme Court continues to debate. In this case, the parents initiated their challenge before the course was actually being taught and the Court decided the parents had not presented adequate evidence that the course would harm/injure their ability to pass on their faith to their children. In essence, the Court issued a kind of non-decision. However, it did comment on the issue of state neutrality in regard to religion.

> *S.L v. Commission scolaire des Chênes,* SCC 2012—Religious parents in Quebec objected to having their children taught that all religions are equal. The Court ruled the challenge premature because the mandatory course was not yet being taught. The Court commented on state neutrality.

The Court noted that while a "gradual separation of church and state in Canada has been part of a broad movement to secularize public institutions"[16] there is no legal or constitutional recognition in Canada of the separation of church and state as a concept, which is found in the U.S. Constitution. In that context, the Court attempted to clarify various ideas expressed in its previous comments on secularism (see in particular the quotes from *Chamberlain v. Surrey School District No. 36* found at the end of Chapter Seven) by referencing a principle it called "state religious neutrality." From the decision:

17. …While it is true that the Canadian *Charter*, unlike the U.S. Constitution, does not explicitly limit the support the state can give to a religion, Canadian courts have held that state sponsorship of one religious tradition amounts to discrimination against others…

21. The concept of state religious neutrality in Canadian case law has developed alongside a growing sensitivity to the multicultural makeup of Canada and the protection of minorities. Already in *Big M Drug Mart*, Dickson J. had stated that "the diversity of belief and

---

16 *S.L.*, Paragraph 10.

nonbelief, the diverse sociocultural backgrounds of Canadians make it constitutionally incompetent for the federal Parliament to provide legislative preference for any one religion at the expense of those of another religious persuasion" (p. 351). In the same way, the Ontario Court of Appeal held in *Canadian Civil Liberties Assn. [Elgin County]* that imposing a religious practice of the majority had the effect of infringing the freedom of religion of the minority and was incompatible with the multicultural reality of Canadian society (p. 363).[17]

The Court noted "that trying to achieve religious neutrality in the public sphere is a major challenge for the state."[18] Secularism, or anti-religion, can be just as religious a doctrine as religion, expressing a position on religious beliefs and failing to accommodate the multiple religious, cultural, and philosophical expressions that enrich Canadian society.

The Court concluded "that, from a philosophical standpoint, absolute neutrality does not exist".[19] However,

following a realistic and non-absolutist approach, state neutrality is assured when the state neither favours nor hinders any particular religious belief, that is, when it shows respect for all postures towards religion, including that of having no religious beliefs whatsoever, while taking into account the competing constitutional rights of the affected individuals affected.[20]

The place of the religious Canadian in Canadian society is equal with that of the non-religious Canadian.

Loyola High School v. Quebec (Attorney General)

Loyola High School is a private English-language Jesuit (Roman Catholic) high school for boys located in Montreal, Quebec. In accordance with Ministry of Education guidelines, Loyola sought an exemption from teaching the ERC course because it already taught a similar course in world religions and ethics. Loyola's

---

17 *S.L.*, Paragraphs 17, 21.

18 Ibid., Paragraph 31.

19 Ibid.

20 Ibid., 32.

course was taught from the perspective of Roman Catholic instruction, although it included the perspectives of historic major thinkers and worldviews. Loyola's request for an exemption was denied by the Minister of Education.

The case eventually reached the Supreme Court of Canada.

Confining ourselves to the issue of state neutrality, I quote liberally from the decision in *Loyola* because the Court's language is too important for us, as religious individuals, to simply read an interpretation of what was said on this point:

> *Loyola High School v. Quebec*, SCC 2015—A private Catholic school in Montreal objected to teaching that all religions are equal. The Court ruled that the school's religious freedom was limited more than necessary to achieve educational goals by the state's classroom instruction requirements.

43. The context before us—state regulation of religious schools—poses the question of how to balance robust protection for the values underlying religious freedom with the values of a secular state. Part of secularism, however, is respect for religious differences. A secular state does not—and cannot—interfere with the beliefs or practices of a religious group unless they conflict with or harm overriding public interests. Nor can a secular state support or prefer the practices of one group over those of another: Richard Moon, "Freedom of Religion Under the Charter of Rights: The Limits of State Neutrality" (2012), 45 *U.B.C. L. Rev.* 497, at pp. 498–99. The pursuit of secular values means respecting the right to hold and manifest different religious beliefs. A secular state respects religious differences, it does not seek to extinguish them.

44. Through this form of neutrality, the state affirms and recognizes the religious freedom of individuals and their communities. As Prof. Moon noted:

> Underlying the [state] neutrality requirement, and the insulation of religious beliefs and practices from political decision making, is a conception of religious belief or commitment as deeply rooted, as an element of the individual's identity, rather than simply a choice or judgment she or he has made. Religious belief lies at the core of the individual's worldview. It orients the individual in the world, shapes his or her perception of the social and natural

orders, and provides a moral framework for his or her actions. Moreover, religious belief ties the individual to a community of believers and is often the central or defining association in her or his life. The individual believer participates in a shared system of practices and values that may, in some cases, be described as "a way of life". If religion is an aspect of the individual's identity, then when the state treats his or her religious practices or beliefs as less important or less true than the practices of others, or when it marginalizes her or his religious community in some way, it is not simply rejecting the individual's views and values, it is denying her or his equal worth. [p. 507]

45. Because it allows communities with different values and practices to peacefully co-exist, a secular state also supports pluralism.

46. This does not mean that religious differences trump core national values...

47. These shared values—equality, human rights and democracy—are values the state always has a legitimate interest in promoting and protecting... Religious freedom must therefore be understood in the context of a secular, multicultural and democratic society with a strong interest in protecting dignity and diversity, promoting equality, and ensuring the vitality of a common belief in human rights.

48. The state, therefore, has a legitimate interest in ensuring that students in *all* schools are capable, as adults, of conducting themselves with openness and respect as they confront cultural and religious differences. A pluralist, multicultural democracy depends on the capacity of its citizens "to engage in thoughtful and inclusive forms of deliberation amidst, and enriched by," different religious worldviews and practices: Benjamin L. Berger, "Religious Diversity, Education, and the 'Crisis' in State Neutrality" (2014), 29 *C.J.L.S.* 103, at p. 115.[21]

The state—including government, the courts, and other government body decision-makers—is effectively required to balance its constitutional interests, in this case its interests in education and state "values," with the requirement of neutrality in regard to religion, and then balance that with the constitutional interests of the religious individual or community.

---

21 *Loyola High School*, Paragraphs 43–48.

Mouvement laïque québécois v. Saguenay

A month after issuing its decision in Loyola, the Court issued a decision in *Mouvement laïque québécois v. Saguenay (City)*,[22] a Quebec case dealing with prayer as part of city council meetings. Distinct from the practice of Parliament, some legislatures, and city councils where there is an opportunity for nondenominational prayer prior to the official opening of the meeting, the Saguenay council included the prayer in its agenda. A citizen of Saguenay who regularly attended council meetings was an atheist. Taking offence at the prayer being offered by the mayor, he and the Mouvement laïque québécois (a secular movement) filed a human rights complaint.

> *Mouvement laïque québécois v. Saguenay (City)*, SCC 2015—This was a challenge about city council meetings being opened with the Lord's Prayer. The Court ruled the city must be neutral in regard to religion.

Quebec is the lone province that is not a signatory to the *Constitution Act, 1982* (which includes the *Charter*) and has its own *Charter of human rights and freedoms*, which the Supreme Court has established should be interpreted with application of the same standards as the Canadian *Charter*. This principle of interpretation is also applied in regard to human rights legislation passed by the federal government, provinces, and territories.

This case was primarily concerned with the standard of review by the appeal court after the Human Rights Tribunal found the prayer to be a violation of state neutrality. While ruling that deference had to be given to the tribunal in making a decision legitimately within its process, the Court commented,

> The state may not act in such a way as to create a preferential public space that favours certain religious groups and is hostile to others. It follows that the state may not, by expressing its own religious preference, promote the participation of believers to the exclusion of non-believers or vice versa.[23]

The state must not demonstrate favouritism for a religious or non-religious community. There must be as robust a recognition of the importance of religion in the life of the individual and religious community as there is for the

---

22 2015 2 SCR 3.

23 *Mouvement laïque québécois*, Paragraph 75.

non-religious. Religious individuals and institutions must be regarded as being of equal worth, and on equal footing, with their non-religious peers in their relationship with government. If the state's constitutional objectives are met through the means of the religious individual or community, then that is as acceptable as meeting those objectives through non-religious means.

As noted in *S.L.*, this balancing is "a major challenge for the state."[24] There are significant players in the state and its citizenry who prefer that Christians *"speak no more to anyone in this name"* (Acts 14:17), i.e. not have influence. And key players in the state are, like Pilate, desirous of *"satisfy[ing] the crowd"* (Mark 15:15).

---

24 *S.L.*, Paragraph 31.

CHAPTER TEN

SHH, DON'T TELL ANYONE

Bear one another's burdens, and so fulfill the law of Christ.

—Galatians 6:2

Therefore, confess your sins to one another and pray for one another, that you may be healed. The prayer of a righteous person has great power as it is working. Elijah was a man with a nature like ours, and he prayed fervently that it might not rain, and for three years and six months it did not rain on the earth. Then he prayed again, and heaven gave rain, and the earth bore its fruit.

—James 5:16–18

But you are a chosen race, a royal priesthood, a holy nation, a people for his own possession, that you may proclaim the excellencies of him who called you out of darkness into his marvelous light. Once you were not a people, but now you are God's people; once you had not received mercy, but now you have received mercy.

—1 Peter 2:9–10

THE CHURCH HAS LONG PLACED GREAT VALUE ON THE IMPORTANCE OF CONFESSING SIN. It is the route to forgiveness.

The Roman Catholic Church has formalized the practice in a way that is known, at least somewhat, even outside its body of adherents. They have confessional booths where the confessor is heard by a priest. The priest has plausible deniability as to the confessor's identity because priest and confessor have separate entrances into the booth, a wall divides them once inside, and the confession is heard through a screen that obscures facial features. Outside of the Roman Church, I'm not aware that such a feature exists in standard Christian practice. But the expectation of confession, and confidentiality in hearing it, remains.

There are few pastors who have not heard a confession that troubles them deeply but which they cannot share. Marty Duren wrote a summary that aligns with my experience and the thoughts shared with me by many in pastoral ministry:

> One of the heaviest burdens of ministry is the burden of knowing: knowing who's hurting, knowing whose marriage is about to implode, knowing whose kid is heading to rehab, knowing who really sent that anonymous note. The burden of knowing cannot be delegated. Nor can your pastor easily offload it when turning into the driveway each evening.[1]

I was a pastor in three different congregations over the course of six years before finishing law school and establishing The Salvation Army's Canadian legal department. During that time I heard a number of confessions, including one concerning a fairly serious criminal offence. I encouraged the confessor to go to the authorities, even offering to go with him, but he felt his conscience was sufficiently clear when the burden shifted to my shoulders. No one was hurt or at risk as a result of what took place, and I bear that confession still. I don't even know if the confessor is still alive.

In the Bible, the expectation of confession and burden-bearing isn't just for priests and pastors. It is for the Church. The Church is you and me, all of us Christ-followers together. There is no Church without *us*. Before the *Charter*, Glen How fought for legal acknowledgement that one did not have to be recognized as part of the clergy to benefit from the military service exemptions in place during WWII. The Jehovah's Witnesses believe that the words of 1 Peter 2:9–10 mean that all men are considered part of the priesthood. It is also the case for some Protestant denominations that there is no clergy category, in the sense of priests and pastors with which most are familiar in the congregational setting.

So what does one do, whether one is recognized formally as clergy or associationally as a member of the priesthood of all believers, when confronted with a confession of criminal behaviour while face to face with the confessor who will not report themselves to civic (state) authorities?

First, if there is a reasonable apprehension that a child is at risk, there are provincial and territorial reporting requirements that obligate the person hearing

---

1   Marty Duren, *Lifeway*, "6 Things Church Members Need to Know About Pastor Burnout." September 16, 2016 (http://www.lifeway.com/pastors/2016/09/16/6-things-church-members-need-to-know-about-pastor-burnout).

the confession to report it to appropriate civic authorities. Most denominations also have a prescribed reporting process to notify clerical (church) authorities in such a situation.

Second, the Supreme Court of Canada spoke to the issue in its 1991 decision in a case called *R. v. Gruenke*.[2]

R. v. Gruenke

Adele Gruenke provided care to an elderly father figure who had assisted her financially to start her own business and included her in his will. They had a platonic relationship, but over time he started asking for sexual favours in repayment for his financial generosity. On one such occasion, the elderly man became forceful and a tussle ensued. Ms. Gruenke's boyfriend was watching from a distance and intervened. The elderly man was found dead in his car the next morning. Two days later, Ms. Gruenke met with her counsellor from the church she attended, confessing her role in "a murder." The counsellor called the pastor for advice, and the conversation moved from the counsellor's home to the pastor's office at the church building.

> *R. v. Gruenke*, SCC 1991—A murder was confessed to a church counsellor and the church's pastor. The court ruled that the confidentiality of "religious communications" was to be considered on a case-by-case basis using the four-part Wigmore Test.

On appeal from Manitoba, at issue before the Court was whether the testimony of the counsellor and/or the pastor was admissible in court or whether the conversations with them were to be considered inadmissible as confidential communications.

The Court distinguished two different kinds of privileged communications, i.e. confidential communications that are inadmissible in court. The first is communications that are excluded as a class for reasons of public policy. The second is communications assessed on a case-by-case basis.

The first category includes solicitor (lawyer) and client communications, which are excluded from the requirement for testifying before the court because their confidential nature is essential to the workings of the judicial system. There is no such provision in law for what was once known as priest-penitent communications to be excluded from the requirement to testify in court. The Court decided that these will be referred to in Canada as "religious communications."

---

2   [1991] 3 SCR 263.

Earlier lower court decisions had recognized a case-by-case analysis standard for priest-penitent privilege. The Supreme Court affirmed that recognition for religious communications, noting "a case-by-case analysis will allow courts to determine whether, in the particular circumstances, the individual's freedom of religion will be imperilled by the admission of the evidence."[3]

The Court recognized that a certain deference is to be given to religious communications in the case-by-case analysis, quoting from an earlier decision of Ontario's Court of Appeal in *Re Church of Scientology and The Queen (No. 6)*:

> Chief Justice Dickson stated in *R. v. Big M Drug Mart Ltd.* ... that the fundamental freedom of conscience and religion now enshrined in s. 2(a) of the Charter embraces not only the freedom of religious thought and belief but also "the right to manifest religious belief by worship and practice or by teaching and dissemination". This protection will no doubt strengthen the argument in favour of recognition of a priest-and-penitent privilege. The restrictive common law interpretation of the privilege may have to be reassessed to bring it in conformity with the constitutional freedom.
>
> In our view, however, while s. 2 of the Charter enhances the claim that communications made in confidence to a priest or ordained minister should be afforded a privilege, its applicability must be determined on a case-by-case basis. The freedom is not absolute.[4]

The move from "priest-penitent" privilege to "religious communications" was explained as being informed by Section 27 of the *Charter*, which requires the *Charter* to be "interpreted in a manner consistent with the preservation and enhancement of the multicultural heritage of Canadians." Additional words from *Big M* show that a "truly free society is one which can accommodate a wide variety of beliefs, diversity of tastes and pursuits, customs and codes of conduct."[5] The result is that the assessment of the communications will begin "with a 'non-denominational' approach. The fact that the communications were not made to an ordained priest or minister or that they did not constitute a formal confession will not bar the possibility of the communications' being excluded."[6]

---

3   *Gruenke*, 290.

4   (1987), 31 C.C.C. (3d) 449, 540.

5   *Big M*, Paragraph 94.

6   *Gruenke*, 291.

The standard applied by the Court is referred to as the Wigmore Test. The Wigmore criteria are so named because they were set out in 1904 by American lawyer and law professor John Henry Wigmore (1863–1943) in his book *Evidence in Trials at Common Law*:

(1) The communications must originate in a *confidence* that they will not be disclosed.

(2) This element of *confidentiality must be essential* to the full and satisfactory maintenance of the relation between the parties.

(3) The *relation* must be one which in the opinion of the community ought to be sedulously *fostered.*

(4) The *injury* that would inure to the relation by the disclosure of the communications must be *greater than the benefit* thereby gained for the correct disposal of litigation.[7]

In the case before him, Chief Justice Antonio Lamer found the circumstances did not indicate that the communications from Ms. Gruenke to her spiritual advisor and pastor were intended to be made with an expectation of confidentiality. Some of the reasons for this conclusion: there was no church policy outlining when communications were to be kept confidential, and there had been no expression during the course of the conversations that what was shared was to be kept in confidence.

This is instructive for the Church. Like the confessional booth, if confidentiality is expected:

- the expectation of confidentiality must be communicated and understood by both confessor and the person hearing the confession;
- confidentiality must be understood to be essential in the relationship between them (perhaps part of church policy);
- the community—undefined but generally regarded as "society," although arguably the religious community—must be of the opinion that the confidentiality in the relationship is to be encouraged for a purpose that benefits the community, not just the confessor; and
- the injury (there's that word again) that would result from disclosure must be greater than what the court would gain by having the

---

7   Ibid., 284.

evidence. This may be the most difficult hurdle as judges tend to think they, not Scripture, are the final decision-makers on this point.

These conditions do not require booth and collar. They can be established in a variety of settings, but the conditions must be established prior to the communications taking place, not assumed, and not after.

CHAPTER ELEVEN

WHAT DO YOU MEAN THERE ARE MEMBERSHIP STANDARDS?

And he said to them, "Follow me, and I will make you fishers of men."
—Matthew 4:19

If your brother sins against you, go and tell him his fault, between you and him alone. If he listens to you, you have gained your brother. But if he does not listen, take one or two others along with you, that every charge may be established by the evidence of two or three witnesses. If he refuses to listen to them, tell it to the church. And if he refuses to listen even to the church, let him be to you as a Gentile and a tax collector.
—Matthew 18:15–17

The brothers, both the apostles and the elders, to the brothers who are of the Gentiles in Antioch and Syria and Cilicia, greetings. Since we have heard that some persons have gone out from us and troubled you with words, unsettling your minds, although we gave them no instructions, it has seemed good to us, having come to one accord, to choose men and send them to you with our beloved Barnabas and Paul, men who have risked their lives for the name of our Lord Jesus Christ. We have therefore sent Judas and Silas, who themselves will tell you the same things by word of mouth. For it has seemed good to the Holy Spirit and to us to lay on you no greater burden than these requirements: that you abstain from what has been sacrificed to idols, and from blood, and from what has been strangled, and from sexual immorality. If you keep yourselves from these, you will do well. Farewell.
—Acts 15:23–29

And they devoted themselves to the apostles' teaching and the fellowship, to the breaking of bread and the prayers. And awe came upon every soul, and many wonders and signs were being done through the apostles. And all who believed were together and had all things in common.

—Acts 2:42–44

Behold, how good and pleasant it is when brothers dwell in unity!

—Psalm 133:1

DIFFERENT CHRISTIAN CHURCHES HAVE DIFFERENT TRADITIONS FOR ADMISSION INTO official church membership. Most churches have two categories of attendees: members and adherents. Apart from having completed the official process for membership, they may be virtually indistinguishable from one another on any given Sunday. That wasn't the case when I made my decision to accept Christ as Saviour and Lord in The Salvation Army in December 1981. Salvation Army members were soldiers, and we were privileged to wear the distinct, dark navy uniform that was known around the world.

In January 1982, I started senior soldier classes (confirmation, membership), working with the *From Mercy Seat to Spiritual Maturity* booklets,[1] The Salvation Army's *Handbook of Doctrine*,[2] and my honking big leather-bound New American Standard Bible with my name engraved in gold leaf on the front—a 1979 Christmas gift from my Aunt Barbara and Uncle Joe from Texas, where everything is honking big and Bibles are leather-bound!

As we neared the end of the twelve-week course and were presented with the *Articles of War* (membership document), I had a problem. The *Articles* left me no way out. I was prepared to make a lifelong commitment to Christ, and expected my service would be in The Salvation Army, but I wasn't sure The Salvation Army and I would last together until the end of my days on planet Earth (which we didn't). So I did what any first year law student might do: I placed an asterisk at the appropriate place and clarified that point in the *Articles of War*. The amendment passed muster and I was enrolled.

In our first church posting, Gloria and I encountered a different membership problem. We had over 150 members on the membership roll, but most were

---

1   The Salvation Army, *From Mercy Seat to Spiritual Maturity* (Territorial Commander, Canada and Bermuda, undated). *From Mercy Seat to Spiritual Maturity* contains three booklets, titled *Saved!*, *Saved to Serve!*, and *Saved to Save!*

2   The Salvation Army, *Handbook of Doctrine* (St. Albans, UK: Campfield Press, 1969).

dead. There was a cultural issue in regard to their removal from the church membership book. Our solution was to transfer the deceased members' names and date of death to a "Promoted to Glory" roll, stroking out their names on the active members roll as "transferred PtG," but not removing them from the book. This gave a more realistic picture of our membership that better aligned with our actual attendance figures.

A few years later, as Legal Advisor to The Salvation Army's Canada and Bermuda Territory, I would review the *Orders and Regulations for Commissions of Enquiry*, the process for holding a hearing into alleged misbehaviour by an officer (clergy), as well as the similar procedures in the *United Church of Canada Manual* and the Roman Catholic *Code of Canon Law*.

The requirements for becoming a member of a church, religious community, and/or para-congregational ministry are important and need to be clearly stated. Also important, as we discovered in Lax Kw'aalams, are the conditions for transfer or removal from membership. And finally, it's necessary to have a process for providing a fair hearing in the event of allegations of misconduct.

A series of Supreme Court of Canada cases deal with just such issues.

Caldwell v. Stuart

Technically, the 1984 decision of the Supreme Court in *Caldwell et al. v. Stuart et al.*[3] is not a *Charter* decision, but it was made after the *Charter* became the law of the land and has had significant impact on *Charter* decisions in later cases. The case was concerned with competing rights under the British Columbia *Human Rights Code*. Mrs. Caldwell was a Roman Catholic teacher who married a divorced man in a civil ceremony. In doing so, she was aware that she contravened two matters of Catholic practice: a Catholic was not permitted to marry a divorced person or to marry in a ceremony performed outside the administration of the Catholic Church. Mr. Stuart exercised the right of the Catholic school, of which he was principal, and chose not to renew Mrs. Caldwell's teaching contract. Mrs.

> *Caldwell v. Stuart*, SCC 1984—A British Columbia teacher was fired by a Catholic school for violating Catholic practices. The Court ruled that the requirement for teachers to be practicing Catholics in good standing was legitimate.

---

3   [1984] 2 SCR 603.

Caldwell claimed she was being discriminated against in employment on the basis of marital status and religion.

In reaching its decision, the Court considered whether the religious practice requirement was a legitimate (*bona fide*) requirement of Mrs. Caldwell's employment, since in all other aspects she was qualified for the job, deciding:

> It is my opinion that objectively viewed, having in mind the special nature and objectives of the school, the requirement of religious conformance including the acceptance and observance of the Church's rules regarding marriage is reasonably necessary to assure the achievement of the objects of the school... the requirement of conformance constitutes a *bona fide* qualification in respect of the occupation of a Catholic teacher employed in a Catholic school... It will be only in rare circumstances that such a factor as religious conformance can pass the test of *bona fide* qualification. In the case at bar, the special nature of the school and the unique role played by the teachers in the attaining of the school's legitimate objects are essential to the finding that religious conformance is a *bona fide* qualification.[4]

The Court also found that Section 22 of the B.C. *Human Rights Code*, which recognized the special nature of religious institutions, should not be interpreted narrowly, as the section "while indeed imposing a limitation on rights in cases where it applies, also confers and protects rights."[5] Thus:

> In failing to renew the contract of Mrs. Caldwell, the school authorities were exercising a preference for the benefit of the members of the community served by the school and forming the identifiable group by preserving a teaching staff whose Catholic members all accepted and practised the doctrines of the Church.[6]

It was significant to the decision that the standards of the religious community, in this case a Roman Catholic school, were identified, known to Mrs. Caldwell, and legitimately required of her, and of others in similar positions, in order for her to hold the position she lost through the violation of those standards.

---

4   *Caldwell*, 624–625.

5   Ibid., 626.

6   Ibid., 628.

Lakeside Colony of Hutterian Brethren v. Hofer

In a 1992 decision,[7] the Supreme Court was again faced with someone being told to leave a religious community. Members of the Hutterian Brethren Church live in colonies and hold property communally, based on their understanding of Acts 2:42–44. As you might expect, they desire to live in peace and harmony with each other, as well as with people not part of their colony. They are governed by a structure of male elders. Colony elders made a decision requiring Mr. Hofer and three others, all named Hofer, to be expelled, thus losing all rights to the farm property in the community. Lest you think the elders had something against the Hofers, two of the elders were also named Hofer. When the expelled Hofers refused to leave, the colony sought assistance from the courts to enforce the order.

> *Lakeside Colony of Hutterian Brethren v. Hofer*, SCC 1992—Several Hutterites were expelled from their Manitoba colony and refused to leave. The Court ruled the colony could establish membership requirements, but removal required following principles of natural justice.

The Court stated that the "courts are slow to exercise jurisdiction over the question of membership in a voluntary association, especially a religious one".[8] Nonetheless, there was precedent for doing so when property rights were at issue, as in this case. The Court noted, "If the defendants were strangers to the colony, then the colony would surely be entitled to an order barring them from the property, since that would be part of the colony's right of ownership."[9] However, members and residents of the colony "have certain rights under the Articles of Association to live on the colony and to be supported by the colony."[10]

The Court found there was no question in regard to the structural legitimacy of the religious community, including membership requirements, following the reasoning in another Hutterite case from 1970. You guessed it, *Hofer v. Hofer*[11] was a case in which members were expelled for converting to another religious faith. In *Lakeside Colony*, however, the Court was faced with determining whether these Hofers had been properly expelled from the colony. It concluded that proper

---

7   [1992] 3 SCR 165.

8   *Lakeside Colony*, 173–174.

9   Ibid., 174.

10   Ibid.

11   [1970] SCR 958.

expulsion from such a religious community cannot be arbitrary, requiring that principles of natural justice be followed.

The content of the principles of natural justice is flexible and depends on the circumstances in which the question arises. However, the most basic requirements are that of notice, opportunity to make representations, and an unbiased tribunal.[12]

Hutterites require the process described in Matthew 18:15–17 to be followed in the exercise of discipline. This New Testament process provides for notice and the opportunity to make presentation and a hearing. The use of tradition and custom in seeking advice from other elders before making a final decision was assessed and found to be acceptable, as all members were aware of it. In the end, the Court found that the expelled Hofers were present at an initial meeting that became their hearing, and at a series of follow-up meetings, but that they had not received notice that their conduct was the purpose for the initial meeting, i.e. that they had been summonsed for the purpose of a hearing. The Hofers got to stay.

Trinity Western University v. British Columbia College of Teachers

Trinity Western University is a private (not publicly funded) Christian university, first opening its doors in 1962. In 1985, TWU established a teacher training program, with four years of a five-year course spent at TWU and the fifth at Simon Fraser University, a public university. TWU applied to assume full responsibility for the five-year teacher education program. The British Columbia College of Teachers rejected TWU's request because the university required staff and students to agree to a Christian Community Standards policy that addressed lifestyle (practice) in addition to beliefs.

> *Trinity Western University v. British Columbia College of Teachers*, SCC 2001—The BCCT refused to grant accreditation to TWU's school of education. The Court ruled that once TWU met educational standards, it was to be accredited. The BCCT's regulation of graduates began after they joined the BCCT.

---

12 Ibid., 195.

The paragraph at the heart of the BCCT's refusal required staff and students:

Refrain from practices that are biblically condemned. These include but are not limited to drunkenness (Eph. 5:18), swearing or use of profane language (Eph. 4:29, 5:4; Jas 3:1–12), harassment (Jn 13:34–35; Rom. 12:9–21; Eph. 4:31), all forms of dishonesty including cheating and stealing (Prov. 12:22; Col. 3:9; Eph. 4:28), abortion (Ex. 20:13; Ps. 139:13–16), involvement in the occult (Acts 19:19; Gal. 5:19), and sexual sins including premarital sex, adultery, homosexual behaviour, and viewing of pornography (I Cor. 6:12–20; Eph. 4:17–24; I Thess. 4:3–8; Rom. 2:26–27; I Tim. 1:9–10). Furthermore married members of the community agree to maintain the sanctity of marriage and to take every positive step possible to avoid divorce.[13]

In *Trinity Western University v. British Columbia College of Teachers*,[14] the Court concluded in 2001 that the B.C. *Human Rights Code* specifically provides for religious institutions, such as TWU, and that TWU could not be required to change its community religious beliefs and practices without violating the university's *Charter* right to freedom of religion. The Court ruled in favour of TWU. The BCCT was required to grant accreditation.

In arriving at its decision, the Court noted that once TWU satisfied the academic requirements of the BCCT, the role of the BCCT was only to regulate the behaviour of TWU's academically qualified graduates *after* they entered the profession. At that point, TWU grads would be regulated under the same provisions applicable to other teachers in the province.

The Court stated:

36. Instead, the proper place to draw the line in cases like the one at bar is generally between belief and conduct. The freedom to hold beliefs is broader than the freedom to act on them. Absent concrete evidence that training teachers at TWU fosters discrimination in the public schools of B.C., the freedom of individuals to adhere to certain religious beliefs while at TWU should be respected. The BCCT, rightfully, does not require public universities with teacher education programs to screen out applicants who hold sexist, racist or homophobic beliefs. For better

---

13 *Trinity Western*, Paragraph 4. Emphasis added.
14 [2001] 1 SCR 772, 2001 SCC 31.

or for worse, tolerance of divergent beliefs is a hallmark of a democratic society.[15]

As a private religious institution, TWU was legally and constitutionally entitled to establish its membership requirements for staff and students. And the BCCT was entitled to establish membership requirements for teachers. Once a student graduated from TWU and became a member of the BCCT, the boundaries for their conduct shifted from TWU's community standards to the BCCT's professional (community) standards.

At the time of writing, TWU is in the courts again. In addition to existing faculties for the professions of education, nursing, and business, TWU made plans to open a law school. Fully satisfying the accreditation requirements of the Federation of Law Societies of Canada, two law societies (government-authorized lawyer self-regulating associations), British Columbia and Ontario, are unwilling to recognize academically qualified graduates of TWU Law, again because of the Christian community covenant. A third law society, Nova Scotia, has withdrawn its challenge.

As the law currently stands, a Christian university is able to identify both the beliefs and practices that make it Christian without being compromised in its academic standing or in regard to professional accreditation after graduation. However, once graduates are regulated by professional organizations they are required to practise in accordance with the profession's standards. This can be readily extrapolated for application in the setting of other Christian institutions and other public professions.

Alberta v. Hutterian Brethren of Wilson Colony

This is one Supreme Court case in which I remain convinced the wrong decision was reached. A significant number of law professors and constitutional law lawyers agree, in addition to the strong dissenting reasons from the justices in the minority of this 4–3 split decision. The conclusion that requires members of the Hutterian Brethren of Wilson colony to submit to government photo identification, for reasons of national security, was arrived at using information that was not before the Court. For that reason, the lawyer for the Hutterian Brethren made the rare attempt to have the Court revisit its decision under a limited appeal provision that would have allowed the Court to do so. The request was denied. In

---

15   *Trinity Western*, Paragraph 36.

the end, the 2009 decision in *Alberta v. Hutterian Brethren of Wilson Colony*[16] strongly affirmed the *Charter*-protected right of an identifiable religious community to establish and maintain its membership standards of belief and practice.

The Hutterites of Wilson Colony had been exempt from photo requirements to hold a valid Alberta driver's license from the inception of the requirement in 1974. While different Hutterite colonies have different understandings of the second commandment, at Wilson Colony it was understood that *"[t]hou shalt not make unto thee any graven image, or any likeness of any thing that is in heaven above, or that is in the earth beneath, or that is in the water under the earth"* (Exodus 20:4, KJV) included photographs. Members of the Wilson Colony would not willingly submit to being photographed.

Alberta v. Hutterian Brethren of Wilson Colony, SCC 2009—An Alberta Hutterite colony challenged new regulations requiring their photos on drivers' licenses. The Court ruled this a minor infringement on religious freedom, and the colony members would have to obtain photo licenses or find other means of transportation.

In 2003, Alberta adopted a new regulation that made photo licenses mandatory, ostensibly for reasons of national security, because the photo would be placed in the province's facial recognition database. Of course, not everyone in Alberta has a driver's license.

As a result, this requires photo identification to hold a driver's license, including the Wilson Colony members, so that the photo can go in the facial recognition database. However, their photos won't be in the database and the Hutterites now find alternate means of transporting their goods rather than violate their religious beliefs. While affirming membership standards rights, the Court indicated:

93. Cases of direct compulsion are straightforward. However, it may be more difficult to measure the seriousness of a limit on freedom of religion where the limit arises not from a direct assault on the right to choose, but as the result of incidental and unintended effects of the law. In many such cases, the limit does not preclude choice as to religious belief or practice, but it does make it more costly.

94. The incidental effects of a law passed for the general good on a particular religious practice may be so great that they effectively deprive the adherent of a meaningful choice: see *Edwards Books*. Or the

---

16   2009 SCC 37, [2009] 2 SCR 567.

government program to which the limit is attached may be compulsory, with the result that the adherent is left with a stark choice between violating his or her religious belief and disobeying the law: *Multani*. The absence of a meaningful choice in such cases renders the impact of the limit very serious.

95. However, in many cases, the incidental effects of a law passed for the general good on a particular religious practice may be less serious. The limit may impose costs on the religious practitioner in terms of money, tradition or inconvenience. However, these costs may still leave the adherent with a meaningful choice concerning the religious practice at issue. The *Charter* guarantees freedom of religion, but does not indemnify practitioners against all costs incident to the practice of religion. Many religious practices entail costs which society reasonably expects the adherents to bear. The inability to access conditional benefits or privileges conferred by law may be among such costs. A limit on the right that exacts a cost but nevertheless leaves the adherent with a meaningful choice about the religious practice at issue will be less serious than a limit that effectively deprives the adherent of such choice...

97. The Hutterian claimants argue that the limit presents them with an invidious choice: the choice between some of its members violating the Second Commandment on the one hand, or accepting the end of their rural communal life on the other hand. However, the evidence does not support the conclusion that arranging alternative means of highway transport would end the Colony's rural way of life. The claimants' affidavit says that it is necessary for at least some members to be able to drive from the Colony to nearby towns and back. It does not explain, however, why it would not be possible to hire people with driver's licences for this purpose, or to arrange third party transport to town for necessary services, like visits to the doctor. Many businesses and individuals rely on hired persons and commercial transport for their needs, either because they cannot drive or choose not to drive. Obtaining alternative transport would impose an additional economic cost on the Colony, and would go against their traditional self-sufficiency. But there is no evidence that this would be prohibitive.

98. On the record before us, it is impossible to conclude that Colony members have been deprived of a meaningful choice to follow or not to follow the edicts of their religion. The law does not compel

the taking of a photo. It merely provides that a person who wishes to obtain a driver's licence must permit a photo to be taken for the photo identification data bank. Driving automobiles on highways is not a right, but a privilege. While most adult citizens hold driver's licences, many do not, for a variety of reasons.

99. I conclude that the impact of the limit on religious practice imposed by the universal photo requirement for obtaining a driver's licence is that Colony members will be obliged to make alternative arrangements for highway transport. This will impose some financial cost on the community and depart from their tradition of being self-sufficient in terms of transport. These costs are not trivial. But on the record, they do not rise to the level of seriously affecting the claimants' right to pursue their religion. They do not negate the choice that lies at the heart of freedom of religion.[17]

I have underlined the section of the decision that introduces concepts vital to the Court's decision that were not in evidence. Treacherously, this decision introduced the idea that a religious community should be asked to pay the cost of accommodating the state, a novel concept, when prior cases have dealt with the question of the state accommodating religious belief and practice. This case stands alone as an aberration on that point. Importantly, there was sound recognition that the determination of belief and practice remained with the religious community.

---

17 *Wilson Colony*, Paragraphs 93–95, 97–99. Emphasis added.

CHAPTER TWELVE

RELIGIOUS FREEDOM IS FOR INDIVIDUALS OF ALL FAITHS

When a stranger sojourns with you in your land, you shall not do him wrong.
You shall treat the stranger who sojourns with you as the native among you, and
you shall love him as yourself, for you were strangers in the land of Egypt: I am
the Lord your God.

—Leviticus 19:33–34

And I charged your judges at that time, "Hear the cases between your brothers,
and judge righteously between a man and his brother or the alien [foreigner] who
is with him…"

—Deuteronomy 1:16

For the Lord your God is God of gods and Lord of lords, the great, the mighty, and
the awesome God, who is not partial and takes no bribe. He executes justice for
the fatherless and the widow, and loves the sojourner, giving him food and clothing.
Love the sojourner, therefore, for you were sojourners in the land of Egypt.

—Deuteronomy 10:17–19

And one of them, a lawyer, asked him a question to test him. "Teacher, which is
the great commandment in the Law?"

And he said to him, "You shall love the Lord your God with all your heart
and with all your soul and with all your mind. This is the great and first com-
mandment. And a second is like it: You shall love your neighbor as yourself."

—Matthew 22:35–39

ATTENDING THE ALL PARTY PARLIAMENTARY INTERFAITH FELLOWSHIP GROUP FOR THE
first time, I got caught up listening to other people introducing themselves and

ended up completely unprepared for my own introduction. This was not introductory remarks to a talk or topic but, "Tell us your name, the organization you represent, and what your faith suggests could be your most important contribution to this group." Simple, right? Not if you're unprepared. Because I had been focused on listening, I found myself thinking about the answer to the third part of the question while answering the first two. "Hi. My name is Don Hutchinson. I'm here on behalf of The Evangelical Fellowship of Canada. The most important contribution I can make to this group is to share the good news of Jesus Christ with you. It would be my hope that, as a result, every one of you would live your life as a follower of Jesus." The Muslim gentleman sitting next to me thrust out his hand in a clear gesture that he wanted to shake mine, while saying, "Finally, an honest Christian. Now we can have genuine conversation about faith."

That worked out better than my expectations as the words were leaving my mouth. In fact, as the words slipped from tongue to teeth to lips to the room, I had felt increasingly awkward and nervous. That welcoming hand was a huge relief! I also received an instant reputation as someone who wasn't afraid to share my faith, about which there were several conversations. But growing up, I had no faith to share. Until I was twenty-one, it didn't occur to me in any thoughtful way that, as Justice Gonthier said in *Chamberlain*, "everyone has 'belief' or 'faith' in something, be it atheistic, agnostic or religious. To construe 'secular' as the realm of the 'unbelief' is therefore erroneous."[1] Canadians' beliefs are dramatically diverse.

Growing up in Scarborough, a suburb of Toronto, in the 1960s and 70s, I still know the names of the first black kid, the first Japanese kid, and the first Pakistani kid I ever met. It didn't occur to me then that we might have different religions. I thought I was a Christian because Canada was Christian. They were in Canada, so they were Christians. The television cartoon *A Charlie Brown Christmas* had a scene explaining the true meaning of Christmas, according to Linus and Luke 2:8–14, although I didn't know Linus was quoting Luke at the time. I watched it every year. Some neighbours went to church and some didn't, and we all got along. Church didn't seem to matter. We were all Canadians, so we were all Christians. Weren't we?

As a teenager, it was exciting to collect the entrance stamps in my Toronto International Caravan passport. For ten days each year, beginning on a Friday night, those of us in Toronto had an amazing opportunity to travel to dozens of foreign countries without leaving the city. Each nationality had a pavilion with food, dance, clothing, and other distinctive cultural features that facilitated them

---

1   *Chamberlain*, Paragraph 137. See Chapter Seven.

sharing their heritage with us. It was amazing! Many of the pavilions were located in heritage parts of the city—Little Italy, Greektown, Chinatown, etc. These were not ghettoes, but focal points of cultural outreach. Multiculturalism has been criticized in many countries, but in Canada—at least in my limited experience—it works because we are neither melting pot (you have to become like us) nor isolationist (you stay over there and we'll stay over here). Still, to me, food and cultural dance didn't suggest any difference in religion.

I vividly recall the dramatic impact that Tim Uppal's testimony had on me, and on a room full of delegates from the Presbyterian Church in Canada who had asked me to organize an evening with MPs for a group attending their June 2008 General Assembly in Ottawa. Using delegate postal codes from the group, I contacted MPs and invited them to attend and share their faith stories. Tim was the only non-Christian MP to attend, and his talk was different. He spoke passionately about his family's move to Canada in pursuit of religious freedom and how important maintaining that freedom for all Canadians was to him. Tim's parents, like mine, had come to Canada in search of a better life. My parents, however, had not been persecuted for their faith. Born in the new home country of his family, Tim carried the passion of their search in his heart and on his sleeve.

As Canadian immigration patterns changed, beginning with the Pearson policies in the 1960s, and official multiculturalism seemed to work better in Canada than many other countries, Canada became increasingly multi-religious as well. In 1982, Canada's multicultural heritage was enshrined in our constitution. How would the *Charter*, or rather the Court, respond to the claims of new religions to which the Court, and many Canadians, were still becoming accustomed?

First, let's turn our attention to a longstanding minority religious community that has faced discrimination overseas and on Canadian soil.

Syndicat Northcrest v. Amselem

In the vein of "no right is absolute," the Supreme Court of Canada's decision in *Syndicat Northcrest v. Amselem*[2] opens with these words:

> 1. An important feature of our constitutional democracy is respect for minorities, which includes, of course, religious minorities… Indeed, respect for and tolerance of the rights and practices of religious minorities is one of the hallmarks of an enlightened democracy. But respect

2   [2004] 2 SCR 551, 2004 SCC 47.

for religious minorities is not a stand-alone absolute right; like other rights, freedom of religion exists in a matrix of other correspondingly important rights that attach to individuals. Respect for minority rights must also coexist alongside societal values that are central to the make-up and functioning of a free and democratic society...[3]

As a side note, Chapter Twenty-Three will point out that in Canada there are no longer any religious majorities. Even though two-thirds of Canadians identified themselves as Christians in the 2011 National Household Survey, the largest religious group is a minority: just under forty percent of the Canadian population self-identifies as Roman Catholic. About one percent identifies as Jewish.

> *Syndicat Northcrest v. Amselem*, SCC 2004—Jewish condominium owners wanted to place prayer huts on their balconies for the religious celebration of Sukkot. The Court ruled in their favour, noting that sincerely held religious beliefs, and practices closely connected with those beliefs, are defined by the individuals who hold them.

This case was from Quebec. You will recall that Quebec has its own *Charter of human rights and freedoms*, which the Supreme Court of Canada has interpreted in a manner consistent with its interpretation of the Canadian *Charter*, as it does with the human rights legislation of all provinces.

Mr. Amselem, along with his family and friends who were involved in this case, were all Orthodox Jews. Judaism, like Christianity and Islam, is not a homogenous religious community but has several expressions of the shared faith. They were owners of units in a high-rise condominium building called Place Northcrest. In September 1996, Mr. Amselem set up a prayer hut (or "sukkah") on his balcony. Sukkot (pronounced sue-COAT) is also called the Feast of Tabernacles. During the feast of Sukkot, many Jews build and live in temporary booths, or sukkahs, in remembrance of when God led them out of Egypt, and they lived in shelters in the wilderness for forty years. However, the condominium agreement prohibited decorations or construction on balconies. Other unit owners complained and the condo corporation, Syndicat Northcrest, took legal action.

In assessing the outcome of the case, the Court was confronted with testimony from a rabbi that the use of a sukkah was not a mandatory requirement for the celebration of Sukkot. It concluded:

---

3   *Amselem*, Paragraph 1.

43. The emphasis then is on personal choice of religious beliefs. In my opinion, these decisions and commentary should not be construed to imply that freedom of religion protects only those aspects of religious belief or conduct that are objectively recognized by religious experts as being obligatory tenets or precepts of a particular religion. Consequently, claimants seeking to invoke freedom of religion should not need to prove the objective validity of their beliefs in that their beliefs are objectively recognized as valid by other members of the same religion, nor is such an inquiry appropriate for courts to make… In fact, this Court has indicated on several occasions that, if anything, a person must show "[s]incerity of belief"… and not that a particular belief is "valid".[4]

And a few paragraphs later:

46. To summarize up to this point, our Court's past decisions and the basic principles underlying freedom of religion support the view that freedom of religion consists of the freedom to undertake practices and harbour beliefs, having a nexus with religion, in which an individual demonstrates he or she sincerely believes or is sincerely undertaking in order to connect with the divine or as a function of his or her spiritual faith, irrespective of whether a particular practice or belief is required by official religious dogma or is in conformity with the position of religious officials.[5]

The condominium owners were found to be sincere in their religious beliefs, with the practice in issue having a nexus, or connection, with the beliefs. Their freedom of religion had been infringed and their religious practice of dwelling in sukkahs on their balconies was upheld.

Multani v. Commission scolaire Marguerite-Bourgeoys

This is another case from Quebec. However, because the decision-maker was a school board, a government agency, the Canadian *Charter* applies.

Mr. Multani and his son, Gurbaj, were orthodox Sikhs. They believed that their religion required a baptized Sikh to wear a kirpan at all times. A kirpan is a

---

4   Ibid., 43.
5   Ibid., 46.

religious object that resembles a small dagger and is made of metal. One day at school, the kirpan fell out of Gurbaj Multani's clothing while he was in the school-yard. The family agreed to secure the kirpan within the boy's clothing. The school board refused this compromise, insisting the kirpan was to be treated as a prohibited weapon.

> *Multani v. Commission scolaire Marguerite-Bourgeoys*, SCC 2006—A Sikh boy's ceremonial knife fell out of his clothes at school and was banned as a weapon. The Court ruled the infringement on religious freedom was significant because the boy was religiously prohibited from being without this symbol of confirmation in his faith.

In *Multani v. Commission scolaire Marguerite-Bourgeoys*,[6] the Supreme Court found that their review of a school board decision, a public de-cision-maker rather than private decision-maker as in *Amselem*, re-quired ensuring proper consideration and application of a *Charter* right by the public decision-maker, in this case the *Charter* right to freedom of religion.

The Court upheld the decision in *Amselem* in regard to the younger Mul-tani's sincerity of belief and the practice of wearing his kirpan having a nexus with that belief. In its consideration of the impact of the school board's decision, the Court ruled:

> 40. Finally, the interference with Gurbaj Singh's freedom of religion is neither trivial nor insignificant. Forced to choose between leaving his kirpan at home and leaving the public school system, Gurbaj Singh de-cided to follow his religious convictions and is now attending a private school. The prohibition against wearing his kirpan to school has there-fore deprived him of his right to attend a public school.[7]

The Court also considered the public safety aims of the school board, finding them to be legitimate, and also found that because the kirpan was not a weapon or intended to be used as such, it was not in violation of the policy. By the time Gurbaj Singh received the decision in his favour, seven years later, he was no lon-ger in school.

---

6   [2006] 1 SCR 256, 2006 SCC 6.

7   *Multani*, Paragraph 40.

S.L. v. Commission scolaire des Chênes

You may recall from Chapter Nine that in *S.L. v. Commission scolaire des Chênes,*[8] parents requested that their children be exempt from participation in the Ethics and Religious Culture course because the course would infringe their freedom of religion through instruction requiring all religions to be treated as equal, including mythologies of the ancient Greeks and Romans. The parents' request was made in accordance with Ministry of Education guidelines. Although the Court issued a "non-decision" in the case, deciding that because the course had not yet started when the exemption request was made there was no infringement to assess, it did offer comments on the nature of the freedom of religion claim.

> *S.L v. Commission scolaire des Chênes,* SCC 2012—Religious parents in Quebec objected to having their children taught that all religions are equal. The Court ruled the challenge premature because the course was not yet being taught. The Court commented on parents sharing their faith with their children.

The Court again affirmed its decision in *Amselem*:

> 22. ...If the person believes that he or she has an obligation to act in accordance with a practice or endorses a belief "having a nexus with religion", the court is limited to assessing the sincerity of the person's belief.[9]

The Court extended that personal belief to align with the "dissemination" part of religious freedom stated in *Big M Drug Mart* (see Chapter Eight):

> 50. In the present case, the allegation that freedom of religion was violated concerned a specific aspect of such freedom, namely the obligations of parents relating to the religious upbringing of their children and the passing on of their faith. The right of parents to bring up their children in their faith is part of the freedom of religion guaranteed by the *Canadian Charter*... Following the analytical approach adopted in *Amselem*, the appellants needed to establish that their religious belief

---

8   2012 SCC 7, [2012] 1 SCR 235.
9   *S.L.*, Paragraph 22.

was sincere and that the ERC Program infringed that aspect of their freedom of religion.[10]

As the Court is inclined to do, it also noted the limitation on parents' rights:

40. Parents are free to pass their personal beliefs on to their children if they so wish. However, the early exposure of children to realities that differ from those in their immediate family environment is a fact of life in society. The suggestion that exposing children to a variety of religious facts in itself infringes their religious freedom or that of their parents amounts to a rejection of the multicultural reality of Canadian society and ignores the Quebec government's obligations with regard to public education. Although such exposure can be a source of friction, it does not in itself constitute an infringement of s. 2 (a) of the *Canadian Charter* and of s. 3 of the *Quebec Charter*.[11]

These are all vital principles to consider in regard to our religious freedom. Yes, in some Canadian provinces it has resulted in Pastafarians from the Church of the Flying Spaghetti Monster having their driver's license photos taken with a colander on their head. More importantly, the Court has established that in religious disputes Canadian courts do not seek to hear evidence from opposing parties about what is legitimate to believe or not believe and what is or is not legitimate action based on that belief.

Can you imagine the Supreme Court being the final authority on matters of religious belief and practice? How would they decide on the issue of holy communion: transubstantiation (the bread and wine of communion become the actual body and blood of Christ) vs. consubstantiation (the bread and wine co-exist with the body and blood of Christ in communion) vs. representation (the bread and wine represent the body and blood of Christ in communion) vs. using grape juice instead of wine vs. those Christians who practise a love feast with a full meal instead of just bread and wine/juice vs. those who do not practise sacramental communion in any manner?

People get upset that Christian clubs are not allowed in some public schools and that Friday prayers for Muslim students are accommodated in others. As noted in Chapter Nine, I think the decision on denying Christian clubs is made in

---

10 Ibid., Paragraph 50.

11 Ibid., Paragraph 40.

error. But we can hardly argue in favour of the Christian clubs and at the same time argue to deny the Muslim prayer opportunity. First, the question of the nexus of practice with belief is individual, which supports both Christian clubs and Friday prayers—both occur on school property but not as school-directed activities imposed on all students. Second, the practice of Friday prayers resulted in students being late returning to class from mosque after lunch, so an accommodation was made to benefit the students and the operation of the school.

It is important for us to realize that a right granted to others is a right granted to me, and a right denied to others is a right denied to me. If I desire to stand against Friday prayers, then I had best be prepared to oppose Christian clubs. A better solution for our children might be to support both and request equal treatment.

I was ten years old when I received my Gideons New Testament in Grade Five. We all got one. Most of my friends considered it to be some kind of rite of passage. Now, many school boards bar the Gideons, because trustees and principals are afraid of human rights claims from those who object to the Christian sacred text—either opposing the school allowing access to the Gideons or demanding access for their own sacred texts. I support the latter, access for all sacred texts. Let a notice go home to parents and let parents decide if their child may receive free religious resources. This doesn't favour one over the other. Treat the sojourners in the land—which, by the way, is all of us who are not a member of Canada's Indigenous people—fairly, and our neighbours as ourselves. And perhaps inform parents that their child is receiving a religious education whether they think so or not. After all, as Justice Gonthier accurately observed, "everyone has 'belief' or 'faith' in something, be it atheistic, agnostic or religious. To construe 'secular' as the realm of the 'unbelief' is therefore erroneous."[12] Religion is about belief and practice. In what, Whom, or whom do you believe? Rejecting all sacred texts is action of the state that favours the non-religious.

Let's not forget the Golden Rule: *"So whatever you wish that others would do to you, do also to them..."* (Matthew 7:12)

---

12 *Chamberlain*, Paragraph 137. See Chapter Seven.

RELIGIOUS FREEDOM IS FOR GROUPS, CONGREGATIONS, AND INSTITUTIONS

Then they returned to Jerusalem from the mount called Olivet, which is near Jerusalem, a Sabbath day's journey away. And when they had entered, they went up to the upper room, where they were staying, Peter and John and James and Andrew, Philip and Thomas, Bartholomew and Matthew, James the son of Alphaeus and Simon the Zealot and Judas the son of James. All these with one accord were devoting themselves to prayer, together with the women and Mary the mother of Jesus, and his brothers.

—Acts 1:12–14

When the day of Pentecost arrived, they were all together in one place... And they devoted themselves to the apostles' teaching and the fellowship, to the breaking of bread and the prayers.

—Acts 2:1, 42

For as in one body we have many members, and the members do not all have the same function, so we, though many, are one body in Christ, and individually members one of another.

—Romans 12:4–5

And let us consider how to stir up one another to love and good works, not neglecting to meet together, as is the habit of some, but encouraging one another, and all the more as you see the Day drawing near.

—Hebrews 10:24–25

IN CHAPTER ONE, I MENTIONED THE EXCITEMENT OF MY FIRST TRIP TO ISRAEL, IN particular the close proximity of the landmarks mentioned in the Bible and the massive size of the fortress at Masada. Remember, the siege mentality at Masada resulted first in the defeat of the Roman garrison and, in time, the suicide of the Jewish zealots.

Another thrill for me was standing in the synagogue at Capernaum, which is likely in the same location where Jesus taught. The synagogue is right across the street from the house where it is thought that Peter's in-laws lived, where Jesus healed Peter's mother-in-law (Luke 4:38–40). There's a glass-bottom church building overtop of the in-laws' place, and did I mention I got to stand in the very synagogue!?

At Masada, our tour group sat in the synagogue where the leaders of the zealots are thought to have worshipped God, and where they eventually held the meeting to discuss their suicide plan.

My excitement wasn't so much about the buildings—or the ruins of them, in this case. It was about the people who had walked there.

Synagogues are houses of assembly, houses of worship, houses of prayer, and houses of education. The Yiddish term for a synagogue is *shul*, which simply means "school," a place to learn about and experience relationship with God. Do you remember the story of when Jesus went to the temple in Jerusalem and angrily overturned the tables of people who were buying and selling in the temple things that better belonged at the street market outside?

He said to them, "It is written, 'My house shall be called a house of prayer,' but you make it a den of robbers."

—Matthew 21:13

Community and communal worship were a central component of Judaism, and they are central to living the Christian life as well. In fact, communal worship is a significant component for most world religions. Together, we learn the beliefs and practices of our faith community—learning from each other about sound relationship, sound doctrine (orthodoxy), and sound practice (orthopraxy).

In the Christian Church, these communities are both congregational (organized around instruction and worship) and para-congregational (organized around a particular expression of common practice that is Christian in nature but frequently does not receive the attention it otherwise might because of our splintered denominational/congregational expression). Perhaps the para-congregational part of the Church is feeding the poor, either at home or abroad, in a way that eludes local congregations, caring for those in need in our society, actively bringing freedom to slaves in either the sex trade or other indentured service, seeking to advance stewardship of the Earth, or other pursuits. The congregational Church may also be engaged in these endeavours, sometimes through the para-congregational ministries and sometimes on the scale that the local congregation is able to execute on its own. Each Christian is part of the Church, the Body of Christ. None of us can do it all or do it alone. When we engage personally, we do our part, that which we are called and equipped by Christ to do. No person or contribution is insignificant when we do our part in the Body of Christ.

All of this takes place through the act of assembly. In the contemporary context, this most often involves organizational structures which establish a whole that is greater than the individuals who are part of it.

As one would expect, the Supreme Court has been asked to address the issue of freedom of religion for these collective groups, congregations, and institutions for the purpose of deciding whether the *Charter* guarantee applies to them or only to their individual participants. The following decisions expand on the reference to the collective aspects of freedom of religion noted by the Court in *R. v. Edwards Books and Arts Ltd.*[1]

Trinity Western University v. British Columbia College of Teachers

We looked at *Trinity Western University v. British Columbia College of Teachers*[2] in Chapter Eleven. The case concerned itself with a private Christian university's application for accreditation for its teachers' college. In making its decision, the Supreme Court gave consideration to the institutional freedom of religion right under the *Charter*.

> *Trinity Western University v. British Columbia College of Teachers*, SCC 2001—The BCCT refused to grant accreditation to TWU's school of education. The Court dealt with TWU as a single institution with a religious identity, not an aggregate of students and professors, deciding in TWU's favour.

25. ...TWU is not for everybody; it is designed to address the needs of people who share a number of religious convictions... It is important to note that this is a private institution that is exempted, in part, from the British Columbia human rights legislation and to which the *Charter*

---

1   [1986] 2 SCR 713. See Chapter Eight.
2   [2001] 1 SCR 772, 2001 SCC 31.

does not apply.[3] To state that the voluntary adoption of a code of conduct based on a person's own religious beliefs, in a private institution, is sufficient to engage s. 15 would be inconsistent with freedom of conscience and religion, which co-exist with the right to equality...

33. ...The diversity of Canadian society is partly reflected in the multiple religious organizations that mark the societal landscape and this diversity of views should be respected...

34. Consideration of human rights values in these circumstances encompasses consideration of the place of private institutions in our society and the reconciling of competing rights and values. Freedom of religion, conscience and association coexist with the right to be free of discrimination based on sexual orientation. Even though the requirement that students and faculty adopt the Community Standards creates unfavourable differential treatment since it would probably prevent homosexual students and faculty from applying, one must consider the true nature of the undertaking and the context in which this occurs. Many Canadian universities, including St. Francis Xavier University, Queen's University, McGill University and Concordia University College of Alberta, have traditions of religious affiliations. Furthermore, s. 93 of the *Constitution Act, 1867* enshrined religious public education rights into our Constitution, as part of the historic compromise which made Confederation possible... Although the constitutional protections were altered by constitutional amendment in Newfoundland in 1998 and eliminated in Quebec in 1997, they remain in effect in Ontario, Alberta, Saskatchewan and Manitoba.

35. Another part of that context is the *Human Rights Act*, S.B.C. 1984, c. 22, referred to by the Court of Appeal and the respondents (now the *Human Rights Code*), which provides, in s. 19 (now s. 41), that a religious institution is not considered to breach the Act where it prefers adherents of its religious constituency. It cannot be reasonably concluded that private institutions are protected but that their graduates are *de facto* considered unworthy of fully participating in public activities.[4]

---

3   Remember that the *Charter* does not apply to private relationships. See Chapter Seven.

4   *Trinity Western*, Paragraphs 25, 33–35.

In recognizing the place of religious institutions in Canadian society, the court dealt with TWU on the basis of both its own status and the status of the graduates from the TWU School of Education.

Congrégation des témoins de Jéhovah de St-Jérôme-Lafontaine v. Lafontaine (Village)

At issue in *Congrégation des témoins de Jéhovah de St-Jérôme-Lafontaine v. Lafontaine (Village)*[5] was whether a Quebec municipality had discriminated against a Jehovah's Witness congregation in their attempt to have commercial land rezoned so they could build a house of worship.

In the course of considering the duty of fairness on the municipality to accommodate the congregation's need, the Court dealt with the congregation as a single institution making the claim to infringement of its freedom of religion, not a collection of its members. The point is subtle but significant. In the end, the decision was made on a technical administrative law note and the request for rezoning was submitted back to the municipality to revisit its decision with the decision of the Court providing guidance and direction as to how to properly do so.

> *Congrégation des témoins de Jéhovah de St-Jérôme-Lafontaine v. Lafontaine (Village)*, SCC 2004—A Quebec Jehovah's Witness congregation wanted to build a new church building, but the city impeded suitable locations. The Court dealt with the congregation as a single entity, setting guidelines for the village to make a decision.

Reference re Same-Sex Marriage

While there had been sporadic attempts at same-sex marriages in Canada beginning in the 1970s, legal challenges to the definition of marriage were commenced in British Columbia, Ontario, and Quebec in 2000.[6] These challenges utilized the equality rights provisions in Section 15 of the *Charter*.

The checkerboard pattern of decisions by provincial courts across the country began to coalesce when the appeal courts of these three jurisdictions all approved of same-sex marriages being performed in their jurisdictions. Following the release of the Ontario Court of Appeal's decision in *Halpern v.*

---

5   [2004] 2 SCR 650, 2004 SCC 48.

6   Buckingham, *Fighting Over God*, 154.

Canada (Attorney General)[7] in June 2003, Prime Minister Jean Chretien held a press conference at which he announced that the federal government would not be appealing the decisions but would instead send a reference case on the issue to the Supreme Court of Canada. The issues for consideration by the Court would ultimately include: jurisdiction of the federal government to define marriage,[8] the jurisdiction of the provincial governments to solemnize marriage (the ceremony and registration),[9] the equality rights provisions in the *Constitution Act, 1982*,[10] and the *Charter*'s Section 2(a) provision for freedom of religion. By not appealing the B.C., Ontario, and Quebec cases, however, their decisions became the law in those provinces. Same-sex marriages were being performed and a potential legal quagmire lay ahead.

While the nationwide assortment of same-sex marriage court actions were taking place, another evangelical Christian group was taking an approach like that of the "moral majority" in the U.S. (see Chapter Nine's reference to the moral majority and the different approach of The Evangelical Fellowship of Canada). The leader of this Canadian expression, Charles McVety, was well tutored by leaders in the moral majority and implemented a Canadian version of their political style of engagement. Careful to protect the registered charity status of Canada Christian College, of which McVety was president and which was accredited with the Ontario Ministry of Training, Colleges, and Universities, the emerging group's activity was carried out through Canada Family Action and other organizations that recognized McVety's leadership. One such organization was the Defend Marriage Campaign, which sponsored the event with the "Adam and Eve NOT Adam and Steve" lawn signs mentioned in this book's introduction.

Following is a quote from me that was reported by Charles Lewis in a *National Post* story about McVety:

> While there are points where Rev. McVety's opinions and those of the broader Canadian evangelical community intersect, it would be a mistake to conclude that either he or his opinions are representative. I've said before that Charles' theological position is at one end of the

---

7   2003 CanLII 26403 (ON CA).

8   *Constitution Act, 1867*, Section 91 (26).

9   *Constitution Act, 1867*, Section 92 (12).

10 *Canadian Charter of Rights and Freedoms*, Section 15.

spectrum of Canadian evangelicalism and his American perspective draws attention and stirs up conversation.[11]

The Evangelical Fellowship of Canada connects with a religious community that spans thirty to thirty-five percent on either side of the theological and political centres of Canada's evangelical population (this is what I call "the evangelical spectrum"). McVety's leadership overlaps, touching down at points with five to ten percent of the theologically and politically right-of-centre portion of that group and then extends beyond, further right of centre, touching down with a further ten to fifteen percent. There are also points where his organizations touch closer to the centre of the spectrum. This is not to suggest any representative size to McVety's influence, as it is not feasible to accurately assess the extent of his organizations' constituency.

McVety has also found alignment on some issues with similarly opinioned representatives in other religious communities. The general alignment and expression of this group of Christian organizations mirrors that of the U.S. religious right: they are pro-Israel, pro-child protection, anti-same-sex marriage, pro-intelligent design, anti-environmentalism, pro-religious freedom, and outspoken on Islamic infiltration. McVety also heads the Evangelical Association that includes several hundred ministry credential holders, many of whom pastor church congregations.

Charles McVety is often found leading in the public square in politically assertive ways that the EFC, as a registered charity and with a substantially larger and identifiable constituent base, cannot.

While McVety was leading the Defend Marriage Campaign, the EFC was making submissions to the courts and Parliament in its more nuanced style. This included a role in getting the *Charter* Section 2(a) freedom of religion question before the Supreme Court of Canada in *Reference re Same-Sex Marriage*.[12]

Reference re Same-Sex Marriage, SCC 2004—The federal government asked the Court to review draft legislation to redefine marriage. The Court ruled that it was within Parliament's jurisdiction, and any change would require recognizing the rights of individuals and institutions who hold to a religious definition.

---

11   Charles Lewis, "Outspoken Evangelical Isn't Afraid to Get into Scraps," *National Post*, November 6, 2010.

12   [2004] 3 SCR 698, 2004 SCC 79.

In its decision in *Reference re Same-Sex Marriage*, the Court manoeuvred its way through the division of powers under the *Constitution Act, 1867* by deciding that Parliament had the constitutional authority to define marriage under Section 91(26), and such definition by Parliament did not intrude on provincial jurisdiction. The Court gave no direction as to whether the federal government should redefine marriage, but it commented on constitutional considerations should Parliament choose to do so.

Dealing with the matter that concerns us, institutional freedom of religion, the Court stated:

53. The protection of freedom of religion afforded by s. 2 (*a*) of the *Charter* is broad and jealously guarded in our *Charter* jurisprudence...

55. The *Proposed Act* is limited in its effect to marriage for civil purposes... It cannot be interpreted as affecting religious marriage or its solemnization... We therefore consider this question as it applies to the performance, by religious officials, of both religious and civil marriages. We also must consider the question to mean "compelled by the state" to perform, since s. 2 (*a*) relates only to state action; the protection of freedom of religion against private actions is not within the ambit of this question. We note that it would be for the Provinces, in the exercise of their power over the solemnization of marriage, to legislate in a way that protects the rights of religious officials while providing for solemnization of same-sex marriage. It should also be noted that human rights codes must be interpreted and applied in a manner that respects the broad protection granted to religious freedom under the *Charter.*

56. Against this background, we return to the question. The concern here is that if the *Proposed Act* were adopted, religious officials could be required to perform same-sex marriages contrary to their religious beliefs. Absent state compulsion on religious officials, this conjecture does not engage the *Charter.* If a promulgated statute were to enact compulsion, we conclude that such compulsion would almost certainly run afoul of the *Charter* guarantee of freedom of religion, given the expansive protection afforded to religion by s. 2 (*a*) of the *Charter.*

57. The right to freedom of religion enshrined in s. 2 (*a*) of the *Charter* encompasses the right to believe and entertain the religious beliefs of one's choice, the right to declare one's religious beliefs openly and the right to manifest religious belief by worship, teaching,

dissemination and religious practice... The performance of religious rites is a fundamental aspect of religious practice.

58. It therefore seems clear that state compulsion on religious officials to perform same-sex marriages contrary to their religious beliefs would violate the guarantee of freedom of religion under s. 2(*a*) of the *Charter*. It also seems apparent that, absent exceptional circumstances which we cannot at present foresee, such a violation could not be justified under s. 1 of the *Charter*.

59. The question we are asked to answer is confined to the performance of same-sex marriages by religious officials. <u>However, concerns were raised about the compulsory use of sacred places for the celebration of such marriages and about being compelled to otherwise assist in the celebration of same-sex marriages. The reasoning that leads us to conclude that the guarantee of freedom of religion protects against the compulsory celebration of same-sex marriages, suggests that the same would hold for these concerns.</u>

60. Returning to the question before us, the Court is of the opinion that, absent unique circumstances with respect to which we will not speculate, the guarantee of religious freedom in s. 2 (*a*) of the *Charter* is broad enough to protect religious officials from being compelled by the state to perform civil or religious same-sex marriages that are contrary to their religious beliefs.[13]

This is a significant example of the Court stating its decision in regard to the rights of individuals. It would also be applicable to congregations, denominations, institutions, and other structures of communal religious expression.

As I finished writing this book, the Supreme Court heard argument in the British Columbia case *Ktunaxa Nation Council and Kathryn Teneese v. Minister of Forests and Glacier Resorts Ltd.*[14] This religious freedom claim by an Indigenous First Nation in regard to proposed development of traditionally sacred (religious) lands may have significant impact on the concepts of individual and group religious freedom, as well as in regard to the sacred space—large or small—that has a nexus with the religious beliefs and practices of the community. Canada's Indigenous peoples are tied to both community and land, believing that the Creator has

---

13 *Ref re Same-Sex Marriage*, Paragraphs 53, 55–60. Emphasis added.
14 SCC File No. 36664, heard December 1, 2016.

placed the community on the land in a specific location for the Creator's reasons. This is similar to the theology regarding the nation of Israel.

Loyola High School v. Quebec (Attorney General)

As you may recall from Chapter Nine, Loyola High School is a private Catholic school for boys located in Montreal. In accordance with Ministry of Education guidelines, Loyola sought exemption from teaching the Ethics and Religious Culture course because it already taught a similar course in world religions and ethics.

> *Loyola High School v. Quebec*, SCC 2015—A private Catholic school in Montreal objected to teaching that all religions are equal. The Court dealt with the school as a school, not just an aggregate of parents, teachers and students, in making its decision in favour of the school's religious freedom.

The decision in *Loyola High School v. Quebec (Attorney General)*[15] is complicated slightly by the Court splitting 4–3 in agreement on the result but differentiating in the analysis to get there. Justice Abella wrote for the majority and Chief Justice McLachlin and Justice Moldaver for the minority.

Justice Abella concluded:

33. Loyola, a non-profit corporation… also argued that its own religious freedom had been violated by the decision. I recognize that individuals may sometimes require a legal entity in order to give effect to the constitutionally protected communal aspects of their religious beliefs and practice, such as the transmission of their faith… I do not believe it is necessary, however, to decide whether corporations enjoy religious freedom in their own right under s. 2 (*a*) of the *Charter* or s. 3 of the [Quebec] *Charter of human rights and freedoms*… in order to dispose of this appeal.

34. In this case Loyola, as an entity lawfully created to give effect to religious belief and practice, was denied a statutory exemption from an otherwise mandatory regulatory scheme. As the subject of the administrative decision, Loyola is entitled to apply for judicial review and to argue that the Minister failed to respect the values underlying the grant of her discretion as part of its challenge of the merits of the

---

15   2015 SCC 12, [2015] 1 SCR 613.

decision. In my view, as a result, it is not necessary to decide whether Loyola itself, as a corporation, enjoys the benefit of s. 2 (*a*) rights, since the Minister is bound in any event to exercise her discretion in a way that respects the values underlying the grant of her decision-making authority, including the *Charter*-protected religious freedom of the members of the Loyola community who seek to offer and wish to receive a Catholic education...[16]

Even though Justice Abella did not find it necessary to determine the issue of corporate religious belief, she did say that the Minister, the decision-maker whose decision was being appealed, had to make the decision in a way that considered the "religious freedom of the members of the Loyola community who seek to offer and wish to receive a Catholic education." This requires assessment of both the individuals and the school which was offering the education. Students graduate and their parents move on, but the school retains a continuing presence which has to be part of the consideration.

Chief Justice McLachlin and Justice Moldaver stated:

83. Like our colleague Abella J., we would allow the appeal. In our view, the Minister's decision cannot be upheld because it failed to protect Loyola's right to religious freedom...

88. We are required to address several issues in deciding this appeal. First, we must decide whether Loyola as a religious organization is entitled to the constitutional protection of freedom of religion. Concluding that it is, we analyze the proper interpretation of the legislative and regulatory scheme at issue in this appeal...

91. In our view, Loyola may rely on the guarantee of freedom of religion found in s. 2 (*a*) of the *Canadian Charter*. The communal character of religion means that protecting the religious freedom of individuals requires protecting the religious freedom of religious organizations, including religious educational bodies such as Loyola. Canadian and international jurisprudence supports this conclusion.

92. This Court has affirmed that freedom of religion under s. 2 (*a*) of the *Canadian Charter* as both an individual and a collective dimension. In *Syndicat Northcrest v. Amselem*... Bastarache J., writing in dissent but not on this point, quoted Professor Timothy Macklem for

---

16 *Loyola High School*, Paragraphs 33–34.

the proposition that religions are necessarily collective endeavours...
It follows that any genuine freedom of religion must protect, not only
individual belief, but the institutions and practices that permit the collective development and expression of that belief...

94. The individual and collective aspects of freedom of religion
are indissolubly intertwined. The freedom of religion of individuals cannot flourish without freedom of religion for the organizations
through which those individuals express their religious practices and
through which they transmit their faith.[17]

Following an examination of supportive international law on this point,
they added:

100. On the submissions before us, and given the collective aspect of
religious freedom long established in our jurisprudence, we conclude
that an organization meets the requirements for s. 2 (*a*) protection if (1)
it is constituted primarily for religious purposes, and (2) its operation
accords with these religious purposes.[18]

More words are needed to allow the Court to express itself rather than offer my summary, but I trust you have found two things in reading them. First,
Supreme Court decisions really aren't that scary to read. Second, you can pick up
on the Court's affirmation of the religious freedom of organizations and generate
ideas on the constitutional protections afforded to us now, as well as any changes
necessary to ensure better protection for the congregational and/or para-congregational ministries with which you are involved.

Christianity is a relational religion—relational with God and relational with
other Christians (and relational with non-Christians, but that's not what this chapter is about). Christianity is lived in community, with all the faults of every human
being who is part of the community. In Canada, our constitution provides protection that encourages the creation of religious communities for worship and service.

---

17 Ibid., Paragraphs 83, 88, 91–92, 94.
18 Ibid., Paragraph 100.

CHAPTER FOURTEEN

THE CHURCH LIKELY CANNOT SERVE BOTH GOD AND GOVERNMENT WITHOUT TROUBLE

*Then the King will say to those on his right, "Come, you who are blessed by my
Father, inherit the kingdom prepared for you from the foundation of the world. For
I was hungry and you gave me food, I was thirsty and you gave me drink, I was
a stranger and you welcomed me, I was naked and you clothed me, I was sick and
you visited me, I was in prison and you came to me."*

*Then the righteous will answer him, saying, "Lord, when did we see you
hungry and feed you, or thirsty and give you drink? And when did we see you a
stranger and welcome you, or naked and clothe you? And when did we see you sick
or in prison and visit you?"*

*And the King will answer them, "Truly, I say to you, as you did it to one
of the least of these my brothers, you did it to me."*

—Matthew 25:34–40

My dad was a dairy farmer in Barbados before he, my mum, and my sisters
moved to Canada. Many years later, in conversation with the old farmer who
became an engineer, I bemoaned my frustration at what was happening to my
beloved Salvation Army.

The Salvation Army is active in more than 120 countries and well known for
its history of practical, charitable expressions of faith in response to need. These
include halfway houses for men leaving prison, homes for unwed mothers (several
of which have become hospitals for women and children), orphanages, schools,
hostels for the unemployed, addiction treatment centres, thrift stores where the
addicted can find employment, and residences for senior citizens, in addition to an
international network of church congregations. In the late twentieth century, as
these good works outgrew The Salvation Army's capacity to fund them, difficult

decisions had to be made, and I was part of the decision-making process. Would we shut down what could not be funded or accept government funding to continue meeting people's real needs? The receipt of government funding eventually resulted in government demands.

As a member of The Salvation Army's Council on Morals and Ethics (now called the Council on Social Issues), I was a participant in some significant discussions. Having originally developed from one home for unwed mothers into a network of premier hospitals for maternal and child health, should the denomination's Grace hospitals accede to provincial funding demands to perform abortions, try to raise the millions necessary annually to run each hospital independently, or transfer our hospitals to government? If transferred, what would happen to the historic name? And should The Salvation Army negotiate to continue its chaplaincy services? When giving addicts a chance to remake their lives, would job training remain part of their fully funded treatment or would they be paid a wage for it in addition to receiving room, food, and counselling? If the thrift store or workshop were to be unionized, what would happen to the job training opportunities? These were difficult questions to which the answers were equally difficult.

The Salvation Army had just entered the process of shutting down some operations or transferring them to the government. In some instances, we formed partnerships with similar Catholic or other Christian entities to maintain the Christian presence. Our employees didn't understand. The unions objected. And I was head of the legal department. Theologically and vocationally, I was frustrated. Emotionally, I was burned out.

I was visiting my dad, who would listen for only so long. That's when the old farmer said it: "If you suck on the government teat, you're only going to get what the government decides to give you."

I don't know a single Christian social service ministry that doesn't put the people it serves second, Christ being first. Christian ministries and government bureaucrats have entered into agreements in good faith, knowing that the ministries were doing a better job than the government because of the heart behind the work. It was ministry unto Him, not simply unto them. Times changed, representatives on both sides of the negotiating tables changed, and government spokespersons increasingly pushed beyond the focus of serving people in need to challenging things they didn't understand or accept about the Christian ethos of the increasingly government-dependent organizations.

The Salvation Army was not the only Christian ministry facing these challenges, and the challenges haven't gone away even as the Supreme Court clarified the relevant law. If lawyers and judges don't grasp the legal and constitutional concepts of state neutrality and religious organizations being dealt with on equal footing with other organizations, how could it be expected of elected officials—municipal, provincial, and federal—and government bureaucrats, who were constantly moving into their positions and then moving on? As you might expect, the pastors and Christian leaders on the other side of the negotiations weren't much better prepared.

One legal decision that myriad Christian ministries took great consolation in, and structured themselves around, was the 1992 direction provided by law professor Errol Mendes, acting as an Ontario Board of Enquiry (predecessor to the Ontario Human Rights Tribunal), in *Parks v. Christian Horizons*.[1] The decision established that religious organizations operating under provisions of Ontario's *Human Rights Code* had to have both a statement of faith and a statement of the lifestyle requirements that could be reasonably expected from employees as a result of the organizations' religious nature. These documents were to be presented and agreed upon as part of the hiring process. Everyone who worked for them, or worked for other Christian ministries that relied on the decision, would know what was expected.

That decision held for nearly two decades, then was carried one step further in the decision of the Ontario Superior Court of Justice, Divisional Court, in *Ontario Human Rights Commission v. Christian Horizons*,[2] often referred to as *Heintz v. Christian Horizons*.

> *Parks v. Christian Horizons*, ON Bd of Enquiry 1992—Employees of a Christian organization contravened conduct expectations by entering into common-law relationships. The board decided that a religious organization required statements of faith and lifestyle requirements that defined their expectations as part of the hiring process.

Christian Horizons was established in 1965 as a ministry serving people with developmental disabilities in a residential setting. It grew into Ontario's largest such service provider. Connie Heintz worked for Christian Horizons for five years, then left because of the fallout from her involvement in a same-sex relationship. She filed a human rights

---

1   16 CHRR D/40.
2   2010 ONSC 2105.

complaint that was decided by the Ontario Human Rights Tribunal in 2008[3] in opposite manner to the decision in *Parks*. The *Heintz* decision was appealed to the Ontario Superior Court system, where a panel of three judges heard arguments from the parties and interveners.

The court affirmed the nature of a religious organization under the *Code*, including the need for statement of faith and lifestyle policies, but deleted the reference to same-sex relationships and added the requirement that each employee job description indicate the *bona fide* (legitimate) rationale for the responsibilities of that particular position to require agreement with the organization's statement of faith and its lifestyle policy.

At that point, Christian Horizons was faced with the dilemma of continuing to fight the issue of religious practice with a branch of the same government from which it received its funding, or accept the general affirmation by the court of its Christian ministry and get on with serving its more than 1,400 residents, in over 180 locations, employing over 2,500 staff. Moving on from the courts would avoid a costly financial battle that could potentially jeopardize future government funding and prevent them from having to spend private charitable support on the legal battle.

Heintz v. Christian Horizons, ON SC 2010—An employee of a Christian organization contravened conduct expectations by engaging in a same-sex relationship. The court ruled that each employee's job description would need to indicate a legitimate work-related rationale for the applicability of statement of faith and lifestyle requirements.

It was a tough call. The leadership at Christian Horizons stepped out of the court system to focus on their clients, staff, and ministry.

I was asked to write an article on this case for the Cardus publication *Policy in Public*,[4] from which the following "Nine Lessons from Someone Else's Experience" are abbreviated. Cardus describes itself as "a think tank dedicated to the renewal of North American social architecture. Drawing on more than 2000 years of Christian social thought, we work to enrich and challenge public debate through research, events, and publications, for the common good."[5]

---

3   *Heintz v. Christian Horizons*, 2008 HRTO 22 (CanLII), 65 C.C.E.L. (3d) 218, 63 C.H.R.R. 12.

4   Don Hutchinson, "How (Not) To Read Heintz vs. Christian Horizons," *Policy in Public*, December 22, 2010 (https://www.cardus.ca/policy/archives/2368/).

5   *Cardus*, "About Cardus." Date of access: January 10, 2017 (https://www.cardus.ca/organization/about/).

1. The View from Outside

As Christians, we must remove our Christ-coloured glasses to fully consider the requirements of Canadian law for the establishment and preservation of Christian community in, by, and for the Christian community. What may appear obvious to faith communities is less obvious to those who do not share the same world-view. Basic documents such as statements of faith, lifestyle positional statements, and well-thought-out position descriptions that identify the job-relevant need for each employee to be part of the Christian community are essential.

2. Self-Define

The second lesson is related to the first. Religious people often fail to realize that it is the responsibility of each community to properly define itself—its beliefs, purposes, requirements of membership, and process for removing members who choose to violate those requirements. Christian communities, including educational institutions, ministry organizations, denominations, and congregations, must not assume that by declaring themselves Christian the way they understand their existence or their biblical interpretation will be understood by all or be determinative in employment, membership, student, or other selection issues. Communities must develop a comprehensive explanation of their existence, including statements of faith and statements of lifestyle and workplace expectations, that defines what they believe, why they exist, and what they expect. These statements and definitions must be understandable by those who share the convictions of the community as well as those who do not.

In short, if we define who we are, what we believe, and what our behavioural expectations are, as well as the consequences for an individual who changes his or her beliefs or engages in incompatible behaviour and the method by which those consequences may be administered, then we will be well-prepared to stand the test of a legal challenge to our existence as a religious community. Of course, no individual or organization in today's Canada can prevent a legal challenge, but we can prepare to successfully defend one.

3. Be Prepared for Disagreement

Religious communities are wise to equip themselves to handle disagreement, dispute, and disappointment. This will help to avoid potential allegations of a poisoned work environment by someone who might otherwise be, or in fact is, subjected to misbehaviour by others in the community as a result of such disagreement, dispute, or disappointment. Having a properly established process and adhering to it will help avoid the question of any failure to follow principles of natural justice if someone is asked to leave the community.

One danger that many Christian ministries may encounter is the temptation to breach the sanctity of the community in order to be compassionate to someone in need, to staff an existing non-leadership position with someone who does not share the community's commitment, or to respond to available finances for staffing by not holding out for the qualified candidate who is also able to agree to the community's faith and conduct standards.

4. Define and Hold to Community Integrity

It is important to protect the structural integrity of every aspect of the community. To do this, you must know corporately who you are and who you wish to be. Then the community must consistently hold to the standards established. Exceptions create openings that may breach the constitution and composition of the community. Such exceptions may also compromise the community if challenged at law.

5. Integrate and Publish Community Requirements

The leadership of a religious community must state and implement, on a person-by-person basis, the truth that existing as a religious community requires each person to know both the importance of community and the connection of community to every member of that community, both in what they believe and in what they do. For employers, position descriptions that do not identify the importance of shared faith and practice, and which do not genuinely connect both to the responsibilities of the individual, will be insufficient. Complete descriptions will meet the requirements of the objective standard of a legitimate occupational requirement such as is found in Ontario and other jurisdictions.

For example, I was part of a large staff at a church which determined that all staff had to share an understanding of faith and practice. In addition to a statement of faith and lifestyle expectations, each position description—from the senior pastor to the junior dishwasher—required the applicant to be able to share a personal testimony of being a Christian, pray with others, lead another person to Christ if asked, and give directions to the washrooms or onsite restaurant. Staff at the church were equipped in these areas. Public announcements were regularly made letting all gathered know that if someone required any of the above, they could look for a person wearing church staff identification—and thus, anyone wearing a church ID was required to exercise those functions. Staff were also required to attend devotions and participate in other religious functions at the church.

6. Choose in Advance Who Tells Your Story

Make sure there are people of character and qualification who are known in advance to be able to explain the religious community, its purpose, and its requirements clearly and unshakeably. This will help both in legal confrontation and if a sounding board is needed to deal with an internal situation. These people are frequently already in your circle of contacts and need not be on the board or staff of the organization. It might be a theologian or a community leader who knows you well. Be aware of them before a problem arises.

7. Canada Has No Separation of Church and State

Canada has no developed constitutional or legal doctrine of the separation of church and state, as formulated by the United States Supreme Court. Instead, Canada has a long history of cooperation between the church and the state, coupled with a sound legal doctrine and definition of religious freedom. In Canada, a distinctly Christian institution may be a religious organization and receive public funding for the provision of a public service.

It is difficult to overstress the importance of Canadian Christians and Christian communities continuing to engage outside the walls of the Church—whether it's the congregational expression, the ministry service organization, or the educational institution—in order to maintain this continuing cooperation. Failure to be involved in the community of Church *and* non-Church is to implicitly accept a creeping standard of confinement to a stained-glass closet, as those who oppose the Church—and all matters of public expression of religion and religiously based beliefs—advocate for the privatization of matters related to faith.

The privatization of faith which is being pursued by those who dislike the Church and its influence would include the prohibition of expressions of faith in the public sphere of life, including the Church's separation from involvement in the public square, exclusion from providing faith-based non-discriminatory public service, and ineligibility to receive public funding for providing services that benefit the general public. We may disagree on the Church's engagement in some of these ways, based on our own beliefs, but we can agree that those who do believe that engagement is important should be free to do so.

8. Rights Talk

We live in a society consumed by the concept of rights. Rights are granted and limited in our society, depending on a variety of circumstances. Christian communities across the country have a recognized right to exist and engage in behaviour related to the beliefs that form the foundation of their existence. Christian institutions have particular rights that permit them to engage in selective hiring, requiring their employees to agree with their mission, beliefs, and behaviours— provided the institution adequately explains the mission, beliefs, and behaviours and why they are essential to the performance of the individual's work, whether it be in a job or vocation.

Section 24(1)(a) of the *Ontario Human Rights Code* is a provision for religious and cultural organizations. It is not a rights exemption, but a granting of rights. Saying that Christian Horizons or other Christian institutions are somehow empowered to discriminate by the section is incorrect. The section grants rights to identifiable communities, including those identified by creed or religious belief, to be selective in their hiring practices without infringing on the rights of an employee or prospective employee who is not qualified under the provisions of that section.

If a candidate or employee is not qualified for the position they seek or hold, there is no infringement of rights in not employing that person. Banks, law firms, car dealerships, and grocery stores are all selective in their employment practices. Religious institutions that engage in selective employment in accordance with the provisions of section 24(1)(a), and similar provisions in other provinces, are operating in compliance with human rights legislation, not with exemption from that legislation.

9. Media Strategy

This brings me to the ninth lesson. Throughout this process, Christian Horizons was under the media's microscope. Organizations must realize that the media is looking for a story. They are not necessarily looking for a nice story, with helpful lessons, but often a soundbite that portrays religious communities as something less than beloved. The media might not be on your side, so assess how best to present a concise and comprehensive, cooperative image to the press. Prepare your talking points, choosing your words carefully. Consider consulting with a media relations expert. Then stick to your talking points, providing your version of the story, not a defence or an explanation, but a concise reason for why your community exists and why you have done right, not wrong.

Don't be afraid of participating in a relationship with the government in order to effect Christian ministry. Do be prepared for the possibility that something might go wrong in the relationship, particularly that the demands of government might exceed the capacity of the Church to comply.

CHAPTER FIFTEEN

SACRED TEXTS ARE NOT HATE SPEECH

Do not think that I [Jesus] have come to abolish the Law or the Prophets; I have
not come to abolish them but to fulfill them. For truly, I say to you, until heaven
and earth pass away, not an iota, not a dot, will pass from the Law until all is
accomplished. Therefore whoever relaxes one of the least of these commandments
and teaches others to do the same will be called least in the kingdom of heaven, but
whoever does them and teaches them will be called great in the kingdom of heaven.
For I tell you, unless your righteousness exceeds that of the scribes and Pharisees,
you will never enter the kingdom of heaven.

—Matthew 5:17–20

ANOTHER CONFESSION: I DIDN'T REALLY WANT TO BE SEEN WITH BILL WHATCOTT WHEN
he came to Ottawa for his hearing. Not many Christian leaders did. Full marks
to Tom Schuck, the lawyer who represented Whatcott all the way through the
process that brought his case with the Saskatchewan Human Rights Commission
to the Supreme Court of Canada. Schuck is a member of Canada's Christian Legal
Fellowship (CLF), a charitable organization whose members have proven to be the
backbone of religious freedom activity in the courts.

It was a privilege to attend my first CLF conference in 1988. At the annual
general meeting it was announced that, after ten years, the board had decided
to wrap up operations. As a naive young law school grad, I asked if CLF would
continue if someone new was prepared to make the effort. About ten minutes
later, I was chair of the board! And very grateful that others stood to give CLF
another try.

Bill Whatcott is not the only person I have felt that way about. I did have
a brief conversation with him, finding out a bit more about who he is and what
makes him tick. But in the role I was in, as someone who represented a broad

swath of the Canadian evangelical Christian community, there was media danger in being tied to the controversial activist.

Single-issue-focused activists in the Christian camp tend to have a deeply personal motivation, know their issue extremely well, and be uncompromising in their position. Unfortunately, they have often studied their topic extensively in the Bible but not situated that topic in a whole biblical context for either their own consideration or that of others. Often the single-issue-focused person treats others as backsliders—as if they were previously Christian and would have found themselves in agreement with the activist's position—who, in the activist's opinion, need a good Bible-thumping to get back on track. This is distinct from those who see others as likely being without biblical understanding, or having a different biblical understanding, who would benefit from receiving a clear and logical, even temperate, presentation of the activist's position.

I admire the passion of these members of the Body of Christ but have found that their frequently all-or-nothing attitude clashes with attainable goals both in politics and in the courts. To be fair, there are some single-issue-focused activists who are first-rate advocates with a solid understanding of Scripture and a full appreciation of the context into which their issue fits.

Charles Ringma expresses my concern succinctly. In his book of daily biblical reflections, *Seize the Day with Dietrich Bonhoeffer*, Ringma's devotional thought for September 19 includes these words:

> In proclaiming the relevance of Christ for our world, we need to make sure that it is Christ's message that we are sharing and living and not simply our convenient version of it.[1]

The gospel message requires us as Christ-followers to identify more than one or two Bible verses that we have interpreted to support our thoughts. We are called to acquire an understanding of the overarching theme of the Bible, and then engage in what the apostle Paul calls *"the ministry of reconciliation"* (2 Corinthians 5:18). Not one dot on an "i" or horizontal line on a "t" will disappear from the Old Testament. But for our righteousness to be greater than that of ancient religious leaders who insisted on adherence to all the Old Testament laws, and the laws they built upon those laws, we need to embrace the whole gospel, the full

---

1   Charles Ringma, *Seize the Day with Dietrich Bonhoeffer* (Colorado Springs, CO: Pinon Press, 2000), September 19.

story that includes creation, the fall of humanity, wandering, redemption, and restoration in Christ. Into that story fits our pursuit of justice.

To learn and live a whole gospel life requires effort on our part. Indulge me with a bit of a bunny trail on that thought before we return to Bill Whatcott.

I encourage you to begin by investing in your understanding of the gospel, set in the whole context of Scripture. Like any other interest you might pursue in life, it's worth making a small expenditure to really get into it. And this investment isn't just about a hobby; it's your life. This is what I call the $100 library. After you have a Bible (not included in the pricing), the other suggested books help with understanding it and placing public policy issues on your heart, and evangelism too, into the whole gospel context:

- My favourite Bible right now cost me $8. I've been using it for three years. It's an ESV (English Standard Version) Deluxe Compact Bible with a minor defect in how some of the pages were cut. I bought it on sale. I like it because it has clear print, it is pocket-size, and I read from it daily.

  What's the best Bible? Which translation is best? The one you will read. I have read several translations and paraphrases, along with complaints theologians have about every single one of them! The Canadian Bible Society (CBS) has a great little resource called "The Bible Explored: A Short History," which gives a brief history of the Bible's translation into English. You can download it for free from their website.[2]

  The CBS also has a program called "Proclamation" that equips one's church or community to orally read through the Bible in ten days. That's the whole Bible read out loud in ten days. Think how much less time it would take to read it to yourself. That's why it's important to have a Bible you enjoy reading.

  Here's a chart that may be helpful in considering which Bible translation interests you. Some effort may be required to find the Bible you will invest in. It may be what your congregation uses or it may take some experimental reading from a friend's collection of Bibles, online, or at a Bible bookstore.

---

2   *Canadian Bible Society*, "The Bible Explored 2: A Short History." Date of access: January 10, 2017 (https://biblesociety.ca/ebook/bible-explored-2-short-history).

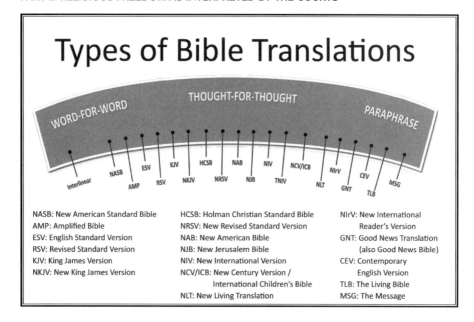

Types of Bible Translations

NASB: New American Standard Bible	HCSB: Holman Christian Standard Bible	NIrV: New International
AMP: Amplified Bible	NRSV: New Revised Standard Version	Reader's Version
ESV: English Standard Version	NAB: New American Bible	GNT: Good News Translation
RSV: Revised Standard Version	NJB: New Jerusalem Bible	(also Good News Bible)
KJV: King James Version	NIV: New International Version	CEV: Contemporary
NKJV: New King James Version	NCV/ICB: New Century Version /	English Version
	International Children's Bible	TLB: The Living Bible
	NLT: New Living Translation	MSG: The Message

- *The Salvation Army Handbook of Doctrine.* This simple, straightforward explanation of the basics from a Wesleyan perspective is still my go-to on foundational, biblically supported beliefs of the Church. You can get a new hardcover copy for $24.50 from The Salvation Army. You can get it used online for less, or download the free PDF version of the 2010 revision. I use the 1969 edition.[3]

- *Knowing God* by J.I. Packer, an Anglican, is the book I buy at used book sales to give to new Christians. This book provides a solid topical foundation and the Bible references are a good way to learn life principles and tie them back to what the Bible says. Because of its popularity, it has been reprinted multiple times in a variety of formats. You can get a brand new paperback for $15–20.[4]

- *What the Bible Is All About* by Henrietta Mears is an overview of the Bible from the perspective of a Presbyterian Sunday school teacher, writing for her class. Billy Graham used to give these away at crusades. You can pick this up new in paperback for $8–10. This book will provide a whole Bible context to your reading and study.

---

3   *The Salvation Army Handbook of Doctrine* (London, UK: Salvation Books, 2010). Access the PDF edition at: https://s3.amazonaws.com/cache.salvationarmy.org/26defc89-e794-4e5a-a567-0793f3742430_English+Handbook+of+Doctrine+web.pdf

4   J.I. Packer, *Knowing God* (Downers Grove, IL: Intervarsity Press, 1973).

Along with *Knowing God*, it will add some Reformed tradition theology to the Wesleyan *Handbook of Doctrine*.[5]

- The *ESV Study Bible*. I have a lot of Bible study resources in my bookcases. This one has become my go-to. Our congregation uses the ESV as our teaching Bible. At our Bible school, I have met and taught students who have multiple university degrees as well as students who do not have a high school diploma. This study Bible serves both well, is a mandatory textbook, and is the sole textbook for several of our courses. It is an excellent resource. You can buy a hardcover (you'll want the hardcover to protect this if you're going to use it as intended) for $35–45.[6]

- *My Utmost for His Highest* by Oswald Chambers. I'm a big fan of daily devotional books. These books usually have a single, pocket-size page per day reflection on a biblical text that challenges the reader to consider how they are growing in their life with Christ. I used this one for years, and revisit it every three to five years, before moving on to others. You can get this classic, first published in 1924, as a brand new paperback for $5–10.[7]

These books are all in the Protestant tradition of *Sola Scriptura*—the Bible alone. They also respect and reflect the historic, traditional understanding of Scripture. Their presentation takes a "What does the Bible say?" approach, for the most part setting aside matters of disagreement on differing traditions and practices. That's the part of the Church I know.

You might also check with your pastor or spiritual mentor to find out if he or she would suggest a modified $100 library. If you are using a different Bible translation, they might recommend a study Bible that aligns with that translation for ease of use.

You don't need bookcases full of Christian books. If you can swing it, you'll benefit from a half-shelf of books you'll read and use as a continuing resource for understanding the narrative of the whole context of the Bible, and the issues of life.

---

5   Henrietta Mears, *What the Bible Is All About* (Ventura, CA: Regal Books, 1985). First edition 1953.

6   *ESV Study Bible: English Standard Version* (Wheaton, IL: Crossway, 2011).

7   Oswald Chambers, *My Utmost for His Highest: Selections for the Year* (New York, NY: Dodd, Mead & Company, 1935).

Saskatchewan (Human Rights Commission) v. Whatcott

Now, back to Bill Whatcott. Whatcott grew up in Toronto, where he shuffled between the home of his alcoholic mother and a series of foster homes after his parents split up. In the process, he suffered varying degrees of abuse and started to engage in a variety of violent and non-violent crimes. Some of the abuse he experienced occurred while in jail or on the streets, where he sniffed glue, used drugs, and lived for a time as a male prostitute before becoming a Christian, then studying nursing at a community college.

> *Saskatchewan (Human Rights Commission) v. Whatcott*, SCC 2013—Bill Whatcott, a self-described Christian activist, was fined by the Human Rights Commission for anti-gay flyers he distributed. The Court found that sacred texts are not hate speech, but how they are used can be.

Whatcott speaks directly, as one might expect from someone who had a tough upbringing and spent more time in jail than school. He is also fixated on the influence of gay activist organizations on key cultural formation institutions, particularly schools and universities, and human rights commissions.[8][9]

In 2002, the *Saskatchewan Human Rights Tribunal* fined Whatcott $17,500 based on the content of some flyers he had distributed, which the tribunal found to incite hatred against people based on their sexual orientation. The flyers shared commentary on morality, sexual behaviour, and public policy, as well as concern for schoolchildren based on advertising by paedophiles in a magazine subscribed to by the public library. They also quoted Scripture.

By the time the case reached the Supreme Court a decade later, in addition to the flyers the section of the *Saskatchewan Human Rights Code* under which Whatcott had been fined was encountering constitutional scrutiny.

In its 2013 decision in *Saskatchewan (Human Rights Commission) v. Whatcott*,[10] the Court enforced a narrow definition of hate speech, eliminating concepts that would align more with the notion of "hurt feelings" and separating them from

---

8   Katherine MacLellan, *The Court*, "Saskatchewan Human Rights Commission v. William Whatcott, et al. (2010), Currently Before the SCC." October 19, 2011 (http://www.thecourt. ca/are-these-flyers-so-offensive-i-shouldnt-have-directed-your-attention-to-them-saskatchewan-human-rights-commission-v-william-whatcott-et-al-2010-currently-before-the-scc/).

9   Bill Whatcott, *Born in a Graveyard: One Man's Transformation from a Violent, Drug-Addicted Criminal into Canada's Most Outspoken Family Activist* (Langley, BC: Good Character Books, 2014), Chapters 1–4.

10   2013 SCC 11, [2013] 1 SCR 467.

punishable hate speech that is intended to expose an identifiable individual or group to detestation or vilification based on prohibited grounds of discrimination. "Detestation" and "vilification" are strong words.

Of vital interest to the Canadian Church is the Court's conclusion that sacred texts, such as the Bible, in and of themselves do not constitute hate speech:

197. With respect to the purported excerpt from the Bible, I would agree with the comments of Richards J.A., at para. 78 of *Owens*, that it is apparent that a human rights tribunal or court should exercise care in dealing with arguments to the effect that foundational religious writings violate the *Code*. While the courts cannot be drawn into the business of attempting to authoritatively interpret sacred texts such as the Bible, those texts will typically have characteristics which cannot be ignored if they are to be properly assessed in relation to s. 14(1)(b) of the *Code*.

198. Richards J.A. found that objective observers would interpret excerpts of the Bible with an awareness that it contains more than one sort of message, some of which involve themes of love, tolerance and forgiveness. He also found that the meaning and relevance of the specific Bible passages cited in that case could be assessed in a variety of ways by different people.

199. In my view, these comments apply with equal force to the biblical passage paraphrased in Flyers F and G that "[i]f you cause one of these little ones to stumble it would be better that a millstone was tied around your neck and you were cast into the sea". Whether or not Mr. Whatcott meant this as a reference that homosexuals who seduced young boys should be killed, the biblical reference can also be interpreted as suggesting that anyone who harms Christians should be executed. The biblical passage, in and of itself, cannot be taken as inspiring detestation and vilification of homosexuals. While use of the Bible as a credible authority for a hateful proposition has been considered a hallmark of hatred, it would only be unusual circumstances and context that could transform a simple reading or publication of a religion's holy text into what could objectively be viewed as hate speech.[11]

---

11 *Whatcott*, Paragraphs 197–199.

This decision provides practical advice to preachers, as well as to other Christians who might engage in witness or social activism based on biblical imperatives. Wisdom is to be exercised in commenting on permissible or prohibited behaviours from a biblical perspective. The use of wisdom will include particular assessment of whether one is exercising religious freedom (e.g. we practise marriage as a monogamous relationship between one woman and one man) or engaging in the marginalization of an identifiable individual or group of people who have their own parallel freedoms (e.g. preaching damnation for those who practise polygamy or same-sex marriage).

Here is the apostle Paul's complementary advice:

God's Spirit makes us loving, happy, peaceful, patient, kind, good, faithful, gentle, and self-controlled. There is no law against behaving in any of these ways.
—Galatians 5:22–23, CEV

CHAPTER SIXTEEN

YOU CAN'T SAY THAT IN THE CLASSROOM (OR IN PUBLIC)

Now this is the commandment—the statutes and the rules—that the Lord your God commanded me to teach you, that you may do them in the land to which you are going over, to possess it, that you may fear the Lord your God, you and your son and your son's son, by keeping all his statutes and his commandments, which I command you, all the days of your life, and that your days may be long. Hear therefore, O Israel, and be careful to do them, that it may go well with you, and that you may multiply greatly, as the Lord, the God of your fathers, has promised you, in a land flowing with milk and honey.

Hear, O Israel: The Lord our God, the Lord is one. You shall love the Lord your God with all your heart and with all your soul and with all your might. And these words that I command you today shall be on your heart. You shall teach them diligently to your children, and shall talk of them when you sit in your house, and when you walk by the way, and when you lie down, and when you rise.

—Deuteronomy 6:1–7

EDUCATION IN THE COLONIES THAT BECAME PROVINCES OF CANADA WAS INITIATED BY and was the responsibility of the Church. A unique form of constitutional provision in the *Constitution Act, 1867* documented this reality. Section 93 acknowledged the nature of education in each province, making it a constitutional requirement to respect the religious nature of the school systems, then directed almost entirely by the Roman Catholic and Protestant churches, without state interference. Similar provisions were enacted as each new province joined Confederation at later dates, right up until Newfoundland and Labrador joined in 1949.

Over time, however, provincial governments encroached into the area of religious education, largely through funding arrangements. These funding arrangements were tied to government supervision through municipal school boards, established under the provincial power over "Municipal Institutions in the Province" found in Section 92 (8) of the *Constitution Act, 1867*.

The provinces started to tie curriculum standards to the funding provided by a mechanism of provincial collection through the income tax system and distribution to school boards. As noted in Chapter Fourteen, the arrangements were made with the best of intentions, but the participants and the culture changed.

Gradually, most religious schools surrendered to a publicly funded education system and its demands. Ontario's public school system, for example, was achieved through negotiation with a variety of Protestant school systems and eventually lost all Christian identity. One Protestant school board remains in the province out of a system where constitutional protection was provided primarily to prevent the Catholic schools from being overrun by the Protestant population and its abundance of schools.

This situation is another lesson about the Church aligning with government to do the Church's work. The result when the Church seeks government assistance has been a fairly constant requirement for the Church to make concessions. In the interest of doing the most good—Christian charity—the Church has let go of the purse strings, then surrendered seats on governing boards, then programs, and eventually identity. One need look no further than the Young Men's Christian Association (YMCA) to see how a Christian ministry for Bible study, fitness, and outreach became the neighbourhood pool and gym.

Christian education both is and is not an answer to the current situation. Teaching the required provincial curriculum from a Christian perspective is valuable, but it is less valuable than teaching a Christian-inspired and developed curriculum. It is also costly in most provinces, either financially to parents or in other prerequisite concessions when government funding of Christian education is involved. For the vast majority of Christian parents who understand their constitutional right to teach their faith to their children, however, the children are being taught from a secular perspective for thirty hours a week, plus homework. The corresponding Christian education is often for one or two hours each week at a church building, plus whatever additional attention parents provide to share their faith outside of Sunday school or youth group.

We can neither undo the past nor limit the work of the Holy Spirit. We learn from the past and reflect on it to assess the impact of present decisions on future generations. In various ways, Canadian Christian parents are able to meet the challenge of providing education in their faith to their children. But they can no longer expect their children to receive a Christian education in a public school (with rare exceptions in some provinces).

There are still strong arguments to be made in regard to parents' rights in the education of their children, as discussed in Chapter Nine, and carried forward as part of this chapter. As decided by the Supreme Court of Canada in *Adler v. Ontario*,[1] the provincial government is not required to fund denominational schools that did not exist at the time of Confederation. The Ontario Court of Appeal's 1997 decision in *Bal v. Ontario*[2] the following year went a step further, agreeing with the Ministry of Education that alternative religious schools receiving public funding were required to discontinue their religious education component or forfeit their funding (remember, teaching a single religion is considered indoctrination, although teaching from a religious perspective is not). While discontinuing funding for all religious schools was a constitutionally enforceable decision of the Government of Ontario, it was not a constitutionally required decision. The difference between the two is why some provincial governments are still providing funding to alternative religious schools and alternative religious instruction for a specified population of students in public schools.

Although the United Nations Human Rights Committee ruled in the 1999 case *Waldman v. Canada*[3] that Canada was in violation of the *International Covenant on Civil and Political Rights* by funding Roman Catholic schools in Ontario but not funding other religiously based schools, the ruling has been unenforceable in Canada.

It is accepted law in Canada that parents cannot force funding for religious education that is not specified in the constitution. And, as noted in *S.L.*, there is still a vital role for parents in regard to the education choices for their children. Recent public demonstrations by parents across the country in reaction to mandated curriculum they oppose demonstrates that, like the parents in *S.L.*, parents are vitally concerned that some curriculum mandates instruction from a secular perspective and is indoctrinational in intent. They rightly consider that such instruction is directed at violating or belittling their religious beliefs.

Home-schooling and different forms of private schooling have become increasingly popular alternatives to the public school system.

In 2007, a Mennonite community near Roxton Falls, Quebec, was put in the position of closing their school and moving their community because they

---

1   [1996] 3 SCR 609.

2   (1997), 34 O.R. (3d) 484 (C.A.).

3   UNHRC Communication No. 694/1996.

were teaching courses in their traditional way, rooted in the Bible, rather than the Ministry of Education's curriculum.[4] This was reminiscent of an early twentieth-century exodus of Mennonites from Saskatchewan for similar reasons.[5]

In 2016, a community of Amish families moved from Ontario to Prince Edward Island for less expensive land, and because they were able to negotiate an agreement with the provincial government in regard to being able to educate their children their way.[6]

The Home School Legal Defence Association of Canada has become the champion of home-schooling and parents' right to determine the education of their children. The constitution provides protection for parents' rights, but it can be a long, hard, expensive court battle to enforce them against the inexhaustible financial resources of a determined and taxpayer-funded provincial government.

The Queen v. Jones

An early *Charter* case on parental rights was the result of an Alberta pastor, Jones, leading a school group in his church basement. For religious reasons, he refused to seek a permit from the Ministry of Education, arguing that to do so would require him to submit the biblical education of his children, and others from the church, to the decision of a secular school board. As a result, Jones was charged with being responsible for the truancy of his own three children. In its 1986 decision[7] (also referenced as *R v. Jones*, "R" standing in for Regina, the Latin word for the Queen), the Supreme Court provided the first *Charter* ruling on parental rights in education, in the context of a claim to the *Charter* right to freedom of religion.

> *The Queen v. Jones*, SCC 1986—An Alberta pastor refused to submit his private home-school-style group to government supervision as required by law. The Court ruled the parents had a right to determine how their children were educated and the state had a right to ensure the quality of education.

---

4   *CBC News*, "Mennonites Leaving Quebec After Government Closes School." August 16, 2007 (http://www.cbc.ca/news/canada/montreal/mennonites-leaving-quebec-after-government-closes-school-1.641343).

5   Buckingham, *Fighting For God*, 46.

6   Sara Fraser, *CBC News*, "Amish 101: What Islanders Can Expect from Their New Neighbours." April 15, 2016 (http://www.cbc.ca/news/canada/prince-edward-island/pei-amish-ontario-1.3536206).

7   [1986] 2 SCR 284.

The starting point for three justices was to assume the sincerity of Jones' convictions. They stated that the Court was "in no position to question the validity of a religious belief, notwithstanding that few share that belief" and acknowledged that, as a result, the requirements of the *Alberta School Act* did interfere with his freedom of religion.[8] Three other justices found no interference with religious beliefs in the provisions of the *School Act*, but still agreed with the result reached by the first three. The decision of the first three will be referenced here as "the Court," since this opinion has carried the day in future cases.

The Court noted:

21. ...while a religious belief that a person has the right to educate his own children is not as strongly asserted nowadays, it is really not that unusual. It would be to negate history to fail to recognize that for many years the individual and the church played a far more significant role in the education of the young than the state. And when the state began to take the dominant role, it had to make accommodations to meet the needs and desires of those who had dissentient views... If the appellant has an interest in, and a religious conviction that he must himself provide for the education of his children, it should not be forgotten that the state, too, has an interest in the education of its citizens.[9]

The decision adds:

23. The interest of the province in the education of the young is thus compelling. It should require no further demonstration that it may, in advancing this interest, place reasonable limits on the freedom of those who, like the appellant, believe that they should themselves attend to the education of their children and to do so in conformity with their religious convictions...

25. ...Those who administer the province's educational requirements may not do so in a manner that unreasonably infringes on the right of parents to teach their children in accordance with their religious convictions...

28. As noted earlier, the province, and indeed the nation, has a compelling interest in the "efficient instruction" of the young. A

---

8 *Jones*, Paragraph 20.
9 Ibid., Paragraph 21.

requirement that a person who gives instruction at home or elsewhere have that instruction certified as being efficient is, in my view, demonstrably justified in a free and democratic society. So too, I would think, is a subsidiary requirement that those who wish to give such instruction make application to the appropriate authorities for certification that such instruction complies with provincial standards of efficiency...

30. ...requiring those who seek exemptions from the general scheme to make application for the purpose. Such a requirement constitutes a reasonable limit on a parent's religious convictions concerning the upbringing of his or her children.[10]

In other words, it is reasonable for the state to expect its standard of education to be delivered to children. If a parent seeks to educate them by a means other than the provincial public education system, or to educate their children in a way other than using the province's preferred curriculum, the province needs to be both aware of the plan and approve of it.

Ross v. New Brunswick School District No. 15

Ross v. New Brunswick School District No. 15[11] concerned itself with the responsibilities of a public school board to provide discrimination-free education to its students. Ross was a teacher who published material, outside of his classroom responsibilities, in which he "argued that Christian civilization was being undermined and destroyed by an international Jewish conspiracy."[12] A Jewish parent filed a human rights complaint against the school board for allowing Ross to teach, and against Ross personally.

> *Ross v. New Brunswick School District No. 36*, SCC 1996—A parent complained about a teacher who published Holocaust denial materials. The Court ruled the school board had a duty to assess activity outside the classroom as part of ensuring that the classroom was a positive place for students.

Although there was no evidence found in regard to direct classroom activity by Ross that could be considered discriminatory, his extracurricular writings did impact students who then demonstrated anti-Semitic actions in the school.

---

10 Ibid., Paragraphs 23, 25, 28, 30.

11 [1996] 1 SCR 825.

12 *Ross*, Paragraph 3.

42. A school is a communication centre for a whole range of values and aspirations of a society. In large part, it defines the values that transcend society through the educational medium. The school is an arena for the exchange of ideas and must, therefore, be premised upon principles of tolerance and impartiality so that all persons within the school environment feel equally free to participate. As the Board of Inquiry stated, a school board has a duty to maintain a positive school environment for all persons served by it.

43. Teachers are inextricably linked to the integrity of the school system. Teachers occupy positions of trust and confidence, and exert considerable influence over their students as a result of their positions. The conduct of a teacher bears directly upon the community's perception of the ability of the teacher to fulfil such a position of trust and influence, and upon the community's confidence in the public school system as a whole.

44. By their conduct, teachers as "medium" must be perceived to uphold the values, beliefs and knowledge sought to be transmitted by the school system. The conduct of a teacher is evaluated on the basis of his or her position, rather than whether the conduct occurs within the classroom or beyond.[13]

The decisions concluded, "A school board has a duty to maintain a positive school environment for all persons served by it and it must be ever vigilant of anything that might interfere with this duty."[14]

The Court found that Ross had been directing discriminatory action toward another religious community and that his claim of a religious right to do so had been justifiably infringed by the school board.

Kempling v. British Columbia College of Teachers

Kempling v. British Columbia College of Teachers[15] is a case that did not make it to the Supreme Court of Canada. The B.C. College of Teachers followed the reasoning in *Ross* to discipline a Christian teacher who, the Court of Appeal agreed, was properly found "guilty of conduct unbecoming a member of the

---

13   Ibid., Paragraphs 42–44.
14   Ibid., Paragraph 50.
15   2005 BCCA 327.

> *Kempling v. British Columbia College of Teachers*, BC CA 2005—A teacher wrote newspaper submissions associating homosexuals with immorality. The British Columbia Court of Appeal found that the BCCT appropriately disciplined him for conduct unbecoming a member.

BCCT" through sharing views in submissions to the local newspaper that "associated homosexuals with immorality, abnormality, perversion and promiscuity."[16]

In its 2005 decision, the Court of Appeal also took into account portions of the decision in *Trinity Western University v. British Columbia College of Teachers*[17] to reassert that teachers are to be compliant with the requirements of their professional association post-graduation.

Trinity Western University v. British Columbia College of Teachers

The *Ross* reasoning endorsed in *Kempling* by the Court of Appeal had also been endorsed in *Trinity Western University v. BCCT* by the Supreme Court. You may recall from Chapter Eleven that TWU was, however, affirmed in establishing

> *Trinity Western University v. British Columbia College of Teachers*, SCC 2001—The BCCT refused to grant accreditation to TWU's school of education. The Court ruled that once TWU met educational standards, it was to be accredited. The BCCT's regulation of graduates began after they joined the BCCT.

its own membership standards. In making reference to the question of teacher conduct, the Court shared the following words, which also reinforce Paragraph 45 from *Ross*, which follows those quoted above. I will begin with the same paragraph from *Trinity Western* quoted in Chapter Eleven and follow it forward in regard to teacher behaviour.

36. Instead, the proper place to draw the line in cases like the one at bar is generally between belief and conduct. The freedom to hold beliefs is broader than the freedom to act on them. Absent concrete evidence that training teachers at TWU fosters discrimination in the public schools of B.C., the freedom of individuals to adhere to certain religious beliefs while at TWU should be respected. The BCCT, rightfully, does not require public universities with teacher education

---

16 *Kempling*, Paragraph 29.
17 [2001] 1 SCR 772, 2001 SCC 31.

programs to screen out applicants who hold sexist, racist or homophobic beliefs. For better or for worse, tolerance of divergent beliefs is a hallmark of a democratic society.

37. Acting on those beliefs, however, is a very different matter. If a teacher in the public school system engages in discriminatory conduct, that teacher can be subject to disciplinary proceedings before the BCCT. Discriminatory conduct by a public school teacher when on duty should always be subject to disciplinary proceedings. This Court has held, however, that greater tolerance must be shown with respect to off-duty conduct. Yet disciplinary measures can still be taken when discriminatory off-duty conduct poisons the school environment. As La Forest J. stated for a unanimous Court in *Ross*, *supra*, at para. 45:

> It is on the basis of the position of trust and influence that we hold the teacher to high standards both on and off duty, and it is an erosion of these standards that may lead to a loss in the community of confidence in the public school system. I do not wish to be understood as advocating an approach that subjects the entire lives of teachers to inordinate scrutiny on the basis of more onerous moral standards of behaviour. This could lead to a substantial invasion of the privacy rights and fundamental freedoms of teachers. However, where a "poisoned" environment within the school system is traceable to the offduty conduct of a teacher that is likely to produce a corresponding loss of confidence in the teacher and the system as a whole, then the offduty conduct of the teacher is relevant.[18]

Teachers, as a profession, exert an influence in school and community. At one time, that influence was expected to be overtly Christian. Now, Christian or other religious expression of public school teachers is limited to that which does not "lead to a loss in the community of confidence in the public school system." This is consistent with development of the concepts of state neutrality noted in Chapter Nine.

Education provided as an alternative to the public school system requires approval from the appropriate governmental body, whether home-schooling or private schooling. Alternative educators would be wise to note that this required

---

18 *Trinity Western*, Paragraphs 36–37.

approval may subject them to review if their teaching might lead to a loss of confidence in the public approval of their education preference.

This transition is consistent with the general societal transition taking place in regard to public expressions of religion generally, which is where we will pick up in the next chapter, outside the courtroom.

PART III
FAITHFUL CHRIST-FOLLOWERS ASK "HOW SHOULD WE THEN ENGAGE?"

Then he said to them, "Therefore render to Caesar the things that are Caesar's, and to God the things that are God's."
—Matthew 22:21

Be subject for the Lord's sake to every human institution, whether it be to the emperor as supreme, or to governors as sent by him to punish those who do evil and to praise those who do good. For this is the will of God, that by doing good you should put to silence the ignorance of foolish people. Live as people who are free, not using your freedom as a cover-up for evil, but living as servants of God. Honor everyone. Love the brotherhood. Fear God. Honor the emperor.
—1 Peter 2:13–17

I swear (or affirm) that I will be faithful and bear true allegiance to Her Majesty Queen Elizabeth II, Queen of Canada, Her Heirs and Successors, and that I will faithfully observe the laws of Canada and fulfil my duties as a Canadian citizen.
—Canada's oath of citizenship

Now who is there to harm you if you are zealous for what is good? But even if you should suffer for righteousness' sake, you will be blessed. Have no fear of them, nor be troubled, but in your hearts honor Christ the Lord as holy, always being prepared to make a defense to anyone who asks you for a reason for the hope that is in you; yet do it with gentleness and respect, having a good conscience, so that, when you are slandered, those who revile your good behavior in Christ may be put to shame. For it is better to suffer for doing good, if that should be God's will, than for doing evil.
—1 Peter 3:13–17

CHAPTER SEVENTEEN

CHRISTIANITY IN CANADA AT 150

O God, why do you cast us off forever? Why does your anger smoke against the sheep of your pasture? Remember your congregation, which you have purchased of old, which you have redeemed to be the tribe of your heritage! Remember Mount Zion, where you have dwelt. Direct your steps to the perpetual ruins; the enemy has destroyed everything in the sanctuary!

Your foes have roared in the midst of your meeting place; they set up their own signs for signs. They were like those who swing axes in a forest of trees. And all its carved wood they broke down with hatchets and hammers. They set your sanctuary on fire; they profaned the dwelling place of your name, bringing it down to the ground. They said to themselves, "We will utterly subdue them"; they burned all the meeting places of God in the land.

We do not see our signs; there is no longer any prophet, and there is none among us who knows how long. How long, O God, is the foe to scoff? Is the enemy to revile your name forever? Why do you hold back your hand, your right hand? Take it from the fold of your garment and destroy them!

Yet God my King is from of old, working salvation in the midst of the earth.
—Psalm 74:1–12

IN *FOR CANADA'S SAKE: THE RE-VISIONING OF CANADA AND RE-STRUCTURING OF Public Religion in the 1960s*, a PhD thesis submitted to Queen's University shortly after the turn of the century, Gary Miedema describes the scene where thousands huddled together in the cold on Parliament Hill as December 31, 1966 was counted down to Canada's centennial celebrations beginning January 1, 1967.

Canada's Centennial Flame was about to be lit, but first, spectators had to stand, sit, or shiver through the pre-requisite ceremony. Prime

Minister Pearson and Opposition Leader John Diefenbaker sat on a podium facing a nine-by-fifteen foot television screen. To their side was a warmly dressed centennial choir, to their rear more officials, including the mayors and reeves of the surrounding municipalities. A pre-recorded address from the Queen to Canadians was played on the screen, though regrettably CBC technicians forgot to pipe in the sound to the throngs on Parliament Hill. Following the presentation of the Queen's address, the Centennial Commission chairman John Fisher rose to recite the Centennial Prayer. "Almighty God, who has called us out of many nations and has set our feet on this broad land, establishing us as one people from seat to sea," the prayer began,

> Gratefully we remember all the way that thou hast led us through one hundred years, to humble us, and to prove us, and to know what was in our hearts… Grant thy blessing upon the joyous celebrations of our Centennial Year, and a deeper worthiness of the dreams that gave us birth; that "…with flame of freedom in our souls and light of knowledge in our eyes" we may magnify thy name among men, one nation, serving thee. Amen.

Next came the Centennial Choir and the singing of the Centennial Hymn. Their breath crystallizing in the cold air, the choristers sang with vigour the final verse.

> Lead us to walk the ways that love has always taken.
> Guide us, O God of Love, and we will shape a spirit
> Worthy a nation reaching for her destiny.
> So may we show the world a vision of Thy goodness,
> Our dream of Man to which all men may yet awaken,
> And share glory still with Thee.

Finally, Prime Minister Pearson, "swaddled in a black cashmere overcoat, red wool scarf, and fur-lined gloves" rose to give his address…[1]

---

[1]   Gary Miedema, *For Canada's Sake: The Re-Visioning of Canada and Re-Structuring of Public Religion in the 1960s* (Kingston, ON: Queen's University, 2000), 147–148.

Seven months later, the Dominion Day celebrations (renamed Canada Day in 1982), with Queen Elizabeth II[2] and Prince Philip in attendance, began in similar fashion. The events fell conveniently on a Saturday, as they will for the sesquicentennial celebration in 2017.

Miedema describes the scene as the crowd gathered, including again the centennial choir. At about 10:00 a.m., Members of Parliament and senators took their place before Prime Minister Pearson and his cabinet joined them, followed by the arrival of Governor General Roland Michener, and finally the Queen and Prince in an open convertible black limousine. Greeting Her Majesty were eight clergymen who then joined the assembled dignitaries.

> The eight clergymen on the dais represented a number of distinctive religious traditions. The Right Rev. Wilfred C. Lockhart, Moderator of the United Church of Canada, the Right Rev. John Logan-Vencta, Moderator of the Presbyterian Church of Canada, His Eminence Maurice Cardinal Roy, Archbishop of Quebec and Roman Catholic Primate of Canada, and the Most Rev. H.H. Clark, Anglican Archbishop of Rupert's Land and Primate of all Canada symbolized the presence of the largest and most historically significant Christian churches in the country.[3]

The "distinctive religious traditions" had something in common. All were Christian.

Although Miedema provides greater detail of the ceremony, his summary paints the picture:

> In the half-hour, nationally televised ceremony that followed, Canadians across the country began their Canada Day celebrations of the country's one hundredth birthday with prayer, Bible reading, and song. "A hundred years ago today," read the distributed programs, "our ancestors witnessed the birth of a new nation. Now a century later, some twenty million Canadians share the heritage of freedom and material

---

2   Queen Elizabeth II is the Queen of Canada. The monarch remains Canada's head of state. The Prime Minister is the head of her government on behalf of the people.

3   Ibid., 2.

prosperity for which, on this historic occasion, all will wish to join in thanksgiving to God."[4]

At one point in the shared recitation of the ceremony, the tens of thousands in the crowd responded in unison with the words, "We rededicate ourselves, O Lord."

The ceremony and ensuing celebration on Parliament Hill that day was years in the planning.

By contrast, in his 1997 book *1967: The Last Good Year*, Pierre Berton reflects on the events of those two significant dates in different fashion. He begins the book with these words:

> The centennial year began with a blaze of glory three hours early so the children could stay up to watch it. I don't mean the sacred flame, flickering at the behest of the Prime Minister on the slopes of Parliament Hill. I mean the full-scale bonfire that lit the winter sky and warmed the hearts of five hundred citizens of Bowsman, Manitoba, a frontier community 250 miles northwest of Winnipeg.
>
> Bowsman's bonfire, fuelled by scores of outhouses, captured the imagination of the country. Here was a genuine centennial project...[5]

The "biffy burning," a celebration of indoor plumbing, was officiated by the local United Church minister Reverend Jim Liles. It was covered by the CBC.

Berton makes passing reference to the Prime Minister's attire that night on Parliament Hill and the lighting of the Centennial Flame, noting, "The ceremony brought tears to the eyes of those who watched it," but not commenting further on the content of the ceremony other than its conclusion with the singing of "O Canada" (which, you may recall, was not yet our national anthem).

Although Berton covers details of Expo '67, Bobby Gimby's contract with the federal government to be the pied piper of "Ca–na–da, we love thee," the Toronto Maple Leafs' last Stanley Cup win (over the Montreal Canadiens in six games), and the expansion of the NHL from six to twelve teams that June, Berton makes no mention of the Canada Day celebration on Parliament Hill, the Queen, or the clergy.

One section of *The Last Good Year* is called "The Big Change." In it, Berton references the dawning of the women's liberation movement in Canada, the

---

4   Ibid.

5   Pierre Berton, *1967: The Last Good Year* (Toronto, ON: Doubleday Canada Ltd., 1997), 10.

changing (for the better) attitudes toward Canada's Indigenous peoples (including the "Indians of Canada Pavilion" at Expo '67), and the seeds of gay pride. The section begins with a reference to legislation introduced by Justice Minister Pierre Trudeau in 1967 that took two years to pass, by which time Trudeau was Prime Minister. Berton writes:

> In 1967, Canadian manners and morals were on the cusp of change. The country was beginning to emerge as from the Dark Ages. The morality laws still belonged to another century. It was almost as difficult to get a divorce as it was to get an abortion. The law still made it a jailable offence to transmit birth-control information. As for homosexuals, they could be jailed—and were jailed, in one case for life—for simply being what they were.[6]

Interestingly, Berton dedicates *The Last Good Year* to his friend Charles Templeton. Templeton had been one of the co-founders of Youth for Christ in 1946. He had toured alongside Billy Graham as one of YFC's evangelists. In 1957, Templeton, like Berton, renounced his faith, declaring himself an agnostic. He became a print journalist, radio and television broadcaster, and was the author of twelve books, one-fifth the number of his prolific author friend Berton who worked alongside him at the *Toronto Star*, in television, and co-hosting the syndicated daily radio show *Dialogue*, where the two debated the issues of the day for eighteen years.

Fewer than fifteen years after the national celebrations had both opened with prayer and songs of worship, Prime Minister Pierre Trudeau opened the final negotiations with the premiers on patriation of the constitution. For several provincial premiers, affirming their legislative primacy over the courts in the document was important and the preamble to the *Charter* was also a matter of discussion and debate.

The historic churches were still strong, although weakening in influence as a result of the *La Révolution tranquille* in Quebec, the cultural revolution nationwide, and, I would add, following the advice proffered by Berton in *The Comfortable Pew*. The evangelical Christian church was growing and beginning to engage in the public square through The Evangelical Fellowship of Canada, which had been established in 1964, and through the media, particularly David Mainse's *100 Huntley Street* television show, which began to air in June 1977.

---

6   Ibid., 110.

Orthodox churches were finding their footing as a result of changing immigration patterns. Members of the Public Service Christian Fellowship encouraged sympathetic Liberal MPs, including Deputy House Leader David Smith (then MP for Don Valley East and later a senator), who drafted a strategy for improved relations between the Liberal government and evangelicals, impressing upon the Prime Minister the importance that the reference to the supremacy of God in the preamble held for the Church in Canada.[7] Several premiers in provinces with a more conservative tone were concerned that a departure from the recognition of the supremacy of God, as referenced in the preamble to Diefenbaker's *Canadian Bill of Rights*, might be politically harmful.

Pierre Trudeau casually stated to his caucus in April 1981, "I don't think God gives a damn whether He's in the constitution."[8] Nevertheless, the preamble was included in the draft, and then the final document. God had not previously been mentioned in the constitution, and recognizing Him in the preamble had no impact on who God is. The constitution, after all, is a secular instrument of the state. On that point, Trudeau was correct.

What the preamble does is recognize something expressed two months later by Trudeau and his immediate predecessor, then Leader of the Opposition and former Prime Minister Joe Clark, on *100 Huntley Street*'s month-long "Salute to Canada."

In his remarks, the Prime Minister stated:

The golden thread of faith is woven throughout the history of Canada from its earliest beginnings up to the present time. Our native peoples lived a rich spiritual life long before the first white man set foot on our soil. Faith was more important than commerce in the minds of many of the European explorers and settlers, and over the centuries, as successive waves of people came to this country, many in search of religious liberty, they brought with them a great wealth and variety of religious traditions and values. Those values have shaped our laws and our lives, and have added enormous strength to the foundation of freedom and justice upon which this country was built...

---

7   Buckingham, *Fighting Over God*, 20.

8   George Egerton, "Trudeau, God, and the Canadian Constitution: Religion, Human Rights, and Government Authority in the Making of the 1982 Constitution," eds. D. Lyon and M. Van Die editors, *Rethinking Church, State, and Modernity: Canada Between Europe and the USA* (Toronto, ON: University of Toronto Press, 2000), 90.

It was in acknowledgement of that debt that the Parliament of Canada later gave its approval, during the Constitutional Debate, to the statement that Canada is founded upon principles that recognize the supremacy of God and the rule of law. Faith played a large part in the lives of so many men and women who have created in this land a society which places a high value on commitment, integrity, generosity and, above all, freedom. To pass on that heritage, strong and intact, is a challenge worthy of all of us who are privileged to call ourselves Canadians.[9]

The following is much of what Mr. Clark shared:

Without any question, we are among the most fortunate nations of the earth, in our freedom, our physical wealth, our respect for the human individual. But there is more than that. In many ways, our Canada is a demonstration of the strength of faith, because, particularly in the early days, the people who reached out to build our country, had very little support except their faith. Their lives were lonely, but they found sustenance and support in their individual religious beliefs, in the sense that their lives were part of a whole, that their struggle would be remembered.

That support of faith is as important today, in modern times, as it ever was, and even more so because the forces of cynicism and doubt are so much more strong today. That's why it is so valuable for us to have occasions like this to remember together the immense good fortune that God has given Canadians, and to reflect on the way that our spiritual heritage has helped define and guide the nature and development of our nation. Not only did people of faith build and keep our Canada, but some of our most important laws reflect that spirit. Our Bill of Rights, written by the late John Diefenbaker, held that the Canadian nation is founded upon principles that acknowledge the supremacy of God, the dignity and worth of the human person, and position of the family in a society of free men and free institutions. Now, we all have personal responsibilities to meet each day in ways

---

9   Pierre Trudeau on *100 Huntley Street*, "Salute to Canada," June 20, 1981. See Appendix IV for the full text of Prime Minister Trudeau's comments. Transcript accessed from the Public Service Christian Fellowship Newsletter, September 1981, 1–3.

that honour our own standards and our own beliefs. I want to take advantage of this opportunity to ask your prayers and your support for all of us who are active in public life in Canada. I ask that we never forget the faith and the vision of the people who originally brought this country together, the Fathers of Confederation, who from the depths of their own profound faith took as their guide a verse from the Psalms of David, the verse that has since become the motto for our nation:

He shall have dominion also from sea to sea, and from the river to the ends of the earth.

We pray today that God's sovereignty over Canada continues to guide us.[10]

Canada was never a Christian nation, but historically it was influenced by Christianity and the various expressions of the Church, for both good and ill. Less than twenty years after it was considered essential to have the churches onside for centennial celebrations, the question being asked had shifted from "How do we include God?" to "Why would we include God?" The first was asked in recognition of societal imperative, the second in light of political pragmatism.

Since April 17, 1982, Canadians have experienced a nation where Christian influence in the governance of the nation, as well as many other aspects of common life in the public sphere, is increasingly contested.

Prior to Canada's House of Commons opening to the public on each sitting day, while the doors are closed, the Speaker leads the House in a prayer. The prayer that follows remained substantially unchanged until 1994:

O Lord our heavenly Father, high and mighty, King of kings, Lord of lords, the only Ruler of princes, who dost from thy throne behold all the dwellers upon earth: Most heartily we beseech thee with thy favour to behold our most gracious Sovereign Lady, Queen Elizabeth; and so replenish her with the grace of thy Holy Spirit that she may always incline to thy will and walk in thy way; Endue her plenteously with heavenly gifts: grant her in health and wealth long to live; strengthen her that she may vanquish and overcome all her enemies; and finally,

---

10 Joe Clark on *100 Huntley Street*, "Salute to Canada," June 20, 1981. See Appendix V for the full text of Mr. Clark's comments. Transcript accessed from the Public Service Christian Fellowship Newsletter, September 1981, 1–3.

after this life, she may attain everlasting joy and felicity; through Jesus Christ our Lord—Amen.[11]

On Friday, February 18, 1994, members of the House of Commons adopted a new morning prayer. The prayer removed reference to God as Father, the Holy Spirit, and the Son, Jesus Christ. The following prayer opened the day on February 21:

> Almighty God, we give thanks for the great blessings which have been bestowed on Canada and its citizens, including the gifts of freedom, opportunity and peace that we enjoy. We pray for our Sovereign, Queen Elizabeth, and the Governor General. Guide us in our deliberations as Members of Parliament, and strengthen us in our awareness of our duties and responsibilities as Members. Grant us wisdom, knowledge, and understanding to preserve the blessings of this country for the benefit of all and to make good laws and wise decisions. Amen.[12]

In an article written in 2000, Brian Stiller noted:

> Last year the Prime Minister's Office [Prime Minister Jean Chretien] forbade the chaplain in Halifax from using the name of Jesus or from reading from the New Testament at the memorial service for the Swissair victims [held on the one year anniversary of the September 1, 1998 crash into the Atlantic Ocean, southwest of Halifax]. What does one do? Bow to the lowest denominator of so-called neutral language and metaphor, or, with taste and sensitivity, offer to others the best of what we know to be true?[13]

Contemporary secularist opinion leaders, and those watching the vote count, may dispute, ignore, or seek to erase the role of the Christian faith in Canada's formation, societal foundations, or present-day public sphere, including the political conversation space known as the public square. Twenty-first-century Canadian

---

11 *Parliament of Canada*, "Daily Proceedings." Date of access: January 11, 2017 (http://www.parl. gc.ca/procedure-book-livre/document.aspx?sbdid=af057bd0-f018-4fb4-bd75-4a2200729f05 &sbpidx=2).

12 Ibid.

13 Brian C Stiller, "God in Our Constitution: Good or Bad?" Date of access: January 11, 2017 (http://www.brianstiller.com/god-in-our-constitution-good-or-bad.html).

Christian opinion leaders may suggest today's reality is more akin to the opening verses of Asaph's Psalm 74, lamenting that God has abandoned the nation and that what was built up is being destroyed. The truth resides with neither extremity.

Yet God my King is from of old, working salvation in the midst of the earth.

—Psalm 74:12

CHAPTER EIGHTEEN

RENDER UNTO CAESAR
(OR AT LEAST PARLIAMENT)

Blessed are those who are persecuted for righteousness' sake, for theirs is the kingdom of heaven. Blessed are you when others revile you and persecute you and utter all kinds of evil against you falsely on my account. Rejoice and be glad, for your reward is great in heaven, for so they persecuted the prophets who were before you.

You are the salt of the earth, but if salt has lost its taste, how shall its saltiness be restored? It is no longer good for anything except to be thrown out and trampled under people's feet.

—Matthew 5:10–13

Tell us, then, what you think. Is it lawful to pay taxes to Caesar, or not?"

But Jesus, aware of their malice, said, "Why put me to the test, you hypocrites? Show me the coin for the tax." And they brought him a denarius. And Jesus said to them, "Whose likeness and inscription is this?"

They said, "Caesar's."

Then he said to them, "Therefore render to Caesar the things that are Caesar's, and to God the things that are God's."

—Matthew 22:17–21

MOST CANADIAN CHRISTIANS, LIKE MOST WESTERN CHRISTIANS, HAVE FORGOTTEN OR simply never considered that the New Testament was written to a persecuted Church. Except, notably, Paul's first letter to the Church at Corinth.

1 Corinthians was written to an affluent church that had become inward-looking and concerned about making sure they fit in with the appearances and behaviour of the culture around them. The Corinthian church's congregational and cultural navel-gazing resulted in division over things like which preacher was better, which sometimes obscure teachings were more interesting and should

be explored in depth, which business techniques were most applicable to church operation and growth, and how much of the behaviour in the city around them was acceptable to embrace by those who identified as followers of Jesus. The apostle Paul had started this church personally. Still it had become so insular and culture-captivated that they had forgotten they were part of a bigger body, the Body of Christ, and that others in that bigger body were suffering for being demonstrably faithful to Jesus. Paul's second letter to them recognizes their course adjustment following the first, and spurs on the whole Church to greater Christ-likeness, including faithfulness in persecution.

The first-century authors of the New Testament were themselves persecuted believers and were writing to a Church that was unwelcome in their world: a minority without political authority; marginalized, not mainstream; persecuted, not honoured; and despised by Jews, who rejected Jesus and His disciples' claim that He was the Messiah, and despised by Romans, who insisted on worship of their gods, including bowing the knee to Caesar, the emperor. In fact, for this latter reason, Christianity was illegal.

Most Canadian Christians, like most Western Christians, have forgotten or simply never considered that Christianity is not a Western religion. We constantly run the risk of making Christ in our own image and subjecting His written Word, the Bible, to the concerns and constraints of our own culture.

Christianity was birthed in the Middle East as a fulfillment of the prophecies found in the sacred text of the ancient religion of Judaism.

Christianity is a contextual religion. The truth that Jesus (Yeshua) is the Christ (Messiah, Anointed One) fits within any culture. This was confirmed by the council at Jerusalem when they welcomed the culturally dissimilar Greeks and Romans without requiring them to become Jewish in order to be Christ-followers (Acts 15).

The truth of Christ-following also stands distinct from all cultures. As Paul wrote twice in his first letter to the Corinthians, *"'All things are lawful,' but not all are helpful"* (1 Corinthians 10:23; also see 6:12,) and the third time, *"'All things are lawful,' but not all build up."* (1 Corinthians 10:23). He was saying, "Yes, there is freedom in Christ but that freedom is *for* Christ: to live a life that honours Him and draws others to Him, not for you to do and have whatever you desire."

The contemporary Canadian Church wrestles with similar issues to that of the first-century Church. How much of Canada's culture can the Church absorb and still be the Church? Is the Church infiltrating the culture or is the culture infiltrating the Church? The Canadian Church has varying degrees of "saltiness" to it. I will set aside the question of being infiltrated by culture, and address the matter of continuing to influence Canadian society.

Most Canadian Christians, like most Western Christians, have also forgotten or simply never considered that Christianity is not a governing religion. When Christianity had an official role in the government of Western nations in the past, it was the result of emperors, monarchs, and legislatures decreeing an official state religion, not the declaration of Christian religious leaders or the Bible. Such state-sponsored arrangements inevitably led to challenges to the orthodoxy (belief) and orthopraxy (practice) of the state church, and in the ecclesiastical authority of the state-sponsored church with religious celebrants.

Christianity has informed and influenced the development of Canadian democracy, including the social contract that holds together the diverse fibres of our national tapestry. It's true that many of our political leaders have been Christians, of varying degrees on the spectrum mentioned in Chapter Six, but Canada is not now, and never has been, a Christian nation. The Bible has been a vital guide, but not our rule.

In Canada, the division between government and faithfully following the One True God is just as it was in Israel when Mary gave birth to Jesus in Bethlehem, and when He was crucified in Jerusalem. This is how it was following His resurrection from the grave and throughout the explosive growth of the early Church, the time of the New Testament authors. So what do they have to say to us about this separation between the state and the Church?

Jesus, of all people, was intimately acquainted with the supremacy of God. He submitted Himself to the authority of the state, not just on the matter of rendering payment of taxes but, a short time later, His very life. Jesus also commissioned the Church not to rule but to represent: to represent Him and to represent our Father, empowered by the Holy Spirit.

All authority in heaven and on earth was, and is, His (Matthew 28:18). In this era, Jesus has chosen not to govern the kingdoms of the world, which for a time have been delivered to another (Luke 4:5–8). His direct challenge to His disciples is not to take control of the governments of the world. Jesus' challenge to us is to make more disciples *and* observe all that He commanded. Love one another. Love our enemies. Feed the hungry. Clothe the naked. Care for widows and orphans...

The image of God, *imago Dei*, is extant in every human being (Genesis 1:26–27). Render to God the things that are God's, that which bears His image. Steward that which He entrusts to us. Generously share the expression of His presence in us with others.

The image of Caesar was on the currency of the state, used for commerce and the payment of taxes. Render to Caesar the things that are Caesar's, that which bears the imprimatur of the state. Participate as a citizen in the life of the state with respect for its authority.

The apostle Paul writes to the church in Rome, and by the Spirit's inspiration to us, *"Let every person be subject to the governing authorities. For there is no authority except from God, and those that exist have been instituted by God"* (Romans 13:1). Paul goes on to describe the role of the state in similar terms to the *Constitution Act, 1867* which sets out the Government of Canada's responsibility to provide peace, order, and good government. Christians are directed to do what is good and subject themselves to the government in good conscience, including paying taxes.

The apostle Peter writes,

> *Be subject for the Lord's sake to every human institution, whether it be to the emperor as supreme, or to governors as sent by him to punish those who do evil and to praise those who do good. For this is the will of God, that by doing good you should put to silence the ignorance of foolish people. Live as people who are free, not using your freedom as a cover-up for evil, but living as servants of God. Honor everyone. Love the brotherhood. Fear God. Honor the emperor.*
>
> —1 Peter 2:13–17

As the Church and its authority is established by God, so too the authority of the state is established by God.

The authority of the Church is the growth of Christ-followers in community so that we would be and make disciples, and that we would be salt, flavouring the world we live in for its good. This is reminiscent of *"the words of the letter that Jeremiah the prophet sent from Jerusalem to the surviving elders of the exiles, and to the priests, the prophets, and all the people, whom Nebuchadnezzar had taken into exile from Jerusalem to Babylon"* (Jeremiah 29:1).

> *Thus says the Lord of hosts, the God of Israel, to all the exiles whom I have sent into exile from Jerusalem to Babylon: Build houses and live in them; plant gardens and eat their produce. Take wives and have sons and daughters; take wives for your sons, and give your daughters in marriage, that they may bear sons and daughters; multiply there, and do not decrease. But seek the welfare of the city*

where I have sent you into exile, and pray to the Lord on its behalf, for in its welfare you will find your welfare.

—Jeremiah 29:4–7

The Church is also to equip us to live lives of righteousness. If we face persecution, just as the illegal Church of the first three centuries of the Church's existence did, that persecution ought to be because of our adherence to following Jesus—being and doing good that benefits other citizens and the state.

The authority of the state is to care for its citizens, those who are Christians and those who are not. This includes providing structure to Canadian society, protection for the people and institutions of that society, and creating the conditions for personal and societal flourishing as described by Jeremiah above.

As citizens of the state and members of the Church, the Body of Christ in the world, we are uniquely situated at the juncture of church and state. Both exert a certain amount of pressure on us for our loyalty with claims that are not always consistent with each other, as well as in areas that are not explicitly spoken to in Scripture.

Our loyalty to both church and state does not require division, but prioritization. We don't just live in both, we are called to participate in both and thus influence both. If you question your ability to influence the Church, simply consider whether you have been influenced by the writing, music, or teaching of anyone in addition to the Bible. Then know that you influence others in the Body of Christ. Similarly, consider who has influenced you in the culture outside the Church, and know that you influence others whether in your neighbourhood, at work, at school, or on the road (yes, driving behaviour).

When Jesus prayed that we not be taken *"out of the world"* but kept from *"the evil one,"* He was advocating for our protection, perhaps our self-protection, as we live life in the state (John 17:15). Jesus knew that we would face both persecution and temptation. When He continued the prayer, noting, *"As you sent me into the world, so I have sent them into the world,"* He was not encouraging separation from society, but our engagement with culture (John 17:18).

When Pilate questioned Jesus about whether He was King of the Jews, Jesus answered,

My kingdom is not of this world. If my kingdom were of this world, my servants would have been fighting, that I might not be delivered over to the Jews [a reference to the religious leaders who had turned Jesus over to the Roman authorities

alleging He claimed a competing kingdom to Caesar's]. But my kingdom is not from the world.

—John 18:36

And yet, has anyone else had greater influence on the politics of this world?

The apostle John informs us that a time is coming when *"[t]he kingdom of the world [will have] become the kingdom of our Lord and of his Christ, and he shall reign forever and ever"* (Revelation 11:15). But that time is not yet.

Now is a time for us to be salt in an otherwise decaying society, a preservative in a dominion that is increasingly unsavoury, adding the savour of life. We are salt in a culturally and politically cold world, safeguarding the narrow path for those who will accept the invitation to tread upon it.

CHAPTER NINETEEN

AMERICAN, BRITISH, CANADIAN, DUTCH, AND GERMAN THINKERS ON PUBLIC FAITH

So all the generations from Abraham to David were fourteen generations, and from David to the deportation to Babylon fourteen generations, and from the deportation to Babylon to the Christ fourteen generations.

—Matthew 1:17

Therefore, if anyone is in Christ, he is a new creation. The old has passed away; behold, the new has come. All this is from God, who through Christ reconciled us to himself and gave us the ministry of reconciliation; that is, in Christ God was reconciling the world to himself, not counting their trespasses against them, and entrusting to us the message of reconciliation. Therefore, we are ambassadors for Christ, God making his appeal through us. We implore you on behalf of Christ, be reconciled to God.

—2 Corinthians 5:17–20

ACKNOWLEDGING THAT THE KINGDOMS OF THIS WORLD ARE DIFFERENT FROM THE kingdom of our God, that there are separate realms of authority for the state and the Church, how should we then engage?

The Old Testament is replete with interesting and sometimes long genealogies: the "begat" sections. They're found in a few spots in the New Testament, too. You know them: Abraham was the father of Isaac, and Isaac the father of Jacob, etc.

The Church also has its genealogy. From Jerusalem sprouted the Eastern Orthodox (e.g. Greek Orthodox), North African (e.g. Egyptian Coptic), and Western Catholic (e.g. Roman Catholic) churches, these three predominant among others in the early Church. The variety of Christian expressions are referred to in the

Nicene Creed (325 A.D.)[1] and the Apostles' Creed (390 A.D.)[2] as the "holy catholic" church, the adjective catholic meaning "universal" or "all-embracing," as
distinct from the Roman Catholic Church alone. These two creeds are primary
expressions of doctrine (belief) that find agreement with almost all branches of
the Church.

Variations in understanding of Scripture and style of worship arose as the
followers of Jesus travelled with the message of God's reconciliation for humanity
in Christ. More recently, in Church-age terms, the Protestant Reformation that
began in force in the 1500s (there were some minor schisms a century earlier)
resulted in a revisiting of theological understanding and traditions in the Roman
and other known denominations of the preceding fifteen centuries, as well as the
development of differing perspectives on engagement between church and state.

Much has been written in this area. And when the much was read, studied,
and considered, more was written. What follows are, like the "begats" in biblical
genealogies, not mini-biographies but summary-snapshots of some of the people
and their theologies that have particularly impacted the Church's public engagement in the latter part of the twentieth century. This group has also helped shape
my thinking for engagement at the beginning of the twenty-first century. These
snapshots may encourage you to explore a more in-depth pursuit of your Christian experience. They may also help explain some things about the status of the
current interaction between the Church and culture.

Notable omissions are entirely my fault. Consideration of who to include
in this non-exhaustive list was determined by my experience. I thought through
the formation of this list from a perspective shared with me by Terry LeBlanc.[3]
Terry is Mi'kmaq/Acadian, with his family roots in the Listuguj First Nation in
Quebec and Campbellton, New Brunswick. These two communities are separated by a short bridge at the narrows of Chaleur Bay and overlap with three
different language and cultural expressions. Terry impressed upon me the benefit
of a particular Indigenous perspective when looking at our engagement on the
issues before us. We are to look back to learn how the issue, or related issues, have
been considered in the past, and then look forward seven generations to consider
the future impact of actions taken today.

---

1   See Appendix I.

2   See Appendix II.

3   Terry LeBlanc is the Founding Chair and Director of the NAIITS (North American Institute
    for Indigenous Theological Studies) and Executive Director of Indigenous Pathways.

I'll proceed in a chronological order by nationality. Again, this list is not exhaustive, simply introductory.

The British

John Wesley (1703–1791) was, like several of those noted in this chapter, the face and name of a movement that included others as vital participants and shapers. Born in England, Wesley was an Anglican clergyman who became a founder of the Methodist (Holiness) movement. He had a personal experience with God, which he described as his heart being "strangely warmed," (Luke 24:32) that propelled him and the Methodists to preach outdoors for the purpose of inviting people to make a personal life conversion that resulted in genuine Christ-following.

The Methodists also held meetings in private homes to study the Bible and pray. This was a significant transition from the pattern that had developed of church taking place in a church building, and membership being extended by birth with confirmation. Wesley also broke with Church tradition by appointing non-clergy as travelling evangelists to preach the gospel. His method of theology is still commonly referenced today as the Wesleyan quadrilateral, asserting that theological authority is understood by:

1. Scripture, the first authority and test of all other truth;
2. Tradition (history), which has developed within the Church and been examined in the writing and expression of the early Church in particular;
3. Reason, the means by which we are assisted by the Holy Spirit in our understanding of Scripture and life; and
4. Experience, the assurance that comes with our personal experience of the scriptural promises.

Wesley's own experience led to a strong teaching of the difference between salvation, accepting Jesus as Saviour, and sanctification, experientially living under the Lordship of Jesus. For Wesley, one's personal Christian experience led to sharing the gospel through evangelism and efforts aimed at cultural influence.

William Wilberforce (1759–1833) was an English Member of Parliament whose elected office made him the face and name of the British movement to end slavery, beginning with the slave trade. This movement went well beyond him alone. John Wesley was also an active abolitionist who, on his deathbed, sent his final letter[4] to Wilberforce, encouraging him not to grow weary in his task and to draw on God's strength to stand even *contra mundum* (against the world) in order to accomplish God's purposes. *Contra mundum* has become a rallying cry for activists of all stripes in the centuries since. In my opinion, the best book on this campaign is Adam Hochschild's *Bury the Chains*,[5] which details the people mix and campaign strategies of the Wilberforce activists, concepts that are still in use today.

In addition to the abolition of slavery, Wilberforce's 1785 personal conversion experience led him to engage in efforts to reform "the manners," as he put it, of British society. He wrote books and participated in establishing organizations that challenged church-goers to effective, Bible-based Christian living and humane treatment of other people and animals. Wilberforce regarded all people as made in the image of God, and all creatures as deserving of our stewardship as part of God's creation. His Christian beliefs led him to participate in establishing the Society for the Prevention of Cruelty to Animals, the Society for the Suppression of Vice (obscene materials, prostitution, adultery, alcoholism, profane cursing, and profaning the Lord's Day), the establishment of the Royal Lifeboat Society (in Canada, we call it the Coast Guard), the Bible Society, and the Church Mission Society to spread the gospel to Eastern nations and Africa, among others. Wilberforce was a model of evangelical Christian engagement with culture.[6]

William Booth (1829–1912) was a travelling Methodist evangelist who, like Wesley and Wilberforce, became the face of a movement. With the support of his wife Catherine, often described as the intellectual theologian to William's practical application of theology, Booth established the East London Christian Mission in 1865. In short order, Booth was selected General Superintendent of several such missions throughout England that together became The Salvation Army in 1878, selecting Booth as its first General.

In 1890, his book *In Darkest England and The Way Out*[7] was a bestseller. In it, Booth set out the foundation for The Salvation Army's church and social mission

---

4   Lex Loiz, *Church History Review*, "John Wesley and William Wilberforce." April 5, 2010 (https://lexloiz.wordpress.com/2010/04/05/john-wesley-and-william-wilberforce).

5   Adam Hochschild, *Bury the Chains: Prophets and Rebels in the Fight to Free an Empire's Slaves* (New York, NY: Houghton Mifflin Company, 2005).

6   William Wilberforce, *Real Christianity: A Paraphrase in Modern English of A Practical View of the Prevailing Religious System of Professed Christians in the Higher and Middle Classes in This Country, Contrasted with Real Christianity*, ed. Bob Beltz (Ventura, CA: Regal Books, 2006). Originally published in 1797.

7   William Booth, *In Darkest England and The Way Out* (Atlanta, GA: The Salvation Army, 1984). Originally published in 1890.

approach to ministry. Booth outlined a means by which the gospel and an ethic of hard work could put an end to poverty and the increasing crisis of homelessness through establishing training centres, homes for fallen women, halfway houses for released prisoners, food aid for the poor, treatment facilities for alcoholics, industrial schools, and legal services and banks to aid the poor. Integrating his plan with the opportunities then available in other parts of the British Empire, Booth proposed a way for people to start life afresh, both in Christ and in a new land.

Booth was actively involved in the campaign that resulted in raising Britain's age of sexual consent from thirteen to sixteen in 1885. Raising the age to sixteen (from fourteen) was not accomplished in Canada until 2008, a result of more than a decade of campaigning by The Salvation Army, The Evangelical Fellowship of Canada, and other affiliates of the EFC.

For Booth, the Bible and its instruction was at the heart of cultural engagement that challenged the Church to actively participate in meeting the needs of the less fortunate in society. Preaching the gospel was combined with living it out in other compassionate expressions. At the time of General Booth's death, The Salvation Army was active in fifty-eight countries, including Canada, where the work was established in 1882.

Clive Staples Lewis (1898–1963) was an Irish-born academic and novelist who left the Church of Ireland at fifteen. An atheist, he became a confirmed Christian in the Anglican Communion when he was thirty-two. His conversion experience was substantially influenced by the theological challenges presented to him by his friend J.R.R. Tolkien, with whom Lewis taught at Oxford. Lewis continued writing and teaching at both Oxford and Cambridge, becoming an amateur theologian and Christian apologist, explaining Christianity and defending it in his writing and debate. His better known Christian fiction includes *The Screwtape Letters* and the seven-volume *Chronicles of Narnia*. His better known non-fiction works include the Christian classics *Mere Christianity*, *The Abolition of Man*, and *The Four Loves*.

C.S. Lewis was convinced that "[t]here is no neutral ground in the universe: every square inch, every split second, is claimed by God and counterclaimed by Satan."[8] He saw the solution as individual conversion, observing that human beings were the primary battleground whose conversion was capable of influencing everything else. Convinced that the way to influence culture, politics, and any other aspect of life was through the conversion of the individual, who would

---

8   C.S. Lewis, "Christianity and Culture," *Christian Reflections* (Grand Rapids, MI: Eerdmans, 1967), 33.

then engage in his or her circle of influence and activity, Lewis wrote, "The application of Christian principles, say, to trade unionism or education, must come from Christian trade unionists and Christian schoolmasters; just as Christian literature comes from Christian novelists and dramatists."[9] This is what he had done, applying his life experience, skills, and conversion to writing, lectures, and radio broadcasts.

The Dutch

Abraham Kuyper (1837–1920) was a clergyman, journalist, theologian, and politician. In addition to many writings, Kuyper founded the *De Standaard* newspaper (1870), the Free University of Amsterdam (1880), and the Anti-Revolutionary Political Party (1879) that carried him to the Prime Minister's chair in the Netherlands, where he served from 1901 to 1905.

Kuyper promoted "principled pluralism,"[10] the idea that multiple religious expressions or worldviews, including humanism, could peacefully and respectfully coexist and participate equally in the culture and politics of the nation, including running their own schools and teaching from their particular religious perspective. As a neo-Calvinist, Kuyper promoted the idea that God is part of every aspect of everyday of life and that government has the responsibility to act in the best interests of all citizens, not just a preferred majority religious community. The concept of sphere theology was important to this understanding and expression. Rather than rights originating with the individual citizen or the state, various elements of society were seen to be sovereign in their own sphere: family, education, church, and state. In Kuyper's theology, there were clear divisions of responsibility between each sphere, with each sphere answerable to God, and the spheres overlapped in the life of the citizen.

Gerald Vandezande (1933–2011) emigrated from the Netherlands in 1950, becoming an advocate for applying Kuyper's principles in the Canadian context. Enormously influential in setting the measured tone of much Canadian evangelical engagement in the public policy arena, Vandezande was a key person in establishing the Christian Labour Association of Canada and Citizens for Public Justice. He authored several books in the social justice disposition, including

---

9   C.S. Lewis, *Mere Christianity* (London, UK: Fontana Books, 1952), 75.

10   Jonathan Chaplin, *Comment*, "The Point of Kuyperian Pluralism." November 1, 2013 (https://www.cardus.ca/comment/article/4069/the-point-of-kuyperian-pluralism).

Justice, Not Just Us: Faith Perspectives and National Priorities.[11] Vandezande was a resource and coach to many in other schools of evangelical Christian thought as they pursued their own engagement in the sphere of public policy.

Some other Canadian institutions that have been particularly influenced by Kuyper's neo-Calvinist theological positioning of the citizen in the spheres of family, church, education, and state are Redeemer University College, the Christian Reformed Centre for Public Dialogue, the Association for Reformed Political Action, and the think tank Cardus (formerly the Work Research Foundation).

The Germans

Dietrich Bonhoeffer (1906–1945) was a German Lutheran pastor and theologian who, along with Karl Barth, Martin Niemöller, and others, was a founding member of the Confessing Church, established to counter the efforts of German Chancellor Adolf Hitler to control the state Lutheran Church. Continuing influence was secured as the result of his writing, and also the circumstances pertaining to his return from the safety of the U.S. to Germany in the midst of World War II. Bonhoeffer was convinced he could not sit out the war. On his return home, he felt pushed by conscience to conspire to assassinate Hitler, which led to Bonhoeffer's execution just days before the end of the war.

Bonhoeffer stressed the importance of personal and collective commitment to Christ, writing, "When Christ calls a man, he bids him come and die."[12] The Christian life, according to Bonhoeffer, was to be lived knowing Jesus as both Saviour and Lord, and lived in community. In the context of following Jesus, Bonhoeffer also understood, "Discipleship means allegiance to the suffering Christ, and it is therefore not at all surprising that Christians should be called upon to suffer."[13]

---

11 Gerald Vandezande, *Justice, Not Just Us: Faith Perspectives and National Priorities* (Toronto, ON: Public Justice Resource Centre, 1999).

12 Bonhoeffer, *Cost of Discipleship*, 99.

13 Ibid., 101.

Dietrich Bonhoeffer formulated a simple question that remains the guiding question for Christian ethics: "Who is Jesus Christ, for us, today?"[14] To live the life of discipleship, to be a Christian living in the world in both profession and practice, the complementary question posed by his writing is, "Who are we, for Jesus Christ, today?"[15]

Martin Niemöller (1892–1984) was a theologian and pastor who has already been mentioned as a contemporary of Barth and Bonhoeffer. Niemöller was initially supportive of the National Socialist (Nazi) Party and celebrated the election of Adolf Hitler. He turned away as quickly as the Nazis turned once they had secured political power, becoming critical of Hitler and Nazi policies. Arrested in 1938, Niemöller was described as "Hitler's personal prisoner."[16]

Martin Niemöller was also a writer. It is perhaps his simplest poem that has left us with the most enduring impact on Christian public engagement:

First they came for the Socialists, and I did not speak out—
Because I was not a Socialist.
Then they came for the Trade Unionists, and I did not speak out—
Because I was not a Trade Unionist.
Then they came for the Jews, and I did not speak out—
Because I was not a Jew.
Then they came for me—and there was no one left to speak for me.[17]

---

14 John G. Stackhouse, Jr., *Making the Best of It: Following Christ in the Real World* (New York, NY: Oxford University Press, 2011), 3. Stackhouse notes that he has only found this quote in secondary sources referencing Bonhoeffer's statement made in the letter "To Eberhard Bethge, 30 April 1944" [Dietrich Bonhoeffer, *Letters and Papers from Prison*, ed. Eberhard Bethge (London, ON: SCM Press Ltd, 1971)]. Stackhouse notes the actual quote in the English translation is, "What is bothering me incessantly is the question what Christianity really is, or indeed who Christ really is, for us today."

15 Stackhouse, *Making the Best of It*, 4. This is in reference to a statement made in Bonhoeffer's *The Cost of Discipleship* (37), which reads: "What we want to know is... what Jesus Christ wants of us."

16 Eric Pace, "Martin Niemoller, Resolute Foe of Hitler," *The New York Times*. March 8, 1984 (http://www.nytimes.com/1984/03/08/obituaries/martin-niemoller-resolute-foe-of-hitler.html).

17 Martin Niemoller, *Holocaust Encyclopedia*, "First They Came for the Socialists..." Date of access: January 17, 2017 (https://www.ushmm.org/wlc/en/article.php?ModuleId=10007392).

The Americans

Following the *Declaration of Independence* in 1776, the *Constitution of the United States* was agreed upon in 1787. It contains an amendment formula, which was used in 1791 to add what is referred to as the *Bill of Rights*. The *First Amendment*, which is often referenced as the separation of church and state, was approved at that time. It reads:

> Congress shall make no law respecting an establishment of religion, or prohibiting the free exercise thereof; or abridging the freedom of speech, or of the press; or the right of the people peaceably to assemble, and to petition the government for a redress of grievances.[18]

The intent of this clause was to limit the power of government in regard to religion, thus ensuring freedom of religion in the United States. Unfortunately, it is the abbreviated phrase "separation of church and state" that has infiltrated the language of Canadians, usually used to suggest that the church should not have influence on the state.

While many Americans have commented on the relationship between church and state, following are some who have particularly impacted thinking in regard to Christian engagement in the public square.

Reinhold Niebuhr (1892–1971) was an American theologian and ethicist whose contribution in this area is often overshadowed by the continued popularity of his younger brother Richard's work, which we will look at next. His books were popular during his lifetime, and continue to have particular influence on American and international politics.[19] A summary of his contribution is a brief reflection on the concept of Christian realism. Niebuhr's work suggests that the best worldview identifies human ability and human limitation, including thorough analysis of the world's resources and theological resources. He promoted a public theology and active political engagement that supported the democratic process.

Niebuhr's realism led him to argue for the necessity of democracy as *the* system for governance in a fallen world, given its checks and balances on power.

---

18   *United State Constitution*, Amendment I.

19   Reinhold Niehbuhr was the author of more than twenty books, including *Moral Man and Immoral Society: A Study in Ethics and Politics* (Louisville, KY: Westminster John Knox Press, 2013; originally published in 1932) and *The Nature and Destiny of Man: A Christian Interpretation, Vol. 1 Human Nature, Vol. 2 Human Destiny* (Louisville, KY: Westminster John Knox Press, 2016; Vol. 1 originally published in 1941 and Vol. 2 in 1943).

He also advanced a political philosophy that continues to impact international relations to move away from idealism toward recognition of realism in the relationships between states, including a contemporary revision of the just war theory (the theological understanding of a nation's right to use force against actual or imminent attack).

One of Reinhold Niebuhr's most enduring writings is a poem which, seen in this light, is an apt summary of his work:

> God, grant me the serenity
> to accept the things I cannot change,
> courage to change the things I can,
> and the wisdom to know the difference.[20]

H. Richard Niebuhr (1894–1962) was also a theologian and ethicist. He focused on studying the way in which human beings relate to God, to each other, to their communities, and to the broader world. His 1951 book *Christ and Culture*[21] continues to be the touchpoint for conversation on how the Church relates to the world in which it is situated, noting five essential points of reference for consideration:

1. Christ AGAINST Culture	Church separated from a hostile culture.
2. Christ OF Culture	No sense of conflict between church and culture.
3. Christ ABOVE Culture	Good values are providentially supplied to shape culture.
4. Christ in PARADOX with Culture	Serving Christ and serving culture despite different sets of values.
5. Christ TRANSFORMING Culture	Evangelism: infiltration and influence of cultural institutions.

---

20 Fred R. Shapiro, *The Chronicle or Higher Education*, "Who Wrote the Serenity Prayer?" April 28, 2014 (http://www.chronicle.com/article/Who-Wrote-the-Serenity-Prayer-/146159/).

21 H. Richard Niebuhr, *Christ and Culture* (New York, NY: Harper & Row, 1951).

In this way, Niebuhr explored the concepts of the absolute sovereignty of God interacting with the subjective relativism of human beings, living in the imperfections and happenings of a fallen world. Richard Niebuhr's explorations were consistently focused on helping Christians understand our moral responsibility to live for Christ in the world in which we find ourselves.

Billy Graham (1918–present) is recognized as perhaps the greatest evangelist of the twentieth century. Holding indoor and outdoor crusades in sports stadiums, broadcasting live and recorded on radio and television, and the author of many books, Graham was also sought out by several American presidents and other influential leaders as a spiritual adviser. Friends with Martin Luther King, Jr., he was a recognized participant in the American civil rights movement, refusing to allow segregation at his crusades. Billy Graham served as the first full-time evangelist for Youth for Christ starting in 1947, travelling throughout the United States and Europe. In 1950, he founded the Billy Graham Evangelistic Association.

Graham considered himself to be a theologically conservative Christian living in a world where theologically liberal Christians had established a foothold in the great institutions of influence within both Church and culture. To strengthen the evangelical presence, Graham pursued both evangelism and the creation of institutions intended to influence both Church and culture. He envisioned and established the *Christianity Today* magazine in 1956, with its variety of related publications, to put print to voice, bringing together renowned conservative evangelical leaders—theologians, journalists, preachers, and financiers—to do so.[22]

Graham's friendship with John Stott (1921–2011), an English evangelical Anglican clergyman, led to establishing the Lausanne Committee for World Evangelization in 1974, which brought together evangelical leaders from around the world to strengthen the global Church for world evangelization and to engage ideological and sociological trends which impact that pursuit. The Lausanne Movement continues to bring evangelical leaders together with other Christian leaders to explore and act on the cause of world evangelization.

Francis Schaeffer (1912–1984) was a pastor, theologian, and philosopher. In 1948, Schaeffer and his family moved to Switzerland, where he established the L'Abri (French for "the shelter") Christian community. The Christian worldview and philosophy training centre and community of L'Abri expanded to locations

---

22 Billy Graham, *Christianity Today*, "Envisioning 'Christianity Today'." Date of access: January 11, 2017 (http://www.christianitytoday.org/ministry/history/envisioningct.html). Excerpted from Billy Graham, *Just As I Am: The Autobiography of Billy Graham* (New York, NY: Harper-Collins, 1997).

in Sweden, France, the Netherlands, the United Kingdom, and the United States. Schaeffer's emphasis was on reaching and training pastors and church leaders to focus on Christ-centred principles, particularly from the perspective of the Reformed theological tradition, for engagement with the Church and, through the Church, culture.

Schaeffer's work was a significant contribution to the rise of Protestant political engagement in American politics in the 1970s and 80s. His 1976 book *How Should We Then Live: The Rise and Decline of Western Thought and Culture* [23] and 1982 book *A Christian Manifesto*,[24] written as a response to the 1848 *Communist Manifesto* and 1933/1973 *Humanist Manifestos*, identified a crumbling culture and morality that Schaeffer proposed could be countered only by a more publicly engaged and assertive conservative Christianity. Schaeffer presented theological arguments for more political participation in pursuit of becoming the dominant worldview. Francis Schaeffer's outlines of what he called "the limits of civil obedience," "the use of civil disobedience," and "the use of force"[25] remain strong themes underlying American political engagement, and informing Canadian engagement. Concepts of Dominion Theology (nation governance based on biblical principles) ring openly in Schaeffer's written voice.

The influence of Francis Schaeffer's thought is seen in much of the Western Church's public policy engagement beginning in the late 1970s, not just in the evangelical church.

Richard John Neuhaus (1936–2009) was actually born in Canada, but moved to the United States as a teenager. Neuhaus followed in his father's footsteps, becoming a Lutheran pastor in 1960. He converted to Roman Catholicism and became a Catholic priest in 1990. The author of several books examining the place of the Church in the contemporary world, in 1990 Neuhaus created a written forum for debate and discussion of that topic in the journal *First Things*, published by the Institute on Religion and Public Life, which he also founded.

In 1995 Neuhaus co-authored *Evangelicals and Catholics Together: Toward a Common Mission*[26] with high-profile evangelical Chuck Colson (1931–2012). The book challenged Protestants and Catholics to deliver a common witness to the

---

23 Francis Schaeffer, *How Should We Then Live: The Rise and Decline of Western Thought and Culture* (Westchester, IL: Crossway Books, 1976).

24 Francis Schaeffer, *A Christian Manifesto* (Westchester, IL: Crossway Books, 1982).

25 Ibid. These are chapter headings for Chapters Seven through Nine.

26 Richard John Neuhaus and Chuck Colson, *Evangelicals and Catholics Together: Toward a Common Mission* (Dallas TX: Word Publishing, 1995).

modern world at the eve of the third millennium. Both men were heavily supported and criticized for the effort.

Richard John Neuhaus' contribution to dialogue within the Church about the role of the Church and Christians engaging with the society in which we live invited many into the conversation who might otherwise have remained silent or secluded within their own denominations and fields of study. He got us reasoning together, as the institutes he established and *First Things* continue to do. Neuhaus saw politics only as a part of a larger public square in which we are called to engage with our neighbours.

Miroslav Volf (1956–present) was born in Croatia, moving to the United States in 1991. He is the director of the Yale Center for Faith and Culture (YCFC) at Yale University. Volf's contributions have included the examination of Christian faith and economics, reflection on the example of the Trinity for community in the Church, the place of Christianity in bringing healing to human community, and the value of interfaith engagement. Since founding the YCFC in 2003, Volf has expressed a particular interest in the contribution of the Christian Church to the common good of humanity, notably in his 2011 book *A Public Faith: How Followers of Christ Should Serve the Common Good*[27] and 2016's *Flourishing: Why We Need Religion in a Globalized World*.[28]

In his introduction to *A Public Faith*, Volf describes his position as "religious political pluralism,"[29] which he describes in regard to the Christian faith in numbered sequence as summarized in the chart below:[30]

1. Christian faith is a prophetic faith that seeks to mend the world.	Christian faith should be active in all spheres of life.
2. Christ was a bringer of grace.	Christian faith is not to be coercive.

27 Miroslav Volf, *A Public Faith: How Followers of Christ Should Serve the Common Good* (Grand Rapids, MI: Brazos Press, 2011).

28 Miroslav Volf, *Flourishing: Why We Need Religion in a Globalized World* (New Haven, CT: Yale University Press, 2016).

29 Miroslav Volf, *A Public Faith*, xi.

30 Ibid., 15–17.

3. To follow Christ means to care for others as well as for oneself.	A vision of human flourishing and the common good is the main thing Christian faith brings into the public debate.
4. The world is God's creation and the Word came to His own even if His own did not accept Him.	The Christian stance toward culture is complex: accepting, rejecting, learning, transforming, subverting, and putting various elements of rapidly changing culture to better use.
5. Christian faith bears witness to Christ.	Christians are witnesses to Christ.
6. Christian faith offers no political blueprint.	Christians desire for others the same freedoms they claim for themselves. Pluralism is embraced.

The course I teach at my church, as part of the applied apologetics "fourth" year of a three-year Bible school, is shaped around Volf's *A Public Faith*, which is a concise, comprehensive, and inspiring text.

The Canadians

John H. Redekop (1932–present) is a Mennonite political scientist who wrote an opinion column in the *Mennonite Brethren Herald* for decades, was a professor of political science at Wilfred Laurier University, served as moderator of the Canadian Conference of Mennonite Brethren Churches, was Chairman of the board for The Evangelical Fellowship of Canada (at a time when that position was called President), and is the author of several books, including *Politics Under God*,[31] which presents a perspective on political engagement that has been described as "Anabaptist realism."

The Anabaptist movement originated in the sixteenth century. Two theological distinctions of Anabaptists are the practice of water baptism only after a confession of faith, including rebaptism of converts who were baptised as infants, and a literal interpretation of the Sermon on the Mount, including living an active

---

31 John H. Redekop, *Politics Under God* (Waterloo, ON: Herald Press, 2007).

lifestyle of peacemaking (Matthew 5:9, conscientious objectors in time of war), refusing to take oaths (Matthew 5:33–37), sharing possessions and the fruits of one's labour rather than storing up treasures on earth (Matthew 6:19–27), and distrusting state authorities, seeing themselves as sheep among wolves (Matthew 10:16). In addition to seeing the Matthew 5 teaching as being instructive about character, Anabaptists are most often found by others to be meek (Matthew 5:5), focused on continually deepening their understanding of living life as Christian (Matthew 5:6), and exhibiting mercy toward others (Matthew 5:7). You know them as Mennonites, Brethren in Christ, Hutterites, and the Amish. Anabaptists are also strong promoters of religious freedom for all, a kind of live-and-let-live philosophy.

While many expressions of the Anabaptist tradition still shun any involvement with politics or political authorities, Redekop regards the distrust of state authorities—church separating itself from the state—as something that was influenced by the historic rejection Anabaptists faced in a time when nations aligned with either a denominational Protestant or Catholic faith that excluded minority religious communities. Anabaptists for centuries experienced varying levels of persecution in the Western world.

Redekop's "Anabaptist realism" recognizes that contemporary democratic government, unaligned with a state religion, is more accepting of multiple religious communities and more cooperative in nature than those that were in place when Anabaptist theology took shape. He suggests that, for the good of society, the Church has an obligation to engage those opportunities presented within the state that do not contravene biblical principles and Christian discipleship. In *Politics Under God*, Redekop develops a practical theology of the opportunities and restrictions for engaging with government. These opportunities are seen to include working with government to facilitate shipping and distributing grain products to the developing world; informed participation in the political process, including prayer, abiding by the law, voting, and seeking political office without compromising one's biblical ethics; holding government to account in its ethical standard; working for the government in positions that do not require the compromise of one's biblical standards; building relationships to encourage politicians in their service to people; and cautious engagement as politicians. Redekop notes, "We do well to remind ourselves that moral indifference can produce devastating results."[32]

Brian Stiller (1942–present) serves as Global Ambassador for the World Evangelical Alliance, a network of churches in 129 nations and the representative platform for more than six hundred million evangelical Christians. Stiller was

---

32 Ibid., 112.

president of Youth for Christ Canada before becoming president of The Evangelical Fellowship of Canada (the EFC) in 1983. From his position at the EFC, Stiller became the face and voice of the Canadian evangelical movement's engagement in the public square.

Whether speaking in a church on Sunday, writing in the EFC's *Faith Today* magazine (which he founded), engaging on his television show or Parliament Hill, or in one of several books, Stiller instilled a homiletic (preaching) style to his communications and those of the EFC. This fit well with the community he was gathering for fellowship and action. The EFC's positions on matters of public engagement were arrived at through a process of consultation that was sensitive to people's theological differences, enabling the EFC to connect with a community that spans thirty to thirty-five percent on either side of the theological and political centres of Canada's evangelical population, a total of sixty to seventy percent of what I call the evangelical spectrum. The EFC also facilitated the formation of relationships with other religious communities at points of alignment on one issue or another. His protégé and current EFC president Bruce Clemenger shepherded this style, gathering evangelical leaders who were missing during Stiller's time at the EFC, and further securing a base that is denominationally representative of greater than half of Canada's identified evangelical membership.

So what does Stiller's homiletic style look like?

1. Clarify: Express the issue being addressed, the position being taken on it, and the reason you are qualified to address it.
2. Verify: Note the biblical basis for speaking to the issue, why it is valid to communicate from that position, and identify relevant cultural comments that align with your position.
3. Amplify: Supplement the information presented with anecdotal (stories), sociological (studies), and/or data (statistics) evidence and any relevant law-related (legislative, judicial from Canada and other nations) presentation supportive of the position.
4. Apply: Apply the information to your position and make a recommendation as to how the recipient of the sermon, article, government, or court submission should proceed.

Stiller has written a number of books on a variety of topics in the tone of practical understanding and application of biblical principles. His books *From the*

Tower of Babel to Parliament Hill: How to Be a Christian in Canada Today[33] and *Jesus and Caesar: Christians in the Public Square*[34] are on my list of essential books to read in preparation for public policy engagement in Canada. He has consistently challenged Christians to be as "the sons of Issachar," who were prepared to advise King David as those *"who had understanding of the times, to know what [the nation] ought to do"* (1 Chronicles 12:32). I have met numerous members of Parliament and provincial legislatures who trace their inspiration for public service to Brian Stiller's eight-hour seminar *Understanding Our Times*, which he delivered hundreds of times from the mid-1980s to the early 1990s.

John G. Stackhouse, Jr. (1960–present) is one who has answered the sons of Issachar call. Stackhouse is an academic and practical theologian who started teaching in 1987, has written several books, and has served as an advisory editor to *Christianity Today* and columnist on Christianity and culture in *Faith Today*. A sought-after commentator on contemporary culture, Stackhouse has written several books. His book *Making the Best of It: Following Christ in the Real World* is on my recommended reading list for any Christian who has a desire to engage culture, whether through evangelism or social activism.

Born in the same year, Stackhouse and I attended Queen's University at the same time, we're both motorcyclists, both committed and informed evangelical Christians engaged in the public sphere, and we still don't agree on everything. Christianity, its evangelical expression, and its leaders have many things in common but we are not a homogeneous group by any means. Stackhouse has stated that Christians on two sides of an argument can both be right or both be wrong and not find agreement.

In *Making the Best of It*, Stackhouse grounds the benefit of what Christians have to share in the twenty-first century with this reminder:

> The most important message we have to tell, of course is the gospel of Jesus Christ. That gospel, however, is nested within the great Story of all that God has done and said, and all that God wants for us. So we have much to say, of different sorts in the public sphere today.[35]

---

33 Brian Stiller, *From the Tower of Babel to Parliament Hill: How to Be a Christian in Canada Today* (Toronto, ON: Harper Collins, 1997).

34 Brian Stiller, *Jesus and Caesar: Christians in the Public Square* (Oakville, ON: Castle Quay Books Canada, 2003).

35 Stackhouse, *Making the Best of It*, 330.

This reality is relevant to the way we engage publicly in evangelism and concerning public policy: how we formulate our positions; the messages we communicate; our choice of language, that we might be understood; and our behaviour, particularly our treatment of those who hold differing opinions, whether they share our worldview or another. Behaving with His story in mind, and mindful that we represent Him as His ambassadors, we will be without cause to apologize for who we are as Christians, citizens engaging on equal footing with our fellow citizens.

Charles Taylor (1931–present) is an active Roman Catholic who is an internationally awarded social science and political philosopher. His seminal work on the philosophy and sociology of religion is his 2007 book *A Secular Age*,[36] in which he explores the transition in the belief system underlying the culture of Western society from Christianity to secularism, including an exploration of the different constructs of secularism.

Taylor has become the preferred philosopher of the Supreme Court of Canada on questions of secularism, particularly as they pertain to freedom of religion. It is beneficial to be familiar with his work. A far more accessible book for the average reader is his 110-page 2011 book co-authored with Jocelyn Maclure, *Secularism and Freedom of Conscience*.[37] Taylor notes that

> it is generally agreed that secularism is a political and legal system whose function is to establish a certain distance between the state and religion, disagreements arise when it comes time to define the term more precisely... [S]ecularism must at present be understood within the broader framework of the diversity of beliefs and values that citizens embrace.[38]

Taylor contrasts rigid, strict, or closed secularism, which tends toward privatizing faith, with his preferred flexible and open secularism, which tends toward accepting and accommodating faith in broad public spaces, so long as that faith is not sponsored by the state. The state is to be neutral, according to Taylor, granting "equal respect to individuals with different worldviews and sets of values."[39]

Charles Taylor's stated position is that "contemporary societies must develop the ethical and political knowledge that will allow them to fairly and

---

36   Charles Taylor, *A Secular Age* (Cambridge, MA: Harvard University Press, 2007).

37   Charles Taylor and Jocelyn Maclure, *Secularism and Freedom of Conscience*, trans. Jane Marie Todd (Cambridge, MA: Harvard University Press, 2011).

38   Ibid., 3–4.

39   Ibid., 19.

consistently manage the moral, spiritual and cultural diversity at their heart."[40] People of varying worldviews and religions must learn to coexist, sharing the public space in a democracy.

Raymond J. de Souza (1971–present) is a Canadian Roman Catholic parish priest, graduate of and chaplain at Queen's University, columnist for the *National Post* and *The Catholic Register*, and editor-in-chief of *Convivium* magazine (*Convivium* is Latin for "life together").[41] De Souza is a sought-after commentator and has written for a number of media outlets, bringing a logical Christian perspective to his remarks on current events. Raymond de Souza is demonstrating a constructive engagement with culture from a confident Christian perspective. Of course, as Father de Souza, both he and those reading or listening to him are well aware that his role is as an ambassador for Christ and His Church.

In the context of looking forward seven generations, I will add someone to this list whose influence is still developing, and whom I expect will impact those who hear her voice.

Cheryl Bear-Barnetson is from Nadleh Whut'en First Nation in British Columbia. She is from the Dakelh Nation and Dumdenyoo Clan (Bear Clan). A multi-award-winning singer and songwriter who has travelled to over six hundred Indigenous communities in Canada and the United States, Bear-Barnetson is a founding board member of NAIITS (the North American Institute for Indigenous Theological Studies) and an associate professor at Regent College, Vancouver. Co-author of *The Honour Drum: Sharing the Beauty of Canada's Indigenous People with Children, Families and Classrooms*,[42] Bear-Barnetson has also written *Introduction to First Nations Ministry*.[43] These are two theologically and culturally sound primers for those with an interest in ministry with Canada's Indigenous peoples.

Some of you may already have been thinking, what about Lesslie Newbigin (1909–1998), author of *Foolishness to the Greeks: The Gospel and Western Culture*,[44] or Jim Wallis (1948–present), author of *Agenda for Biblical People*[45] and *Living God's*

---

40 Ibid., 110.

41 *Convivium* (www.convivium.ca).

42 Cheryl Bear-Barnetson and Tim Huff, *The Honour Drum: Sharing the Beauty of Canada's Indigenous People with Children, Families and Classrooms*, (Lagoon City, ON: Castle Quay Books, 2016).

43 Cheryl Bear-Barnetson, *Introduction to First Nations Ministry* (Cleveland, OH: Cherohala Press, 2013).

44 Lesslie Newbigin, *Foolishness to the Greeks: The Gospel and Western Culture* (Grand Rapids, MI: Eerdmans, 1988).

45 Jim Wallis, *Agenda for Biblical People* (New York, NY: Harper & Row, 1976).

Politics: A Guide to Putting Your Faith into Action?[46] Or what about or Cornelis Van Dam, author of *God and Government—Biblical Principles for Today: An Introduction and Resource,*[47] or Richard Twiss (1954–2013), author of *One Church, Many Tribes?*[48] The list could go on substantially longer.

Others of you have been thinking, "Please don't truncate and mess with the positions of any more great contributors to Christian public engagement."

My hope is that this, the longest chapter, whets one's appetite to explore further, and sufficiently informs others to prepare a context for what follows.

Next, let's consider some steps to take in preparing for our own public space engagement with the broader culture in which we live.

---

46 Jim Wallis, *Living God's Politics: A Guide to Putting Your Faith into Action* (New York, NY: HarperOne, 2006).

47 Cornelis Van Dam, *God and Government—Biblical Principles for Today: An Introduction and Resource* (Eugene, OR: Wipf & Stock, 2011).

48 Richard Twiss, *One Church, Many Tribes* (Bloomington, MN: Chosen Books, 2000).

CHAPTER TWENTY

JUST THE TRUTH, THE WHOLE TRUTH, AND NOTHING BUT THE TRUTH

I said in my alarm, "All mankind are liars."
—Psalm 116:11

Jesus said to him, "I am the way, and the truth, and the life."
—John 14:6

And Jesus said to him, "Why do you call me good? No one is good except God alone. You know the commandments: 'Do not murder, Do not commit adultery, Do not steal, Do not bear false witness, Do not defraud, Honor your father and mother.'"
—Mark 10:18–19

Love is patient and kind; love does not envy or boast; it is not arrogant or rude. It does not insist on its own way; it is not irritable or resentful; it does not rejoice at wrongdoing, but rejoices with the truth.
—1 Corinthians 13:4–6

I REMEMBER THE FIRST PHONE CALL. THEN THE NEXT. THEN THE EMAILS. ONTARIO'S Human Rights Commission had imprisoned a pastor from Windsor for preaching a message that had been secretly taped and then filed with the Commission. The message was on marriage being between one woman and one man. He had not said a word about same-sex marriage. To a lawyer, this story was absurd. To the pastors who were reaching out to me in a panic, this was a serious matter. What could they preach? Who was recording their messages?

In Ontario, the truth is that the Human Rights Commission promotes human rights but doesn't act like a court. The Human Rights Tribunal is the court-like body that decides on human rights complaints. The *Human Rights Code*, and similar legislation in other provinces, does not authorize a jail sentence for anybody. It does authorize fines for violations, training programs, and corrective measures after a hearing that complies with the principles of natural justice (described in Chapter Eleven). And as you read in Part II, preaching the "for" perspective on the gospel, the whole gospel, is the way to go. It's when we get into preaching the "against" side on social policy, or individuals or groups of people, that caution is required. Sometimes we need to step back, rethink, and realize that there is a positive "for" way to address the issue that concerns us.[1]

Calling someone who would likely know the answer to such a question (about a pastor being imprisoned for preaching on marriage) was the right thing to do. Circulating the rumour to people who would not was the wrong thing to do. And not just because it meant I received multiple enquiries!

One of the reasons I wrote this book is to help inform and encourage pastors, other leaders, and the person in the pew with an awareness of where we as Christians stand in Canada. There are rumours of persecution, and then there's reality. We need to search out the truth before we decide whether to share the story. This is particularly true with the twenty-first century explosion of internet-based new media and social media "sources."

Another reason for writing this book is to direct us back to *the* Book. Self-help and commentary books abound, and may actually be very helpful, but they cannot replace the Bible in terms of developing our relationship as Christ-followers with Christ and one another. As we briefly consider the truth about what persecution is and how we might assess, perhaps even pre-empt, its development in Canada, let me begin with words found near the end of Canadian Glenn Penner's book *In the Shadow of the Cross: A Biblical Theology of Persecution and Discipleship*:

> God's priority is not so much to answer the questions that His people may have about why they are persecuted but to give them a revelation of Himself.[2]

Penner makes this statement in the context of John's record of letters from Jesus to seven churches, which we call the Book of Revelation. These words echo the sentiment I have found in the works of authors who have experienced or

---

1 We'll look at this a bit more in Chapter Twenty-Four.

2 Glenn Penner (1962–2010), *In the Shadow of the Cross: A Biblical Theology of Persecution and Discipleship* (Bartlesville, OK: Living Sacrifice Books, 2004), 251.

observed persecution, and the words I have heard from the lips of those who know what it is to stand for Christ in the face of social marginalization, societal hatred, political criminalization, and living daily with the reality that they might be beaten, imprisoned, or put to death because of their commitment to living for Jesus.

These few pages do not offer a complete understanding of persecution. They barely scratch the surface as an introduction. Hopefully, they provide some context for insight into the current Canadian situation, and encouragement to explore what it means for us to be faithful.

In his 1997 book *Their Blood Cries Out: The Worldwide Tragedy of Modern Christians Who Are Dying for Their Faith*[3]—a book still considered by many to be the best primer for understanding the persecution of members of the global Church—Canadian Paul Marshall notes his use of the term persecution to be "the denial of any of the rights of religious freedom."[4] Marshall uses the word denial in its strictest sense, a refusal, rejection, and disavowal of any rights of religious freedom. *Their Blood Cries Out* is a stunning introduction to the stresses, strains, and horrors being faced by Christians in nearly a third of the world's countries, and the appalling lack of interest shown by too many in the Western world.

Marshall begins where we will begin, noting that two concepts in particular are the starting points for understanding human rights.

First, *imago Dei*, the simple truth that *all* people are made in the image of God. God made us in His image. This is reinforced in Genesis 1:27 by stating this truth twice as God's creation process for man and woman, after having stated the same thing in Genesis 1:26 as the intention for the creation of human beings. Second, Marshall comments on God's interaction with Cain after Cain killed Abel. Genesis 4:10 tells us, *"And the Lord said, 'What have you done? The voice of your brother's blood is crying to me from the ground.'"* God recognized the injustice of what Cain had done. Cain killed his brother because Abel's offering to God was the firstborn of his flock, the firstfruit as it were, the first. Cain's offering was the equivalent of a random five, ten, or twenty in the plate, rather than an intentional, valuable to him first-choice selection as his expression of worship. Abel was killed in violation of his religious freedom, his worship of God in belief and practice.

The various international declarations and national constitutional statements on human rights, including religious freedom, find their origins in these biblical principles.

---

3   Paul Marshall, *Their Blood Cries Out: The Worldwide Tragedy of Modern Christians Who Are Dying for Their Faith* (Dallas, TX: Word Publishing, 1997).

4   Ibid., 248.

Human dignity is not something to be achieved. We all have it, because we are image-bearers. As image-bearers, we have a desire to worship. Some worship themselves. Others worship false gods. We worship God, Him whose image we bear. Jesus recognized the freedom of choice in worship when He warned His followers that we cannot worship both God and money (Matthew 6:24) and when He watched the rich young ruler walk away from Him (Matthew 19:16–22), just as others turned away from Him (John 6:66).

Human rights, including religious freedoms, are equally as applicable to the Christian citizen as to any other. These rights are freedoms that *all* people are to be able to enjoy as long as their practice of religion is peaceful.

Even though good has come from persecution, persecution is not good. It is the unjust treatment of another human being or group of human beings. In almost all instances it is not lawful, even when authorized by government, for persecution either violates constitutions or international agreements when it occurs.

So, what does persecution look like?

There are different lists in circulation that summarize the stages of persecution. One of the most frequently used outlines five stages. The stages are not mutually exclusive, nor do they necessarily take place as a progression. But they do suggest warning, danger, and abuse points.

The starting point for persecution is clear: an individual or group is identified as a problem by another individual or group. The five-stage summary follows.

The first stage is stereotyping the group. Generalizing a quality that describes a whole group is stereotyping. If an example hasn't already come to mind, here is a single word: evangelical. Toss that one into the ring and most Canadians have a gut reaction, either for or against.

The second stage is vilification. This is the word the Supreme Court of Canada used as the point of definition for hate speech in its 2013 decision in *Saskatchewan (Human Rights Commission) v. Whatcott*:

> 41. …Representations vilifying a person or group will seek to abuse, denigrate or delegitimize them, to render them lawless, dangerous, unworthy or unacceptable in the eyes of the audience. Expression exposing vulnerable groups to detestation and vilification goes far beyond merely discrediting, humiliating or offending the victims.[5]

---

5 *Whatcott*, Paragraph 41.

The third stage is marginalization. Once it has been determined that the general characteristic (stereotype) of an individual or group is bad, and they are unworthy of general acceptance (vilification), the next step is to make them unwelcome. Treating others as insignificant and outside the scope of acceptability delegitimizes their participation in societal dialogue.

The fourth stage is the one at which official state action is required. The individual or group is criminalized for their beliefs or practices. Note that it is not usually the practises alone that are criminalized (some religious and cultural communities are constrained from criminal actions for the sake of the actions alone, e.g. child mutilation) but practices that occur only because they have a nexus with the belief of the identifiable individual or group (e.g. singing Christian songs in a public gathering).

The fifth stage is outright persecution. This may take place through social hostility, not officially sponsored by the state but often sanctioned by the state, or political hostility that is endorsed by state officials (e.g. people are beaten by neighbours simply because of their religious beliefs and the state takes no restrictive or punitive action with the neighbours, or perhaps the state authorizes such action if someone speaks publicly about a minority faith belief).

Stages four and five are the stages where the risk of death becomes a present reality.

Sometimes the stages are reduced to three: discrimination, persecution, and martyrdom. However, I think the nuance of the five-stage model is a better way to measure increases on a spectrum of persecution that is recognizable under Canadian and international law.

Another list of persecution stages is shared by The Voice of the Martyrs Canada, a ministry that works with the global Church in nations where persecution is taking place. It recognizes a persecution scale that is explained using Scripture:

Ridicule (2 Chronicles 36:16) ▶ Harassment (2 Corinthians 7:5) ▶ Discrimination (John 15:18–21) ▶ Attacks (Acts 16:22) ▶ Imprisonment (Revelation 2:10) ▶ Torture (Matthew 10:17) ▶ Martyrdom (John 16:1–4).[6]

Glenn Penner became the chief executive officer of Voice of the Martyrs Canada shortly after he wrote *In the Shadow of the Cross*. Penner's words in regard

---

6 I encourage you to look up the Scripture references.

to the churches to whom John's letter (Revelation) was sent are illuminating in consideration of challenges faced by the Canadian Church today:

> When faced with persecution, some churches, like the one in Ephesus, in their zeal to defend the faith, become bastions of strict, unloving orthodoxy (2:1–7). Others, like the church in Smyrna, need to be encouraged not to give in to fear in the face of suffering (2:8–11). The scourge of false doctrine creeping in from the outside endangers some faithful churches, like the one in Pergamum (2:12–17). Yet others, like in Thyatira, struggle to maintain ethical and moral purity, especially when the culture demands compromise in order to continue to make a living (2:18–29). The church in Sardis illustrates that persecuted Christians are not immune from spiritual deadness (3:1–6), while some churches, as in Philadelphia, need to be encouraged to look beyond their own neediness to the opportunities that God has placed before them (3:7–13). The Laodicean church might well represent the church that, like in Corinth, forgets that this world is not all there is. Such churches deal with opposition by assimilation into the culture and adopting the trappings of success. They forget that the time to sit on thrones is in the future (3:21) and not today. The task of Christ's Church is to carry the cross in the pursuit of the goals of the kingdom of God. By pursuing the goals of this world, the Laodiceans may have removed the offense of the cross, but they had incurred the offense of Christ.[7]

I find it reassuring that the early Church was just as flawed and prone to the human condition as we are in twenty-first century Canada. Jesus' words to John for the seven churches were about faithfulness, not perfection. When signs of persecution become evident, at whatever stage, it is crucial that we, the Church, look to Jesus. The promises found in John's letter for those who overcome persecution through faithfulness to Jesus are wonderful. As my pastor Jason Boucher says, "God isn't just good. He's amazing!"

When we hear stories of persecution, especially living in a social media world where tweets, posts, and blogs are often circulated with a single click, we have an obligation to do our best to verify the truth of the story before we pass it along. Often we can do that by only sharing from sources that have developed a

---

7   Penner, *In the Shadow*, 252.

good reputation for truth. Other times, we can verify stories by means of a simple internet search.

In the next chapter, we'll consider some of the ways in which the Church can respond to signs of persecution and to actual persecution, whether isolated incidents or widespread.

CHAPTER TWENTY-ONE

FREEZE, FLIGHT, FORTITUDE, INFILTRATE, OR FIGHT?

I lift up my eyes to the hills. From where does my help come? My help comes from the Lord, who made heaven and earth.

—Psalm 121:1–2

SOMETIMES OUR *CRI DE COEUR*, THE PASSIONATE CRY OF OUR HEART, IS "WHERE ARE You, God? Don't You see what I'm going through? Don't You see what others are going through? Where are You?" It aligns closely with "What should I do? What do You want from me? What do You want me to do? What should I do, oh God?"

These heart cries line up with the intimate plea of Jesus to His Father in the garden of Gethsemane on the night He was betrayed. Jesus *"fell on his face and prayed, saying, 'My Father, if it be possible, let this cup pass from me"* and His own heart's answer came in the same breath of prayer: *"nevertheless, not as I will, but as you will'"* (Matthew 26:39).

The simple response is that the answer to our heart's cry is found in Jesus. The more complex version is that the answer to our heart's cry is found in our relationship with Jesus, the depth of that relationship being our preparation for the moment when we are confronted with a vital decision.

I am a motorcyclist. I'm also a safety nut, even making a cameo appearance at the end of a motorcycle safety video. No, I wasn't lying in the middle of a road! I spoke the simple words "Keep an eye out for motorcycles." Gloria finds these two words together, "motorcycle safety," to be incongruous. For her, the idea of being safe on a motorcycle is a prayer thing because motorcycles are inherently unsafe. For me, riding Big Red (that's my motorcycle's name) is a preparation thing. I buy my riding gear by exploring the slide rating (how far can one slide on pavement at what speed before the material wears through) and the various safety ratings of the padding in jackets, pants, and boots, even the impact dispersion ratio of a helmet. Gloria doesn't want to hear about that stuff when I'm evaluating a potential purchase. We are both all too aware that on a motorcycle my bumpers are my knees, and friends in the medical profession have referred to motorcycles as "donor cycles."

Having and wearing proper riding gear is one part of preparation. A second part is regular inspection and maintenance of one's motorcycle. Another part of safety preparation, neglected by too many, is practising riding skills. Taking courses, particularly defensive habits and emergency actions, watching videos, and practising the skills they teach has resulted in on-road action that saved my life more than once. I'll give Gloria this point: prayer doesn't hurt.

On one occasion, I was riding to Georgia with a friend from Ontario, Ken, to be with my dad for Father's Day. We were in Virginia, south of Roanoke, before crossing into North Carolina, when I took the lead. As I rounded a beautiful scenic curve, I found the road littered with gravel. Two wheels, a big bend in the road, and gravel is not a good combination. Big Red started to slide to the outside of the corner against my will. I eyed the yellow line in the middle of the road, geared down, opened the throttle (gas), and counter-steered as hard as I could. I felt a solid bump and bounce before finding myself upright in the middle of my lane, headed straight in the direction I wanted to go. My heart was pounding. I kept going for about ten minutes before pulling off into a gas station. My heart was still pounding. My heart is pounding now as I write this!

When Ken and I started to chat about what had happened, he told me, "I thought I was going to be calling Gloria to tell her I was bringing you home in a box and Big Red on a flatbed."

"Yeah, that gravel was pretty bad," I said, still shaking.

"Didn't you see the gulley?" Ken asked. "You went off the road and hit the gravel shoulder before bouncing back into the middle of the lane. I was sure you were either headed for the forty-foot drop off the side or into the cement monument that was about ten feet in front of you."

I had seen neither. From Ken's vantage point, slowing behind me as I slid, he took it all in, including the scenery. My training and practice kicked in as soon as I saw the gravel in the road. Look where you want to go. Increase your traction. Steer (at that speed, counter-steer) where you need to go. And yes, I prayed. To this day, I'm certain the bump and bounce left a squashed guardian angel somewhere on the side of the road.

When we face persecution, at any stage, that's how it goes. What's our preparation like? How close and deep is our relationship with Christ? Have we equipped ourselves to be faithful when challenged? Are we ready to face the test, perhaps with our lives on the line?

Just as the mission on my motorcycle was to keep Big Red on the road, headed for a Father's Day celebration in Macon, the mission in the Gospels is to carry Christ with us and share His message with others in word and deed, headed to a meeting in heaven. The biblical responses to persecution depend on stage and state. By that, I mean the stage of persecution being encountered and the nature of the laws and social conditions in the nation-state in which the persecution is being perpetrated.

Let's look at five biblical responses to encountering persecution in its various stages.

1. Freeze

This may be a brief or more prolonged time of discernment. We discern through reflection on and understanding of Scripture, prayer, and relationship with others about the circumstance in which we find ourselves. Sometimes these means of discernment will take place in rapid succession, or even while we are engaged in one of the other responses. There may not be time to seek wise counsel from elders in the faith. You may find that the situation is immediate and requires a reflexive response based on your preparation.

Lifting your eyes to where your help comes from may result in hearing a response from the Lord if you have developed the habit of listening for and to Him in prayer, not just speaking. There are several books on conversational prayer techniques. Such techniques include journaling (writing out your prayers), *Lectio Divina* (reflecting on the Scripture and asking God to share His thoughts on the passage), prophetic prayer (asking God to share His words of encouragement for others when you are praying for them in person), and more. Years ago, I was in a meeting where Jack R. Taylor encouraged praying along the following lines before regular Bible reading: "Holy Spirit, You knew when You inspired the writing of these words that I would be reading them today. Through them, what do You have to say to me today?"

As part of the conversation with His disciples at the Last Supper, Jesus told the assembled disciples,

When the Spirit of truth comes, he will guide you into all the truth, for he will not speak on his own authority, but whatever he hears he will speak, and he will declare to you the things that are to come.

—John 16:13

After His resurrection, Jesus told them, *"But you will receive power when the Holy Spirit has come upon you, and you will be my witnesses in Jerusalem and in all Judea and Samaria, and to the end of the earth"* (Acts 1:8).

Throughout the New Testament, we read examples of the Holy Spirit guiding those who witnessed for Jesus. We also read of times when they prayed together and reflected on the guidance of Scripture and the wisdom found through having discussions with mature leaders.

One important way to assess whether we're following the guidance of the Holy Spirit is to compare our intent and proposed action with Scripture. Another is to listen to the advice of those who have demonstrated their trustworthiness as Christ-followers.

2. Flight

In a private meeting with the twelve, Jesus told them that persecution would come and concluded His description of the expected persecution with these words: *"When they persecute you in one town, flee to the next, for truly, I say to you, you will not have gone through all the towns of Israel before the Son of Man comes"* (Matthew 10:23). Key to this course of action is being faithful to the mission. For example, the continuing mission of sharing the gospel was why Paul escaped from the plot to kill him in Damascus (Acts 9:23–25).

We also read of an occasion when Jesus slipped through a hostile crowd (John 8:59) until the time for completing His mission in the flesh had come.

I have a friend who jokingly suggests that a group of us might flee to a small South American mountain village if things get rough in Canada. Unfortunately, we have examples of this in our past. In the 1920s, thousands of German-speaking Mennonites left Manitoba for Mexico when the government ordered that education be provided in English only. The Mexican government promised that they could run their own schools and have their conscientious objection to military service respected.[1][2] A decade ago, a Mennonite community outside a small town in Quebec faced a similar situation when the government ordered them to close their self-run school and send their children to public schools.[3]

When persecution arises, at whatever stage, it is essential to identify its impact and consider whether suffering is required to accomplish God's purposes in the circumstance.

In earlier stages of persecution, a different kind of flight may take place that aligns more with fortitude. We see this in Canada with the growth of home-schooling and private Christian school movements. Children are not removed from the world, or the nation for that matter, but receive their education in a setting intended to fortify their faith to prepare them for the encounters of adulthood.

3. Fortitude

Fortitude is the most common response of today's persecuted Christians. In many nations, as for the Jews with Israel and Canada's Indigenous peoples, Christian people have a strong bond with the land. The most common request from Christians facing persecution is that we pray for them to have the strength to remain, and to remain faithful.

It is hard not to be so afraid in the face of persecutors as to tell one's persecutors, as Peter fearfully did, "I don't know Him" (Luke 22:54–62). There is a strong temptation to keep one's head down and stay hidden. However, those who encounter social or political hostilities have said that in the midst of persecution, there are truly only two options for the Christ-follower: confess Christ or deny Him.

The mission remains the focus.

In February 2015, forty-two men stood on the shore of the Mediterranean Sea in Libya. Twenty-one were in orange jumpsuits. Those twenty-one refused to deny Christ. With the cross tattooed on their right wrists, an act of confirmation in Coptic Christianity, the video broadcast of their deaths sparked both a fresh compassion for Copts in Egypt and an increase in devotion among the Copts and

---

1   Buckingham, *Fighting Over God*, 46.

2   David Agren, *Maclean's*, "Mennonites in Mexico Looking for New Home, Again." January 8, 2013 (http://www.macleans.ca/society/life/wandering-once-more/).

3   *CBC News*, "Mennonites Leaving Quebec After Government Closes School." August 16, 2007 (http://www.cbc.ca/news/canada/montreal/mennonites-leaving-quebec-after-government-closes-school-1.641343).

other Egyptian Christians. It also generated an increased interest in Christianity among other Egyptians.[4]

More recently, Syrian church leaders are encouraging Christians from the region to stay, or at least stay near enough to return to their historic homelands, once the Syrian conflict concludes. They see the place of the Christian community as continuing to contribute to the life and culture of the region as they have done since the first century, from the year following Jesus' death and resurrection.[5]

4. Infiltrate

The word infiltrate literally means "to filter in." Christians are encouraged to live fully as part of Canadian society. In business, Christian principles provide a strong ethic. In public service, the committed Christian has the opportunity to influence other people's lives by example. In the arts, Christian expression presents witness to a world that worships celebrity.

There is nothing sinister about being the tentmaker with an excellent reputation (Acts 18:3) or the respected businesswoman known citywide simply by her first name (Acts 16:14).

We need to be careful not to hide our faith. We also have to be thoughtful about the appropriate time for our actions to be accompanied by words of testimony.

5. Fight

There are times when it is appropriate to fight for one's legal rights. Paul did so on several occasions (Acts 16:37, 22:25, 25:10–11). Again, the focus in the fight is the mission of Christ, furthering the interests of the kingdom of God.

At times our legal rights, including freedom of religion, particularly in the Canadian context, are constitutionally promised. Chapters Eight through Sixteen give examples of such court fights. There are also battles in the public square— public marches, rallies on policy issues, and presentations to parliamentary

---

4   Jayson Casper, *Christianity Today*, "How Libya's Martyrs Are Witnessing to Egypt." February 23, 2015 (http://www.christianitytoday.com/ct/2015/february-web-only/how-libyas-martyrs-are-evangelizing-egypt.html).

5   *WorldWatch Monitor*, "Syrian Christian Spearheads 'One Million Voices' Petition to Support Church to Stay in ME." November 8, 2016 (https://www.worldwatchmonitor.org/2016/11/4717348/).

committees, to name a few. Our rights to association and peaceful assembly are rights Paul did not have.

In the setting of a courtroom or the public square, it is worth noting again the words of Justice Gonthier found at the conclusion of Chapter Seven.

At this point, I think it's appropriate to reflect on some basic principles of civil disobedience. Civil disobedience is generally considered to be the publicly expressed refusal to obey certain laws, regulations, or commands of the government in order to draw attention and seek change to government policy that is considered morally offensive. It is not usually a rejection of the political system as a whole.

The biblical principle of submission to government authorities is repeatedly stated in the New Testament (Matthew 22:20–22, Romans 13:1–7, Titus 3:1, 1 Peter 2:13–14). It is reflected in Western democracy's expectation that citizens will generally adhere to the laws of the land—from traffic laws to the prohibition on taking the life of another person. This social contract is crucial for us to live together as a society.

But what if laws are inherently evil or harmful to our common good? And how does one assess whether laws are good or evil?

For Christians in Canada, our first public effort in dealing with a harmful law is to seek to amend or replace it using democratic means. Similarly, we approach unjust laws in other nations first through diplomatic means.

Civil disobedience may be justified when all other peaceful options have been tried, and failed.

A prominent American example of twentieth-century civil disobedience led by a Christian pastor stands out. Martin Luther King Jr. led non-authorized marches and other acts of civil disobedience in pursuit of change to American laws that discriminated against black Americans. King was imprisoned for his efforts and had known that was a possibility before his first engagement. He led a massive march and rally in Washington, D.C. which ultimately resulted in passage of the U.S. *Civil Rights Act of 1968*, which became law just days after his assassination. He knew the risks. He pursued the goal.

On what basis did this Christian leader, who had an earned doctorate in Christian theology, make the decision to break the law in the ways he did?

There is a biblical basis for using civil disobedience, particularly to oppose policies that dehumanize, oppress, or brutalize people. Here are some examples of civil disobedience found in Scripture:

- the Hebrew midwives saved the lives of Hebrew boys whom Pharaoh had ordered to be put to death at birth (Exodus 1:15–22, the story of Moses' birth);
- Shadrach, Meshach, and Abednego refused to obey Nebuchadnezzar's law requiring all citizens to worship a golden statue (Daniel 3, the fiery furnace story);
- Daniel, one of three presidents in Babylon, refused to pray only to King Darius for a period of thirty days (Daniel 6, the lion's den story);
- the wise men disobeyed Herod's directive to return and tell him where Jesus was born, having had it revealed to them that Herod intended to kill the child (Matthew 2:1–12); and
- the story of the Good Samaritan (Luke 10:25–37), in which Jesus endorsed breaking the religious law to help someone in dire need.

John H. Redekop identifies seven considerations for a Christian community before engaging in civil disobedience. I pose them here as questions:

1. Has the religious community made a careful and balanced assessment of the situation, including the risks of potential harm that might result from the civil disobedience?
2. Is what's at stake of great moral seriousness?
3. Has a specific goal been clearly identified that is indisputably of benefit to the common good?
4. Have all other reasonable steps been exhausted?
5. Will the behaviour planned to challenge the policy in question still demonstrate a general respect for government and the principles of lawful behaviour?
6. Will only suitable means, that make sense to non-sympathetic observers, be used?
7. Are participants prepared to accept the consequences for breaking the law that may be imposed as a result of their civil disobedience?[6]

These questions address the situation in which Dr. King accepted the responsibility and risks of becoming leader of a movement.

---

6   John H. Redekop, "Christians and Civil Disobedience: A Background Paper by the Religious Liberty Commission of The Evangelical Fellowship of Canada," Revised August 2001. See also: Redekop, *Politics Under God*, Chapter Eleven.

Two well-known first-century Christian leaders engaged in principled civil disobedience. When ordered to stop teaching about Jesus, Peter and John stated, *"We must obey God rather than men"* (Acts 5:29). This was not a general statement authorizing Christians to engage in civil disobedience when preaching is restricted by government. It was the resolution of a genuine dilemma between obedience to God for the good of others and obedience to authorities. These men were numbered among the disciples when Jesus told them to be His witnesses in Jerusalem (Acts 1:8). They had been in prison for doing so and were prepared to go back in order to obey Jesus' directive to them.

Civil disobedience usually takes one of two peaceful forms. Direct civil disobedience is an actual violation of an offending law, usually to bring it to consideration by the public, government, and the courts. Indirect civil disobedience is an act, such as a rally or a march that may break traffic laws or municipal permit bylaws, intended to draw attention to the offending law.

In addition to the general principle of submitting to government authority, Christians are urged to pray for those in authority and lead quiet lives (1 Timothy 2:1–2). Prayer is an appeal to the authority that Jesus said is above that of government, and it is the first action for Christians considering a challenge to an immoral government policy. Civil disobedience is the last.

Another way to fight is financially, by supporting organizations that are structured to engage government and/or the courts for our freedoms. My rule of thumb is to note the issue God has laid on my heart, pray about it, investigate each organization I consider supporting—its history, effectiveness, and character of leadership—and then decide. Gloria and I have supported some organizations with a monthly contribution, to assist with regular operating costs, and other organizations based on an issue-by-issue assessment.

CHAPTER TWENTY-TWO

HUMILITY AND PRAYER ARE ACTION AND THE BEGINNING OF ACTION

Therefore, since we have been justified by faith, we have peace with God through our Lord Jesus Christ. Through him we have also obtained access by faith into this grace in which we stand, and we rejoice in hope of the glory of God. Not only that, but we rejoice in our sufferings, knowing that suffering produces endurance, and endurance produces character, and character produces hope, and hope does not put us to shame, because God's love has been poured into our hearts through the Holy Spirit who has been given to us.

—Romans 5:1–5

So if there is any encouragement in Christ, any comfort from love, any participation in the Spirit, any affection and sympathy, complete my joy by being of the same mind, having the same love, being in full accord and of one mind. Do nothing from selfish ambition or conceit, but in humility count others more significant than yourselves. Let each of you look not only to his own interests, but also to the interests of others. Have this mind among yourselves, which is yours in Christ Jesus, who, though he was in the form of God, did not count equality with God a thing to be grasped, but emptied himself, by taking the form of a servant, being born in the likeness of men. And being found in human form, he humbled himself by becoming obedient to the point of death, even death on a cross. Therefore God has highly exalted him and bestowed on him the name that is above every name, so that at the name of Jesus every knee should bow, in heaven and on earth and under the earth, and every tongue confess that Jesus Christ is Lord, to the glory of God the Father.

Therefore, my beloved, as you have always obeyed, so now, not only as in my presence but much more in my absence, work out your own salvation with fear and trembling, for it is God who works in you, both to will and to work for his good pleasure.

—Philippians 2:1–13

FEAR AND TREMBLING. I USED TO WONDER HOW WE WERE TO WORK OUT "WITH FEAR and trembling" a faith that is based in grace. Our salvation may not come via works, but staying faithful to Jesus takes effort. Fear and trembling before God, of whom I am in awe. Fear and trembling from the temptations that come from living out our faith in a way that offers various rewards for doing good, including opportunities to wield worldly power. Fear and trembling as one becomes increasingly aware of the cost of engaging in a spiritual battle. Fear and trembling from standing for Jesus in a world that is seemingly on its knees before every other god but wants nothing to do with Him.

What does it look like to stand in His grace, especially knowing that standing in His grace will produce suffering, endurance, character, and hope? In answer, Paul shares with the Philippian church the magnificent summary found above of what it is to be like Jesus. For me, this motivates prayer along the lines found in this contemplative Salvation Army chorus:

To be like Jesus!
This hope possesses me,
In every thought and deed,
This is my aim, my creed;
To be like Jesus!
This hope possesses me,
His Spirit helping me,
Like him I'll be.[1]

But how to get there?

Among the opportunities missed during my lifetime was a declined invitation to meet Henri Nouwen (1932–1996) and hear him speak. I was enamoured with The Salvation Army, where I had come into relationship with Jesus. I read almost everything written by the great Salvation Army authors.

Beyond The Salvation Army, my reading extended to a select few influential Protestant writers. I was a bit snobbish, ignorant really, about post-Reformation

---

1   John Gowans and John Larsson. "To Be Like Jesus," in *Spirit*, Salvation Army Publishing & Supplies Ltd., 1975.

Catholic authors. After all, if they hadn't gotten the idea of justification by faith right, what did they have to offer? This question betrays the prejudice I held because of my limitations in understanding the fullness of the Body of Christ, not adequately grasping the concept of separate parts and one Body, with the various gifts given for the common good (1 Corinthians 12:7, 12–27). It wasn't until years after his death that Nouwen would begin to mentor me through the gift of his collected writings. One of these, *In the Name of Jesus*,[2] is helpful to us here.

Henri Nouwen had it all in worldly professional terms. As a priest, he was highly respected. As a professor, he was sought after, teaching at the University of Notre Dame, Yale Divinity School, and Harvard Divinity School. He contributed to a variety of publications and had authored several books. But he knew, even with Jesus, that something was missing in his life, or at least the way he was living his life. Nouwen left Yale to take a six-month trip among the poor of Bolivia and Peru. When he returned, he landed at Harvard. Four years later, Nouwen left Harvard to spend time with Canadian Jean Vanier at L'Arche in France, and found his place. He lived the last decade of his life as a member of the L'Arche Daybreak community north of Toronto, serving as pastor to the support staff, family, and developmentally disabled residents there.

In the Name of Jesus is a remarkable little book that describes the transition that can take place in the desires of one's heart, making it possible to move from the pursuit of being a sought-after teacher to the humility needed to be a washer of disciples' feet.

Shortly after joining The Evangelical Fellowship of Canada's public policy team in October 2006, I made a visit to Ottawa. My first day was rushed, but that evening I decided to take a walk up to Parliament Hill in the brisk October air. As I walked north on Metcalfe Street, the Peace Tower grew into the Centre Block and then the West and East Blocks, with the Langevin Block on my right. I touched a cornerstone of the Langevin Block, the office building which houses the Prime Minister's office, before heading across the street. I could sense the power of the place and it was intoxicating. I had a problem.

There is a path that circles the Parliamentary precinct and makes its way to the Supreme Court of Canada building. I walked around that path, including the Court, three times that night, praying that the power of the place would not draw me in. I didn't return to my hotel room until I felt a sense of peace.

---

2 Henri Nouwen, *In the Name of Jesus: Reflections on Christian Leadership* (New York, NY: The Crossroad Publishing Company, 1989).

I'm not sure who I shared the story with that encouraged me to read *In the Name of Jesus*, but it was a game-changer for me. I had been reintroduced to Nouwen at the turn of the century through his book *The Return of The Prodigal Son*,[3] which impacted me deeply and caused me to read a small collection of Nouwen's writings. It was easy to find my copy of *In the Name of Jesus*. Through this large-print, double-spaced, easy-to-read 100-page book, I found myself being counselled by a man who had experienced, understood, and overcome temptation similar to mine.

In the book, Nouwen compares two events, one at the beginning of Jesus' three and a half years of ministry and the other at the end. Reflecting on the temptations faced by Jesus while alone in the desert with the devil (Matthew 4:1–11), Nouwen pinpoints three temptations of twenty-first-century Christian leaders. After demonstrating to the reader in simple, real, and direct terms that this is not an academic exercise, he presents solutions for a Christ-follower in the context of another conversation, the one between Peter and Jesus on a beach in Galilee after Jesus' resurrection (John 21:15–22). The temptations come in private but the solutions, Nouwen suggests, can only be found in the community of the Body of Christ.

"Jesus' first temptation was to be relevant: to turn stones into bread."[4] Do we concern ourselves with whether we are able to impress people with our accomplishments—Bible memorization, evangelism, public policy success, or other areas? This is the desire to be relevant. The first question Jesus posed to Peter had nothing to do with Peter's accomplishments. It was simply, "Do you love Me?" Are we in love with Jesus? If so, what does that look like?

Being in love requires being in relationship. The first communing we have to do with the community of the Body of Christ is with Christ Himself, the Head of the Body. Christ being the Head is not to suggest that we lack or set aside our own intellectual capacity, but to recognize that He is the way, the truth, and the life (John 14:6). Nouwen encourages us to develop the practice of contemplative prayer, reflecting on Him whom we love, speaking with Him, and listening for His voice.

My friend Rob gives simple instruction on prayer that meets many of us where we're at. If we enjoy having conversation with friends over coffee, or some other beverage of choice, he suggests we set two seats in the same way we might

---

3   Henri Nouwen, *The Return of The Prodigal Son: A Story of Homecoming* (New York, NY: Image/ Doubleday, 1992).

4   Nouwen, *In the Name of Jesus*, 30.

for conversation with a friend. Set two beverages if it helps. Then engage in conversation with your Friend.

Nouwen notes:

> Christian leaders cannot simply be persons who have well-informed opinions about the burning issues of our time. Their leadership must be rooted in the permanent, intimate relationship with the incarnate Word, Jesus, and they need to find there the source for their words, advice and guidance.[5]

We must avoid allowing our opinions, our sense of relevance, to stand ahead of the directions in His Word or the depth of our relationship with Him. Doing so inevitably leads to pride and divisiveness.

The second temptation Jesus faced was to throw Himself from the pinnacle of the temple, calling on the angels to lift Him up so He wouldn't be harmed. In short, "to do something spectacular, something that could win him great applause."[6] Doesn't everybody want to be the hero? The centre of attention? Jesus' second comment to Peter, *"Feed my sheep"* (John 21:17), had nothing to do with Peter's popularity. The flock belongs to Jesus (John 10:16). Peter was privileged, by Jesus' direction, to proclaim the gospel along with others who were working together with Him to do the same.

Ministry in the Body of Christ is mutual, with Jesus and with others. It's not about us. And we can't do it alone. We are called to live out the vulnerable servant leadership that Jesus modelled, even to the point of washing the feet of others as circumstance requires, both literally and metaphorically.

Like Peter, Nouwen says we must humbly confess our failings and seek forgiveness from the ones we have injured, from Christ, and from His Church. Nouwen wisely suggests that this confession occur in an appropriate way, most often not in public but in a truly safe place.

So what is a safe place? My friend Barry says, "Every pastor needs a pastor." He's right, and it extends to every member of the Body of Christ. We all need someone, preferably a small group of someones, we can trust to keep confidence and help us process the trials of life and celebrate the victories.

Jesus' third temptation was the temptation to power: to rule the kingdoms of the world. Nouwen writes:

---

5   Ibid., 45.

6   Ibid., 53.

One of the greatest ironies of the history of Christianity is that its leaders constantly gave in to the temptation of power—political power, military power, economic power, or moral and spiritual power—even though they continued to speak in the name of Jesus, who did not cling to his divine power but emptied himself and became as we are. The temptation to consider power an apt instrument for the proclamation of the Gospel is the greatest of all.[7]

He goes on to note that "power offers an easy substitute for the hard task of love."[8] Jesus' closing words in this part of the conversation put Peter on notice that he who had done what he wanted and gone where he wanted in his youth would find that as he grew older *another will dress you and carry you where you do not want to go* (John 21:18). The servant-leader, like Jesus, is one who is willing to be "led to unknown, undesirable, and painful places. The way of the Christian leader is not the way of upward mobility in which our world has invested so much, but the way of downward mobility ending on the cross."[9] Humility.

To engage with others as Jesus did, to understand the signs of the times in the culture in which we live, as Jesus understood the signs two millennia ago, we must set aside time for deep theological study and reflection. Theology is just an impressive-sounding word for reading, studying, and thinking with God as our focus. Jesus loved His Father, reflected on that love, and followed Him. That made Jesus a godly servant and a godly leader. Paul made this plea to us:

I appeal to you therefore, brothers, by the mercies of God, to present your bodies as a living sacrifice, holy and acceptable to God, which is your spiritual worship. Do not be conformed to this world, but be transformed by the renewal of your mind, that by testing you may discern what is the will of God, what is good and acceptable and perfect.

—Romans 12:1–2

Are we willing to transition from leading to being led? From being a Christian leader to a Christ-follower?

---

7   Ibid., 76.

8   Ibid., 77.

9   Ibid., 81.

In meetings and in personal conversation, Jack Frost (1952–2007) would pose the question, "Are you a sent one or a went one?"[10] Are we bullishly pursuing our own goals or are we communing with God, family, and those with whom we are in close relationship to make sure we are on the right track? The most intimate of these conversations, Frost suggested, takes place at the kitchen table with one's spouse and the Lord.

When I was growing up, important (and not so important) conversations took place at the kitchen table. That's where family and friends informally gathered, closest to the fridge, cupboards, stove, and kettle, with a large window that looked out onto the backyard and a ravine. Conversations about faith and future, without smartphones in hand, are nurtured in environments where everything that's needed for relaxed, extended chitchat is in one comfortable room. My one political campaign was planned and orchestrated from a dining room table, only because the kitchen table wasn't big enough.[11]

Tim Huff (1964–present) is a Canadian who has spent a life of Christian service with those whom society might consider less fortunate, but whom God sees as equally made in His image. Author of three books that speak to adults about Christian compassion and service, Huff is also the author and illustrator of the Compassion series of children's books. I commend to you *The Cardboard Shack Beneath the Bridge: Helping Children Understand Homelessness*,[12] *It's Hard Not to Stare: Helping Children Understand Disabilities*,[13] and *The Honour Drum: Sharing the Beauty of Canada's Indigenous People with Children, Families and Classrooms*,[14] all the books that have been published in the series to date. Written in accessible language with illustrations, these books are designed for inspiring kitchen table conversation, dialogue that brings your family together not to talk about you but to talk about others in the world we share. In an era of fast food (even meals at home may involve a microwave and eating alone) and 24/7/365 connection to office, games, media, and social media, we need to be more intentional than in the past about establishing opportunities for these kinds of formative and transformative conversations.

---

10 Jack was a personal friend. I hosted him a number of times when he was in southern Ontario. This is something he said as a speaker in meetings and in conversation over coffee.

11 Alas, there are no silver medals in municipal politics.

12 Tim Huff, *The Cardboard Shack Beneath the Bridge: Helping Children Understand Homelessness* (Pickering, ON: Castle Quay Books, 2007).

13 Tim Huff, *It's Hard Not to Stare: Helping Children Understand Disabilities* (Pickering, Castle Quay Books, 2013).

14 Cheryl Bear-Barnetson and Tim Huff, *The Honour Drum: Sharing the Beauty of Canada's Indigenous People with Children, Families and Classrooms*, (Lagoon City, ON: Castle Quay Books, 2016).

Jesus lived His life focused on following His Father so that He might properly lead and serve others. In the garden of Gethsemane, wrestling with the sacrifice that lay before Him, Jesus twice *"fell on his face and prayed, saying, 'My Father, if it be possible, let this cup pass from me; nevertheless, not as I will, but as you will'"* (Matthew 26:39; see also Luke 22:42).

Sometimes our engagement in life, evangelism, community service, or public policy is compromised by a lack of depth in our relationship with Jesus. Do you remember the story of Jesus walking on the water to the disciples who were in a boat? Peter got out of the boat and was doing okay while he was focused on Jesus, but he started to sink when distracted by the wind and waves (Matthew 14:22–33).

In 1980, I had the privilege to travel to New Zealand. While there, we went to St. Faith's Anglican Church in Ohinemutu, Rotorua. We experienced a church building that blends indigenous Maori Christian design with a clear glass window facing a lake. On the window is an image of Jesus. With the lake in the background, it looks like Jesus is walking on the water. The day we were there was quite breezy and the waves were cresting beneath Jesus' feet. This image was fixed in my memory when I visited Israel. This was the Jesus I envisioned walking on the Sea of Galilee when I looked offshore at Capernaum. This was the Jesus, and these were the waves, that drew a soon-to-sink Peter out of the relative safety of the boat.

It's easier to walk on water when the stream is five centimetres deep and frozen than when battling the wind and waves of the ocean's depth. Preparation is important. Don't let your faith be shallow, harsh, and cold. Pursue that dangerous ocean-deep faith that equips you to tack and jibe as the wind of the Holy Spirit *"blows where it wishes"* in your life (John 3:8).

Sometimes our engagement in life, evangelism, community service, or public policy is compromised by a lack of depth in our relationship with others. Establishing the necessary depth is attained when we let our interactions be shaped by prayer and God's written Word. This was the experience of the early Christ-followers with each other, something we'll explore more in Chapter Twenty-Four.

Having considered here the importance of the depth of our engagement with Christ in preparation for our engagement with culture, the next chapter will offer a statistical look at some key indicators of the breadth of the Church in Canada.

CHAPTER TWENTY-THREE

LIES, DAMNED LIES, AND STATISTICS

The Lord spoke to Moses in the wilderness of Sinai, in the tent of meeting, on the first day of the second month, in the second year after they had come out of the land of Egypt, saying, "Take a census of all the congregation of the people of Israel, by clans, by fathers' houses, according to the number of names, every male, head by head. From twenty years old and upward, all in Israel who are able to go to war, you and Aaron shall list them, company by company."

—Numbers 1:1–3

I, John, your brother and partner in the tribulation and the kingdom and the patient endurance that are in Jesus, was on the island called Patmos on account of the word of God and the testimony of Jesus. I was in the Spirit on the Lord's day, and I heard behind me a loud voice like a trumpet saying, "Write what you see in a book and send it to the seven churches, to Ephesus and to Smyrna and to Pergamum and to Thyatira and to Sardis and to Philadelphia and to Laodicea."

—Revelation 1:9–11

"THERE ARE THREE KINDS OF LIES: LIES, DAMNED LIES, AND STATISTICS."[1] IN *CHAPTERS from My Autobiography*, Mark Twain (whose real name was Samuel Langhorne Clemens) attributed this expression to Benjamin Disraeli in reference to Twain's own beguilement with figures. I suspect that if Twain was alive today, he would add a fourth kind of lie: Canadian weather forecasts! But I digress.

In today's Canada, quoting Bible verses won't get you far in court, before a parliamentary committee, or standing on the steps of a Canadian legislature with a public address system. The Bible has lost that place of authority in our society.

---

1   Mark Twain, *Chapters from My Autobiography*, Chapter XX. Published in the July 5, 1907 edition of the *North American Review*, No. DCXVIII.

The void has been filled with experiential testimony and statistics. In the land of those focussed on personal rights, personal experience carries much weight. And the experience of many—gathered through the collection and sharing of statistics—can be of greater influence.

I was pleased to see the return of the long-form census in 2016, after it was temporarily replaced by the National Household Survey in 2011. The data from mandatory reporting of the whole population is usually more reliable than the data from voluntary reporting by a portion of the population. All levels of government—school board, municipal, provincial, and federal—rely on this information to make important policy and spending decisions.

The Canadian census provides data on the extremely reliable end of the statistical spectrum, because its sample size (the number of people answering) is the whole population. This makes it more of a snapshot than a sample. At the other end of the spectrum are social media, television, and radio surveys that are substantially less reliable because of selection bias; the results are determined only by people who have a vested interest in the subject matter and there are limited or no controls on participation. If the survey is important enough to someone, they might contact a list of friends or organizations and invite them to skew the results. These are often referred to as junk statistics, because the population represented by the sample is unknown. They have little value.

A good pollster will provide reliable statistical information based on key factors. They will be cautious about the use of controls to validate a representative sample. They will make the effort to compose questions that don't lead toward a desired result and are testable through asking related control questions. It is also valuable to have the same questions asked in polling done periodically over time. Good pollsters regularly assess their polling methods to take into account changing technology.

Statistics, not just those gathered in the census, now inform key influencers and decision-makers in almost every aspect of Canadian life. Academics and parliamentarians alike will base major studies and reports on their analysis of collected data, or the synthesized analysis of that data by others.

Statistics may be used effectively, but statistics are not as neutral as simple numbers and are susceptible to being manipulated in a way that favours the argument being made. It's important to ask good questions about the data collection and the statistical analysis. Who paid for the survey? Who shaped the questions? What are the specific questions? In what order were they asked? How many people were surveyed? How were they surveyed? Where did they live? What was the gender breakdown? Marital status? Religious affiliation? What data was included or left out of the final analysis? What is the margin of error or range of accuracy in the data?

The failure to verify the validity of statistics may result in the repetitive sharing of lies.

In 1948, Alfred Kinsey published *Sexual Behavior in the Human Male.*[2] Kinsey noted that in interviews with over 5,500 American men, ten percent admitted to being homosexual. The now-mythic statistic propelled a movement that was first oriented toward securing human rights, then political clout, followed by marriage equality, and now the effort to require religious conformity. Statistics Canada reported in 2015 that just under 1.7 percent of Canadian adults identify as homosexual (gay or lesbian) and 1.3 percent as bisexual, a number that is up from 1.1 percent homosexual and 0.9 percent bisexual in the 2010 report based on its every-five-years Canadian Community Health Survey. Neither statistic approaches the Kinsey percentage, which was long ago debunked in the U.S. by asking good questions to verify or discredit its validity. The repetition, however, influenced the psyche of the Western world.[3] [4]

The importance of statistics in the formation of public policy cannot be underestimated.

In the opposite public policy vein, the Government of Ontario took legislative action effective January 1, 2012 to amend Ontario's *Freedom of Information and Protection of Privacy Act* to forbid the release of statistics on the number of publicly funded abortions performed in the province, the only medical procedure in the province to receive such hidden-from-public-view status.

What might *reliable* statistics tell us about the Church in Canada, and the current condition of our ability to influence Canadian culture?

Statistics Canada, in a broad general survey of the current situation, tells us the following about changes in Church status early in the twenty-first century:

---

2   Alfred Kinsey et al., *Sexual Behavior in the Human Male* (Bloomington, IN: University Press, 1975). Originally published in 1948.

3   *Statistics Canada*, "Same-Sex Couples and Sexual Orientation... by the Numbers." June 25, 2015 (http://www.statcan.gc.ca/eng/dai/smr08/2015/smr08_203_2015#a3).

4   *Statistics Canada*, "Gay Pride... by the Numbers." July 8, 2011 (http://archive.is/jqUDg).

2001 National Census	2011 National Householder Survey
Christian 75%	Christian 67.3%
Roman Catholic 43%	Roman Catholic 38.7%
Protestant 29%	Protestant 25.9%
Other Christian 2.6%	Other Christian 2.7%
Muslim 2%	Muslim 3.2%
Hindu 1%	Hindu 1.5%
Sikh 1%	Sikh 1.4%
Buddhist 1%	Buddhist 1.1%
Jewish 1.1%	Jewish 1.0%
No Religion (Nones) 16.5%	No Religion (Nones) 23.9%

The term "rise of the Nones" is used to describe the increasing number of people who are religiously unaffiliated. As it has become more societally acceptable not to belong to a church, many Nones have likely replaced the least-committed Christians, those extending one end of the Church spectrum, as well as the commitment spectrum of other religious communities. Some Nones are agnostic, claiming neither faith nor disbelief in God. Some are atheist, claiming disbelief in God. And many simply haven't given consideration to what they do or don't believe. Some statistical reporting is based on data that separates None from agnostic, atheist, and "spiritual."

Like the Nones, Christian denominations and theological traditions are not monolithic in their beliefs or behaviour. They do hold to a shared set of core beliefs in doctrinal statements, such as the Apostles' Creed.

To drill down a little deeper into the stats on Canadian Christianity, we must look at other data and analysis.

The contemporary Protestant Christian expression breaks down into two major components: traditional or mainline denominations (Anglican, Presbyterian, United, etc.) and evangelical (Baptist, Mennonite, Pentecostal, etc.). In addition to Protestant and Catholic are the Orthodox Christian expressions

(Greek, Russian, Syrian, etc.). The reliable data available on Protestantism offers a telling story.

The traditional denominations are identified by name in Statistics Canada's census questions.

David Ewart is a United Church of Canada minister who surveyed his denomination, reviewed internally collected data, and also looked at the census. Ewart's 2009 report *United Church of Canada People Trends as of 2007* notes that "1965 was the peak of Membership in the United Church of Canada. From 1945 to 1965, our membership increased by 42% from 750,000 to 1,064,000."[5] However, this represented a percentage decline from six percent to 5.4 percent of the Canadian population. Ewart continues, "In 2007, our Membership is 1.6% of the Canadian population. If the trend for the past 10 years continues unchanged, then by the years 2010, 2015, 2020, and 2025 our Membership will be: 1.4%, 1.1%, 0.8%, and 0.4% respectively."[6]

Gordon Haynes is a Presbyterian minister whose *The Haynes Report: The Life and Mission Agency Research Project 2011–2012*, published by the *Presbyterian Record* in 2013, demonstrates a similar trend in the Presbyterian Church in Canada beginning in the late 1950s and early 1960s.[7]

Brian Clarke and Stuart Macdonald are professors at Knox College, University of Toronto. They report a similar trend, with membership peaking in the early 1960s, for the third *Comfortable Pew* denomination in their 2010 *Working Paper: Anglican Church of Canada Statistics*.[8] In addition, their *2011 Working Paper: United Church of Canada Statistics* confirms Ewart's work and 2011 *Working Paper: Presbyterian Church in Canada Statistics*[9] confirms Haynes'.

While several evangelical denominations are identified by name in the census questions, evangelical Protestant Christians have also been statistically identified using other means.

---

5   David Ewart, "United Church of Canada People Trends." February 2007 (http://www.davidewart.ca/UCCan-People-Trends-Updated-Feb-2007.pdf).

6   Ibid., 1.

7   Gordon Haynes, *The Presbyterian Record*, "The Haynes Report." June 1, 2013 (http://presbyterianrecord.ca/2013/06/01/the-haynes-report/).

8   Brian Clarke and Stuart Macdonald, *Working Paper: United Church of Canada Statistics*. January 6, 2011 (http://individual.utoronto.ca/clarkemacdonald/clarkemacdonald/Welcome_files/unitedchurch.pdf).

9   Brian Clarke and Stuart Macdonald, *Working Paper: Presbyterian Church of Canada Statistics*. January 6, 2011 (http://individual.utoronto.ca/clarkemacdonald/clarkemacdonald/Welcome_files/presbyterianchurch.pdf).

Reginald Bibby is a Canadian sociologist who described this category as Conservative Protestants in his 1987 book *Fragmented Gods*.[10] Analyzing Statistics Canada's census data, Bibby concluded that about seven percent of the population fit the evangelical category, which he refers to as "Conservative Protestant." Statistics Canada uses religious code values in the census to identify religious affiliation. An update on his data following the 2001 census put the number at eight percent.

George Rawlyk (1935–1995), a Canadian historian, used a different means of analysis referred to as the Christian Evangelical Scale (CES), which was developed by pollster Andrew Grenville. Following Rawlyk's death, Grenville has continued his research in this area as a research innovator and executive with a number of research firms, also working with The Evangelical Fellowship of Canada on regular periodic polling on the subject. The CES suggests that about twelve percent of Canadians are evangelicals. The discrepancy may be accounted for by the CES identifying evangelicals who may be members of mainline and Catholic denominations, where there are identifiable pockets of evangelically aligned individuals.

The CES measures belief and behaviour, roughly based on David Bebbington's "quadrilateral," four characteristics of British evangelicals described in his 1989 book *Evangelicalism in Modern Britain*.[11] The four characteristics are:

- Conversionism, the belief that lives need to be changed;
- Biblicism, a particular regard for the Bible;
- Crucicentrism, a focus on the atoning work of Christ on the cross; and
- Activism, the gospel expressed in service to others.

Distinct from the twelve percent of the Canadian population described as evangelical Protestant Christians, the CES has also captured seven percent of the population who are members of the Roman Catholic Church. In reference to the CES, the combined statistic of nineteen percent has been described as "Evangelically Aligned Christians."[12]

The 2011 National Household Survey indicates that of 2.1 million immigrants to Canada over the preceding decade, the most significant immigration

---

10 Reginald Bibby, *Fragmented Gods: The Poverty and Potential of Religion in Canada* (Toronto, ON: Irwin Publishing, 1987).

11 David Bebbington, *Evangelicalism in Modern Britain* (London, UK: Routledge, 1989).

12 Rick Hiemstra, "Counting Canadian Evangelicals," *Church and Faith Trends*, October 2007, 1.

growth in the Christian Church was in the Roman Catholic (475,000) and Orthodox (110,000) communities. The mainline Protestant denominations experienced a combined total immigration growth of fewer than fifty thousand members during the same timeframe. By comparison, Pentecostals experienced immigration growth of forty-one thousand and Baptists of thirty-five thousand, mostly in Ontario and Western Canada Baptist conferences. Bibby goes into greater depth on immigration growth in his free downloadable 2012 ebook *A New Day: The Resilience and Restructuring of Religion in Canada*.[13]

A survey done by Ipsos Reid for CanWest Global, with results published in the *National Post* on April 16, 2006, provides a snapshot of encouragement for continuing Church engagement. The poll revealed that six in ten Canadians believe in Jesus Christ and four in ten considered themselves converted Christians who had committed their lives to Christ. One in five indicated they attended church at least once a week, and another one in five once or more monthly. Paired with answers to the following questions from a complementary Ipsos Reid poll, Christians generally, and evangelicals in particular, are encouraged to feel comfortable sharing their faith through evangelism and public policy engagement:

- I think evangelical Christians make an important positive contribution to Canadian society: Agree 56%, Disagree 36%.
- I think it is a good thing if persons with strong religious beliefs express their views on political issues: Agree 53%, Disagree 46%.[14]

A 2013 Angus Reid poll conducted in conjunction with The Evangelical Fellowship of Canada indicates the numbers are reversing somewhat with only a third of Canadians seeing evangelical Christian contribution as positive.

The same 2013 survey reveals that increasingly both religious and non-religious Canadians, over eighty percent, are inclined to see religious beliefs as a private matter to be practised in their homes and places of worship.[15]

---

13 Reginald Bibby, *A New Day: The Resilience and Restructuring of Religion in Canada*. September 12, 2012 (http://www.reginaldbibby.com/images/A_NEW_DAY_Sept_12_2012.pdf).

14 Andrew Grenville shared this in his session, "Knowing Your Political Culture & Public Attitudes" at the Navigating the Faith-Political Interface seminar in Toronto, May 11, 2007. It is from an Ipsos Reid complementary poll to the "Religion Alive and Well" poll done for CanWest Global, April 2006.

15 From a presentation by Rick Hiemstra at Laurentian Leadership Centre of Trinity Western University, Ottawa, October 12, 2016.

I think both of these trends are reversible. It will require Christian expression that is seen, and seen as positive. One of the reasons that Christian public expression is being challenged may well be our own inattention to the Bible and its teaching.

Rick Hiemstra's 2014 report *Confidence, Conversation, and Community: Bible Engagement in Canada, 2013*[16] was commissioned by the Canadian Bible Forum (Bible League of Canada, Canadian Bible Society, Every Home for Christ, Gideons Canada, OneBook, Open Doors Canada, Scripture Gift Mission Canada, Scripture Union Canada, and Wycliffe Canada) and The Evangelical Fellowship of Canada. Hiemstra reports that fourteen percent of Canadians read the Bible at least once a week, with the vast majority of Canadian Christians seldom or never picking up the sacred text that is foundational to our faith. Only eighteen percent of Canadians strongly agree that the Bible is the Word of God. Those who do "are ten times more likely to read the Bible frequently (at least a few times a week) and six times as likely to attend religious services weekly as those who just moderately agree."[17] Only one in seven Canadians and one in four Christians regard the Bible as relevant to daily life. Two-thirds of Canadians think the Bible is roughly equivalent to other sacred texts in its teachings.

The attitude of Christians to the Bible is perhaps the most significant obstacle that needs to be overcome in the Canadian Church. Can you imagine a historian who doesn't read history books? Would you go to a doctor who doesn't consider the study of medicine relevant to her life and work? Hiemstra writes that only one in five Christians reflects on the meaning of the Bible to life regularly more than once a week. One in ten Christians (one in seventeen Canadians) have conversation with others about the Bible outside of church services, with six in ten of those who have such conversations reading the Bible at least a few times each week.

Frequency of church attendance and frequency of Bible reading and Bible conversation are interrelated. Evangelicals represent forty-three percent of regular Bible readers, with fifteen percent Catholics and thirteen percent traditional Protestants. Those who attend church weekly are more likely to read the Bible than those who attend monthly, and those who attend monthly are more likely than those who attend only occasionally.

---

16 Rick Hiemstra, *Confidence, Conversation, and Community: Bible Engagement in Canada, 2013* (Toronto, ON: Faith Today Publications, 2014). The report is also available at www.bibleengagementstudy.ca.

17 Ibid., 5.

Rick and I observed a similar trend in our 2009 paper *Canadian Evangelical Voting Trends by Region, 1996–2008.*[18] Frequency of church attendance, which the Bible Engagement Study links with Bible reading, influenced issue awareness based in moral/biblical concerns. Shifting voting trends were based on that awareness. Issue priorities for Christians aligned with frequency of attendance at religious services. Similarly, Hiemstra observed that financial giving and volunteering for both Christian and non-Christian causes were impacted by frequency of church attendance in his 2009 report *Evangelical Giving and Volunteering.*[19] Quite simply, of all Canadians, frequent church attenders are more financially generous and more generous in giving their time for the benefit of others.

In November 2015, I was privileged to travel to China to visit the world's largest Bible printing facility and to have conversations with leaders of the state-registered Protestant and Catholic churches. In 2006 and 2008, I had met in Canada and the U.S. respectively with leaders from China's unregistered church movement. Both sides of the Chinese Church, registered and unregistered, shared something: a key catalyst to their growth has been obtaining, reading, studying, and discussing the printed Word of God in their own language. One result of this growth and study has been that every province of China now has Christian social services serving the neediest of the nation. On a beautiful evening in Nanjing, we enjoyed cake prepared in a Christian bakery staffed by the developmentally disabled.

Obedience to Scripture and service for Christ go hand in hand for the committed Christ-follower. Fulfillment is found in the experiences of loving God and loving one's neighbour. The inspiration to do so is found in the Bible and a caring Christian community. Following Christ is an everyday occurrence in life, regardless of one's occupation, not just a Sunday morning activity.

The Church has been in a state of growth for two millennia. In the course of that time, some parts of the Church have declined, not been renewed, and disappeared; witness the seven churches in John's Revelation. The trend evidenced by the traditional Protestant churches in Canada is neither fatal to the Canadian Church nor irreversible. Hope for reversal is found in the potential for renewal of commitment to Christ and His written Word, the Bible. These churches were considered evangelical in their nature at one time, hence the remnant of evangelically aligned congregations, some of which have departed to join evangelical

---

18 Don Hutchinson and Rick Hiemstra, "Canadian Evangelical Voting Trends by Region, 1996–2008," *Church and Faith Trends*, October 2009, 1.

19 Rick Hiemstra, "Evangelical Giving and Volunteering," *Church and Faith Trends*, October 2009, 1.

groupings such as the Anglican Network in Canada, Congregational Christian Churches in Canada, Associated Gospel Churches, and others. Evangelical Christians and churches are also called to a continued commitment to Christ and His Word as they face the same cultural influences confronting the traditional churches. A similar call extends to the Catholic and Orthodox communities. Christ called the seven churches of Revelation, just as he calls the various churches in Canada, to remain faithful.

The sheer number of Christians in Canada suggests a great opportunity for influence on the culture. The only true such influence, however, will be found in and through allegiance to Christ, following Him in every area of life, not just faithful church attendance. Be in the world, but not of it (John 17:1–26).

CHAPTER TWENTY-FOUR

CASUAL CHRISTIANS IN CONFRONTATION OR COMMITTED ENCOUNTER WITH CULTURE

I do not ask for these only, but also for those who will believe in me through their word, that they may all be one, just as you, Father, are in me, and I in you, that they also may be in us, so that the world may believe that you have sent me.

—John 17:20–21

From now on, therefore, we regard no one according to the flesh. Even though we once regarded Christ according to the flesh, we regard him thus no longer. Therefore, if anyone is in Christ, he is a new creation. The old has passed away; behold, the new has come. All this is from God, who through Christ reconciled us to himself and gave us the ministry of reconciliation; that is, in Christ God was reconciling the world to himself, not counting their trespasses against them, and entrusting to us the message of reconciliation. Therefore, we are ambassadors for Christ, God making his appeal through us. We implore you on behalf of Christ, be reconciled to God. For our sake he made him to be sin who knew no sin, so that in him we might become the righteousness of God.

—2 Corinthians 5:16–21

The brothers immediately sent Paul and Silas away by night to Berea, and when they arrived they went into the Jewish synagogue. Now these Jews were more noble than those in Thessalonica; they received the word with all eagerness, examining the Scriptures daily to see if these things were so. Many of them therefore believed...

—Acts 17:10–12

AFTER SPEAKING AT A CONFERENCE FOR CHRISTIAN LEADERS, I WAS TAKING QUESTIONS about what I had shared. One leader asked where my ideas about public engagement and community ministry, distinct from evangelism, had come from and how he could communicate these ideas within his denomination. It took a few seconds for me to digest the question, and then to realize the narrowness of my own experience. I had made my decision to accept Jesus as Saviour and Lord of my life in The Salvation Army at twenty-one years of age. Hands-on expression of serving the "least of these" (Matthew 25:37–40), demonstrating faith by works (James 2:14–18), and waiting tables (Acts 6:2–3) had been part of my introduction to Christianity. I did not have the experience of growing up or getting my spiritual formation in a church setting that was focused on worshipping Jesus with music, study, prayer, and fellowship but without the culture engagement components. I admitted my disadvantage and did not criticize his experience. It was simply different from mine.

Each of us is as different as the diversity of our experiences. We each have varying degrees of exposure to the numerous expressions of the Church, the Body of Christ, in Canada. We have common and differing traits in our spiritual DNA, as it were.

Before turning to our engagement with culture, let me share a few thoughts on our engagement with other Christians.

On the night He was betrayed, Jesus washed His disciples' feet. For them it was a disquieting experience of loving service. The disciples understood the role of a house servant to wash the dusty feet of guests, but the paradigm shift of having their feet washed by their Master Rabbi, the Son of God, left some speechless. One refused the service, until he understood its purpose. Afterward Jesus challenged them, and us, with a new commandment:

> *A new commandment I give to you, that you love one another: just as I have loved you, you also are to love one another. By this all people will know that you are my disciples, if you have love for one another.*
>
> —John 13:34–35

This was a clear message about Christ-follower loving Christ-follower as a witness to those outside the Church.

Later in the evening, Jesus prayed for our unity, that we *"may all be one, just as you, Father, are in me, and I in you, that they also may be in us, so that the world may believe that you have sent me"* (John 17:21).

Jesus knew our diversity would be just as great as, and greater than, that of the twelve in the upper room with Him. It's not about sameness. Unity is our diversity collected in common purpose. That may involve divergent expressions and pursuits, but with the common purpose of bringing glory to God. May our pursuits be based not purely in personal preference, or theological sameness, but in kingdom purpose. His purpose.

A well-known Latin phrase reads, *In necessariis unitas, in non necessariis libertas, in utrisque caritas* ("In essentials, there should be unity; in non-essentials, liberty; in both cases, charity [love]"). The origins of this phrase have been attributed variously to Augustine, Bishop of Hippo Regius in North Africa, who is recognized as a saint by both Roman Catholics and Anglicans; Rupertus Meldenius, a Lutheran theologian who taught in the German university city of Augsburg; and others. No attribution is required to recognize that this simple statement defines the starting point of effective engagement for Christians with each other. First, let us discontinue the quarrelling about who belongs in the Body of Christ because we may disagree on non-essentials. Beyond the essentials, there needs to be a demonstration of grace. We can, do, and will have conversations about our differences, but let them be civil conversations, grounded in love. Some will judge this a most liberal understanding of theological divisions. Others will deem it a starkly conservative interpretation of the red letters found in some Bibles, the words of Jesus.

The price of admission to the Church was paid on a cross on Mount Calvary. It makes no difference whether one belongs to a church that focuses on being able to state the date and time of one's decision to follow Christ or a church in which members cannot remember a moment in life when they didn't aspire to do so. What matters is that we do desire to follow Him.

From that point of accepting each other, even though there may still be points of disagreement, let's turn to opportunities for engagement with culture. Some engagement will be alongside persons from your part of the Body. Other engagement will be enhanced by joining with those who may or may not be part of your Body expression. I encourage you to think about public engagement both inside your experience box and outside of it.

Let's begin with Jesus' advice to the twelve in His talk on being prepared for persecution and still engaging culture: *"Behold, I am sending you out as sheep in the midst of wolves, so be wise as serpents and innocent as doves"* (Matthew 10:16).

As former Member of Parliament Preston Manning has admonished, that means we should not be "vicious as snakes and stupid as pigeons."[1]

Sometimes our "vicious" approach to evangelism or public policy engagement is the result of what Miroslav Volf refers to as "thin" Christianity. I referred

---

1   Preston Manning, "Lessons from the Life and Teachings of Jesus," *Navigating the Faith-Political Interface* (seminar), Toronto. May 11, 2007.

to it as casual Christianity in Chapter Six. We may be zealous in our faith and engagement, but that engagement may be more emotional or lightly connected to church than from a devoted connection with Jesus. Volf suggests that the answer to this potentially coercive expression of Christianity is a "thick" faith, a committed practice of our religion in an authentic and growing relationship with Jesus and His Church.[2]

When Paul shared the gospel at Berea, the Bereans listened to his message with eagerness and searched the Scriptures to verify that what he was saying was true (Acts 17:10–12). My friend Bill has long spoken of the importance of not just being a Christian, but being a Berean. By that he means that we need to have a developing relationship with Jesus and with the Bible. The Bible is the record from which, in community, we deepen our faith, find guidance, and receive correction when required. It's not about quantity, how long we've been a Christian, but the quality of our relationship with Christ, His Church, and His written Word.

Volf writes:

> The cure against Christian violence is not less of the Christian faith, but, in a carefully qualified sense, *more* of the Christian faith. I don't mean of course that the cure against violence lies in increased religious zeal; blind religious zeal is part of the problem. Instead, it lies in stronger and more intelligent commitment to the Christian faith as faith.
>
> …the more the Christian faith matters to its adherents as faith that maps a way of life, and the more they practice it as an ongoing tradition with strong ties to its origins and history, and with clear cognitive and moral content, the better off we will be.[3]

Are we making the effort to develop our relationship with Jesus, to work out our salvation with fear and trembling? (Philippians 2:12)

Jesus is the One who sends us into the world. Paul reminds us that being sent by Him means we *"are ambassadors for Christ, God making his appeal through us"* (2 Corinthians 5:20). We represent the One who has sent us.

It has been said that we are in a culture war. The role of an ambassador is to negotiate on behalf of Him whom she or he represents. Christ has made us ambassadors of the ministry of reconciliation, reconciling the world—men and women, culture and society—to God.

---

2   Volf, *A Public Faith*, 39–41.

3   Ibid., 40.

Paul highlights for us that we are not engaged in warfare against those who are *"flesh and blood"* (*imago Dei*), but we are in a war *"against the rulers, against the authorities, against the cosmic powers over this present darkness, against the spiritual forces of evil in the heavenly places"* (Ephesians 6:12). This is a spiritual battle for which the ultimate victory has been won through a blood-stained cross, an empty tomb, and a poured-out Holy Spirit.[4] But the effects of the battle continue to reverberate in our world, a world where we serve as ambassadors for the King who has come and is coming again.

Bruce Clemenger of The Evangelical Fellowship of Canada tells the story of how he was sitting on a panel before a committee of the Senate, the upper house of Canada's Parliament, when it struck him that there was a communications gap between the witnesses, all of them Christian leaders, and the senators. He observed that the religious leaders were speaking to the senators as if the senators were backslidden—had at one time been Christians, accepting the principles of Christianity, among those who had loved and were now lost—rather than as if the senators were lost—had no depth of knowledge about or relationship with Jesus and the biblical principles being presented. This was a remarkable observation.

Remember, I assumed for two decades that I was a Christian because I am a Canadian. These Christian leaders were making the same mistake. The understanding that we are ambassadors to the lost should result in change to our communication technique. When put into practice, Clemenger's observation is helpful to the one delivering the message, and respectful of the one receiving it. Are we attentive to know how best to engage in the conversation? Bob Dylan didn't just inform us that the times, they were a-changin'; he also noted that "the answer is blowin' in the wind." What is wind? In the Hebrew, *ruach*; in the Greek, *pneuma*. Wind. Breath. Spirit. Are we listening to the Spirit, He who fills, equips, and sends us? (Luke 12:12, Acts 1:8)

Jesus and the early Christ-followers spoke differently to different audiences.[5][6]

---

4   My pastor, Jason Boucher, has conveyed this thought using the words "a blood-stained cross, an empty tomb, and a poured-out Holy Spirit" on so many occasions that it has become integrated with my own vocabulary.

5   Tony Campolo and Mary Albert Darling, *Connecting Like Jesus: Practices for Healing, Teaching, and Preaching* (San Francisco, CA: Jossey-Bass, 2010), 172–173. generally in regard to cross-cultural communication as Western Christians in Western culture, L. Newbigin, *Foolishness to the Greeks*, Op. cit.

6   Generally in regard to cross-cultural communication as Western Christians in Western culture, see: Lesslie Newbigin, *Foolishness to the Greeks: The Gospel and Western Culture* (Grand Rapids, MI: Eerdmans, 1988).

To a faithful and expectant Jewish people, Jesus delivered a message of hope and words that clarified their expectations. To fishermen, He spoke of becoming fishers of men (Matthew 4:19). To farmers, He spoke of seedtime and the harvest (Mark 4:1–9).

To the religious leaders of Jesus' day, Jesus often delivered a challenge to be faithful to God, God's revelation, and God's people rather than the rules and regulations of a religion that had created hurdles on the path of those seeking to follow God. In fact, the religious leaders were the only people Jesus ever referred to with harsh words: "hypocrites," "blind guides," "whitewashed tombs," and a "brood of vipers" (Matthew 23:13–33). It was also in regard to their decision to permit business in the prayer court of the temple that Jesus gave His lone public demonstration of physically aggressive behaviour, turning over tables of commerce, with none of that force directed toward people (Mark 11:15–19).

To the political masters of Rome, and their courts of law, Jesus and His disciples were consistently respectful. Respect, however, does not require compromise of one's faith to the arena of political or public opinion.

In Athens, Paul spoke to academics and philosophers in a way that appealed to their intellect, quoting from one of their own well-known philosophers and a Greek poet to make his point about Jesus (Acts 17:16–34).

For those of us who fit the category of Gentiles, we find ourselves unexpectedly included as recipients of the gospel, the good news of Jesus Christ (Matthew 10:5). Like the Syrophoenician woman who approached Jesus seeking her daughter's healing from a demon, we are nourished by "the children's crumbs" as they fall from the table (Mark 7:24–30). Both Peter and Paul were initially shocked that God's plan included the Gentiles, we who may receive the Messiah (Christ) and His Holy Spirit into our lives without first converting to Judaism.[7]

All of these messages were delivered from a foundation of love of neighbour, love for and understanding of the audience.

How we speak to others, and how we listen to them, makes a difference. It's important to know the people with whom we are in conversation. If they shared our background, they probably wouldn't need persuading. And if we are to persuade them, we will need to be genuine. The best way to be understood as genuine is to genuinely build a relationship over time, not just be critical disagree-ers, vocal do-it-my-way-ers on public policy, or Bible-thumpers in evangelism. We need

---

7   Peter's shock is expressed in Acts 10. Paul, in Romans 9, shares the theological process he went through to grasp the inclusion of the Gentiles as followers of the Messiah. See also Paul's comments in Galatians 1:15–21, where he recounts a three-year process.

to be authentically engaged with people as real people ourselves. Conversation is about listening and speaking. Even if it's short, perhaps only a one-time opportunity, our attention to both listening and speaking will sow seeds, encourage growth, and perhaps even reap a harvest. If the conversation is extended over time, it will continue from a place of friendship and acceptance of one another, even if there's lack of agreement on the topic of conversation.

When we converse, including in the public policy arena, we will find that not much has changed in two thousand years. People are interested in themselves. Ask good questions about them, even in initially establishing the relationship—"Tell me your story. How did you become interested in doing this?"—and more questions demonstrating interest. People are also interested in stories, studies, and relevant statistics. Stories. Studies. Statistics. Or, in other words, testimony of personal experience, dependable observations of social and behavioural evidence, and reliable and authoritative data.

It's not difficult to think of Jesus telling stories or Matthew, Mark, Luke, and John recording their experiences with Jesus. We may be less likely to reflect on the knowledge He shared that came from observation, such as the preferred location to build a house, the proper use of a lamp, or the best seeding practices to reap a harvest. On the data side, He recounted the number of lepers healed and the number who gave thanks, and requested the disciples who had been sent out in pairs to report back to the group on their experience. This was authoritative information in His day, expressed according to what was required in the setting and for the desired purpose. We need to provide considered authoritative information that does the same in our day and setting. Be strategic. Determine the desired outcomes, who needs to be persuaded, and how best to reach them.

Evangelism has not been a major component of my life. Don't get me wrong, witness has. So has community service. There are few in my circle of contacts, Christian or not, who are unaware of the One I follow. One of the pleasures I have had in life was several years of travelling Canada to speak with Christian leaders. A significant part of the experience was travelling with my friend David Macfarlane.

As we arrive at the point where I would like to give you some words of advice about evangelism, let me instead encourage you to live a life of witness, and refer you to my friend David's book *Ignite Your Life: How to Brighten Your Days by Living for Significance and Legacy* for evangelism insights.[8]

---

8   David Macfarlane, *Ignite Your Life: How to Brighten Your Days by Living for Significance and Legacy*
    St. Catharines, ON: Thisway Communications, 2012).

Macfarlane, a motivational, creative-thinking evangelist, writes as he speaks. *Ignite Your Life* poses the personal and congregational questions we need to ask, presents ideas he and others have used successfully, and offers the kick in the pants some of us require to get started building our legacy for Jesus—whether through evangelism, community service, or both. The book is full of stories, humour, and biblically based thoughts that get our own thinkers thinking.

Here are the opening words:

A boy, who was seldom taken to church, was asked by a Sunday school teacher on one of his infrequent visits: "What is a saint?" Remembering the colourful stained-glass windows of saints he had seen while visiting a historic-cathedral, the boy answered, "A saint is someone that the light shines through."

The other kids laughed… but maybe he had it right! A saint—a person of faith, a genuine follower of Jesus—is someone through whom the light should shine, not just in church on the weekend, but every day![9]

When it comes to stepping into the public square on matters of public policy, much has already been shared in these pages. It's important to accept that there are various opinions on this subject within the Body of Christ, from the Amish who disengage from culture almost completely to Roman Catholics and both traditional and evangelical Protestants who have a history of political engagement. It's also important to remember that the original commission given to those made in *imago Dei* is to be stewards of the Earth and all life. This is hands-on work!

John Redekop summarizes his approach to practical, biblically based citizenship in these words:

Christian citizenship is part of Christian discipleship. It is part of living consistently, responsibly, and obediently in a sinful society. While discipleship must never be fused, or confused, with good citizenship, it certainly should transform it just as much as it transforms all other aspects and dimensions of living. The ethical guidelines in our citizenship activities are exactly the same as for all other arenas of our involvement, including business, education, management, labor unions, the various professions, farming, and any other honourable pursuit undertaken by

---

9   Ibid., 2.

Christians. In politics, as in all other areas of life, Christians practice loving servanthood and, having decided to get involved, do so only to the extent that Christian discipleship permits.[10]

So what might our citizen involvement look like?

1. Be informed. Maintain a general knowledge of current events, including what's going on at the municipal, provincial, and federal levels of government. Track more closely with issues of particular importance to you. Do this by following one or more (emphasis on more if you can do it) trustworthy (be discerning) news sources, including perhaps organizations that engage on issues from a biblical perspective. Be wary of trusting what shows up on social media feeds and alt-media websites. Also, benefit from good resources. Some have been referred to in this book. Others include:
   a. *The Gospel Imperative to Advocacy* from the Canadian Council of Churches,[11] the largest ecumenical Christian body in Canada with twenty-one church denominations as members, including the Canadian Conference of Catholic Bishops and six denominations also affiliated with the EFC.
   b. The Canadian Conference of Catholic Bishops[12] has resources from a variety of its commissions and committees available on its website.
   c. The Evangelical Fellowship of Canada (EFC)[13] has a section on its website that is dedicated to biblical understanding and action on social issues. The EFC has forty-three denominational affiliates.
   d. Citizens for Public Justice[14] produces worship and action guides on a variety of issues.
   e. The Association for Reformed Political Action[15] has resources on a number of issues and has an "easymail" feature to facilitate contacting public officials on matters of interest to you.

---

10 Redekop, *Politics Under God*, 34.

11 The Canadian Council of Churches (www.councilofchurches.ca).

12 The Canadian Conference of Catholic Bishops (www.cccb.ca).

13 The Evangelical Fellowship of Canada (www.theefc.ca).

14 Citizens for Public Justice (www.cpj.ca).

15 The Association for Reformed Political Action (www.arpacanada.ca).

    f. Cardus[16] is a Christian think tank that does research designed to impact the culture. The culture shapes the political environment.

    g. The Christian Reformed Church in Canada's Centre for Public Dialogue has a Biblical Advocacy 101 toolkit that is simple and downloadable. It's also available in Canadian and American advocacy editions.[17]

    h. And there are more. Denominationally based or local organizations that engage their municipal or provincial governments also provide opportunities to get involved. For Christian charities, the Canadian Council of Christian Charities maintains a list of charities that meet its standard of certification for financial accountability.[18]

2. Pray. Being informed will benefit you in praying for government and all other policy participation.

3. Vote. Be informed in your voting. It's not just about voting for your parents' political party or basing your decision on mainstream media or social media likes or dislikes. With ready internet access, it is relatively easy to find summaries of or complete copies of the party platforms at the provincial and federal levels. At the municipal level, you're going to have to check for local information from candidates.

4. Share your views with elected representatives. Email, phone, and in-person encouragement are welcome by almost all public officials, as is reasonable disagreement. But don't be the constant complainer. Build relationships. For Members of Parliament and the Senate, no postage is required if you decide to send them a letter.[19]

5. There were no political parties in Jesus' day. Whether or not you join one is up to you. By doing so, you may be able to influence the policies or candidates of that party. You might even become a candidate!

6. If not a political party, you might find a place to make your contribution by participating with one or more organizations that engage the political process well on your behalf. Your participation in prayer, finances, and/or time will be appreciated.

---

16 Cardus (www.cardus.ca).

17 *Faith Alive*, "Biblical Advocacy 101 Toolkit." Date of access: January 12, 2017 (http://www.faithaliveresources.org/Products/810830/biblical-advocacy-101–toolkit.aspx).

18 The Canadian Council of Christian Charities (www.giveconfidently.ca).

19 Address your letters to them at Parliament of Canada, Ottawa, ON, K1A 0A9.

Whether in politics, evangelism, business, or school, committed Christ-followers have lots of opportunities to engage our culture. Our Christ-like participation will have a positive impact for Him, and may also keep our public spaces open for us to engage a more accepting populace.

> *And let us not grow weary of doing good, for in due season we will reap, if we do not give up. So then, as we have opportunity, let us do good to everyone, and especially to those who are of the household of faith.*
>
> —Galatians 6:9–10

Witnessing to the gospel is essential to being Christian. The World Council of Churches, the Pontifical Council for Interreligious Dialogue (at the Vatican), and the World Evangelical Alliance released *Christian Witness in a Multi-Religious World: Recommendations for Conduct* in 2011. It is reproduced in its entirety in Appendix VI. Almost every Christian expression on the planet is represented within those three bodies. Here, in list form, are the ten principles they agreed on:

1. Act in God's love.
2. Imitate Jesus Christ.
3. Demonstrate Christian virtues.
4. Perform acts of service and justice.
5. Use discernment and wisdom.
6. Reject violence.
7. Endorse freedom of religion and belief.
8. Mutual respect.
9. Renounce false witness.
10. Build relationship.[20]

That really does sum it up.

Jesus' sense of personal fulfillment and contentment came from following His Father, exercising His authority in spiritual things, and exerting His influence in the things of this world through servanthood and leadership. He even let the twelve closest to Him over His three and a half years of public engagement make

---

20 *Christian Witness in a Multi-Religious World: Recommendations for Conduct*, World Council of Churches, Pontifical Council for Interreligious Dialogue, World Evangelical Alliance, June 28, 2011.

their own decisions about who He was for them, and who they were for Him. Then he left it with them for their lifetimes.

Today, He has left it with us, those who seek to experience full redemption and are committed to being increasingly conformed to His present likeness, as one Body with one Head, until we pass it to the next generations or until He returns, whichever comes first.

CHAPTER TWENTY-FIVE

THE CHURCH AS CHARITY

Bring the full tithe into the storehouse, that there may be food in my house. And thereby put me to the test, says the Lord of hosts, if I will not open the windows of heaven for you and pour down for you a blessing until there is no more need.
—Malachi 3:10

Each one must give as he has decided in his heart, not reluctantly or under compulsion, for God loves a cheerful giver.
—2 Corinthians 9:7

What good is it, my brothers, if someone says he has faith but does not have works? Can that faith save him? If a brother or sister is poorly clothed and lacking in daily food, and one of you says to them, "Go in peace, be warmed and filled," without giving them the things needed for the body, what good is that? So also faith by itself, if it does not have works, is dead.

But someone will say, "You have faith and I have works." Show me your faith apart from your works, and I will show you my faith by my works.
—James 2:14–18

EARLY IN MY TIME AS A PASTOR, I HAD RESTLESS NIGHTS BECAUSE OF A CHRISTMAS GIFT. Gloria and I were opening family Christmas cards when inside one of them we found a ticket for a big-prize lottery. In the church denomination we belonged to at the time, gambling was strictly prohibited. My sleep-reducing dilemma was twofold. If we won the big prize, we would be rich. At the same time, it would be public and we would be in serious trouble for gambling! I harboured a desire to win and was sure that my sins would find me out (Numbers 32:23). But, I thought, if we won, we would give at least ten percent to the Church, the Malachi minimum noted above. The odds of winning the lottery would have required extra-earthly intervention, but in my restless mind, to win was to get caught. That frightened me. There's only one person who drives that kind of fear: the one who tempted Jesus in the desert. My resolution came when Gloria's repeated efforts finally sank in and I accepted that we had done nothing wrong. We hadn't bought the ticket. And we hadn't encouraged the purchase of the ticket. Ah, sleep.

Alas, the Church did not benefit from our winnings, which ended up being as imaginary as my fears. The resulting lack of wealth has not interfered with our support for individuals, congregational and para-congregational ministries, and other philanthropic endeavours. We support because we enjoy it![1] For us, the issue of giving at least ten percent of our income to support Christ's work through the local church was settled a long time ago. We tested Him and found Him to be true. We gave that amount cheerfully, and then found that cheerful giving spurred further growth in our generosity.

Why do you support your church financially? Why do you help other para-congregational ministries or individuals? I revisit these questions often.

A favourite charity circulates its lottery prize brochure every year. Every year I wrestle with the thought, *Hey, it's not gambling if it's supporting a good cause.* But as Gloria reminds me, the charity gets about fifty cents on the dollar as compared to one hundred cents if we donate directly.

On a walk through the mall before Christmas, have you ever spent time thinking about whether to stick a bill in The Salvation Army's plastic bubble or whether it's a better idea to mail a cheque so you get the receipt? How about when opening mail early in the new year? Have you experienced a moment of disappointment when the envelope from a charity you support contains a request for special assistance instead of the anticipated tax-deductible donation receipt? Me, too.

There are not many Canadians who remember a time when we couldn't benefit personally from income tax deductions or credits by contributing to a registered charity. There's nothing wrong with reducing taxes or maximizing charitable capacity by getting those receipts in exchange for our cash. But if the receipts become determinative of our generosity, we might have a problem. The ability to provide or receive a charitable donation receipt is a benefit granted by the federal government. However, the giving imperative is biblical.[2]

---

1   I learned to enjoy it. Gloria was ahead of me on that one.

2   Like all government benefits, being a registered charity for purposes of the *Income Tax Act* requires adhering to the regulations established by the Canada Revenue Agency for issuing of receipts, annual reporting, limitations on political activities, etc.

The *Income War Tax Act* was introduced by Canada's federal government in 1917 as a temporary measure to help pay for the expense of Canada's military contribution to the Great War, regrettably later renamed World War I. Religious, charitable, agricultural, and educational institutions were exempt from taxation under the Act.

In 1930, as part of the effort to temporarily encourage charitable compassion during the Great Depression, the Act was amended to include a deduction from taxable income for all donations to any charitable organization up to a limit of ten percent, the biblical tithe. The *Income War Tax Act* was replaced after World War II with the *Income Tax Act* in 1948. The charitable donation deduction remained.

It was not until 1967, Canada's centennial year, that the Minister of National Revenue introduced a central registry for charities issuing receipts to those claiming the deduction. Those charities that registered were required to provide an annual report on their finances and operations. In 1988, the deduction was changed to a tax credit.[3]

A definition of what constitutes a charity does not appear in Canadian income tax legislation. It has been generally accepted that the concepts developed in the 1601 *Statute of Charitable Uses* in England and the decision of the British House of Lords in its 1891 decision in *Pemsel v. the Commissioners for Special Purposes of the Income Tax*,[4] are definition enough. They are summarized as:

a. the relief of poverty,
b. the advancement of religion,
c. the advancement of education, and
d. other purposes beneficial to the community as a whole in a way which the law regards as charitable.

The advancement of religion has historically been presumed to be of public benefit because of the moral, theological, and ethical framework that religion has provided to the Western world, informing and inspiring its underpinnings and traditions. In our historically Christian-influenced culture, the Church was considered to make a vital contribution to the character and participation of citizens and to the community.

---

3   Buckingham, *Fighting Over God*, 179–181.

4   *John Frederick Pemsel v. the Commissioners for Special Purposes of the Income Tax*, House of Lords, July 20, 1891, as reported in *Law Reports, Council of Law Reporting* (London, UK: Wm. Clowes and Sons Ltd., 1891), 531–592.

Carl Juneau, the former Assistant Director of Communications for the Charities Directorate at the Canada Revenue Agency, stated and answered a question on the place of religion in Canadian society in 1999, less than two decades ago:

> Why is *any bona fide* religion charitable?
> ...In essence what makes religion "good" from a societal point of view is that it makes us want to become better—it makes people become better members of society.[5]

Within a decade of that statement, the Canada Revenue Agency was undertaking a review to consider what constitutes "advancing religion" in the twenty-first century. Such assessment can open the door for those who want to press the issue about whether or not "advancement of religion" should be a charitable object. Why should it? The definition of charity is old. It is ripe for reconsideration in a culture that demonstrates less respect toward religion, let alone seeing any public benefit in religion. For many voices, by 2008 when the review was initiated, religion and religious organizations were perceived more as taking than giving. Perhaps those voices were simply the loudest and least informed, but they were heard. The benefit of the charitable donation tax credit keeps money out of the public purse, establishing the government and societal basis to continue asking the question, "What is the societal return on investment that justifies this benefit for religious organizations and individuals?"

The perception of the Church by Canadian society in the twenty-first century is different than it was even at the close of the twentieth. Some regard the Church as a relic while others see the Church as opposed to the progress of an advancing contemporary Canadian culture. Still others wonder where the public presence of the Church in community has gone. These ideas may be more the fault of failure to adequately communicate by the Church than actual Church absence.

The 2007 Canada Survey of Giving, Volunteering and Participating conducted by Statistics Canada revealed that the core group of those who volunteered their time in religious and non-religious organizations were also weekly religious service attendees.

> The frequency of attendance at religious services is linked to all forms of prosocial behaviour measured by the CSGVP, including volunteering.

---

5   Carl Juneau, *Church & The Law Update*, "Is Religion Passé as a Charity?" March 22, 1999 (http://www.carters.ca/pub/update/church/volume02/chchv2n5.pdf), 5–6.

Those who attended religious services on a weekly basis were much more likely to volunteer than those who did not (66% vs. 43%). Similarly, weekly attendees who volunteered tended to volunteer more time (232 hours vs. 142 hours). Weekly attendees accounted for 17% of Canadians but contributed 35% of total volunteer hours in 2007.[6]

In fact, twenty-three percent of Canadians who volunteer 170 hours or more per year are regular religious service attendees.[7] Let's use the apostle Paul's term and call this "cheerful giver factor one." Religious participation motivates volunteerism. Recently retired World Vision Canada CEO Dave Toycen writes, in his book *The Power of Generosity*, that "being generous is about more than money; it involves our time, influence and expertise as well."[8]

Similarly, Statistics Canada notes in regard to charitable financial donations,

> ...weekly attendance at religious services or meetings is a strong indicator of potential membership in the top donor category. Weekly attendees have a higher probability of being top donors (49% of weekly attendees are top donors compared to only 15% those who do not attend weekly). These top donors are highly important contributors. Although they only make up 8% of the population, they contribute 39% of all donations.[9]

The 2004 survey results indicated another relevant breakdown of the data from the same series of questions. Nineteen percent of Canadians who attended religious services weekly provided seventy-four percent of all donations to religious charities and twenty-two percent of all donations to non-religious charities.[10] Let's call this "cheerful giver factor two." Giving to congregational and

---

6   Michael Hall, David Lasby, et al., *Caring Canadians, Involved Canadians: Highlights from the 2007 Canada Survey of Giving, Volunteering and Participating*, Statistics Canada, Catalogue No. 71–542–XPE (Ottawa, ON: Statistics Canada, 2009), 43.

7   Ibid., 41.

8   Dave Toycen, *The Power of Generosity: How to Transform Yourself and Your World* (Toronto, ON: HarperCollins Publishers Ltd, 2004), 120.

9   Hall, et al., *Caring Canadians, Involved Canadians* (2007), 20.

10   Michael Hall, David Lasby, et al., *Caring Canadians, Involved Canadians: Highlights from the Canada Survey of Giving, Volunteering and Participating*, Statistics Canada, Catalogue No. 71–542–XIE (Ottawa, ON: Statistics Canada, 2006), 13. This information was not presented clearly in the 2007 survey, so I elected to use the comparable 2004 numbers on this point.

para-congregational charities flows over into giving to non-religious charities. But the figure many will latch onto is that in 2007 forty-six percent of all charitable giving in Canada went to religious charities.[11] Their question will be simple. What does Canada get for it?

We need to do a better job of telling our story. These two factors are important. The Church is still shaping people's character. Also important are the stories and statistics about Church participation in meeting community needs. Congregational participation in the Out of the Cold program nationwide, offering meals and accommodations to those in need of a place to stay warm during winter months, and para-congregational hostels and shelters are critical to the care of Canada's most vulnerable. The network of food banks from shore to shore to shore in Canada are either operated or heavily supported by the Church. Emergency and disaster relief, both domestic and international, would be crippled without the participation of the Canadian Church. There are other significant social service expressions from soup kitchens, soup trucks, clothing and furniture depots (often giving them away for free), and providing homes for those with disabilities and hospices for people near death.

As contradictory as it seems to the notion of humble service, if the media and general population don't see our community contribution, it doesn't exist. Perception becomes reality, and the likelihood of losing one's tax-deductible (or tax credit) status is enhanced.

If the advancement of religion were to no longer be recognized as a charitable object, the question would become, what is the risk of the Church's dependence on registered charity donation receipts? Some smaller denominations and independent churches in Canada have opted to be ready for what they see as an eventuality by not registering as a charity, and teaching tithing and cheerful giving as simply the financially unrewarded (at least by the government) lifestyle of a Christ-follower.

This leads to "cheerful giver factor three": giving without getting anything in return, not even a tax receipt.

There was no donation receipt for the widow who put two small copper coins in the offering box at the temple. Jesus observed her gift with these words:

> *Truly, I say to you, this poor widow has put in more than all those who are contributing to the offering box. For they all contributed out of their abundance, but she out of her poverty has put in everything she had, all she had to live on.*
>
> —Mark 12:43–44

---

11 Hall, et al., *Caring Canadians, Involved Canadians* (2007), 15.

This was sacrificial giving. The widow gave without reservation or reward.

On September 7, 2016, I heard a remarkable story. A small group of us were assembled to hear Bishop Hannington Bahemuka of the Charismatic Episcopal Church of Uganda. His story has been verified. In 2001, rebels who opposed the Ugandan government raided his village, located in the Bundibugyo district. The people were forced out and ended up in a refugee camp.

In the camp, there were children who had been orphaned by the unfolding events. As winter arrived, Bishop Hannington challenged the people of his community to give their extra blankets to the children who were without; as it got colder, he challenged them to take the children into already crowded tents. As time moved on, he set up schools for the children.

When they were able to return home, the people found that their war-torn village had been destroyed. Someone suggested making contact with a Western aid agency. Hannington spoke to his people about the need to be cheerful givers, noting that they had established the village and that they had from their own resources all that was necessary to rebuild, as provided them by God. Like Nehemiah and the wall of Jerusalem, the people started rebuilding, working together to build houses and community facilities.

When it came time to rebuild the church, a woman with crippling disabilities offered her only chicken. The chicken's eggs were both her source of food and income. Hannington declined the offer. Valerio challenged him not to rob her of the joy of being a cheerful giver or of making a contribution to the reconstruction of her church. Humbled, Hannington accepted the chicken. The cheerful-giver-oriented people of the village met Valerio's needs, having agreed among themselves that no one would go hungry or unhoused in the village of cheerful givers.

Here are the four points Bishop Hannington shared with us as the principles for cheerful giving:

1. Everything belongs to God.
2. God puts everything into the hands of man.
3. God has put resources in every place.
4. God calls on us to meet the needs of one another.

Wow! Simple and true. Do we live like it? We can, with or without the donation receipts. The receipts themselves are neutral. It's the role they play in our giving about which we need be mindful.

Toycen notes that "there is a difference between a rightful place in our lives and one that dominates and becomes obsessive. Money can be part of the problem or part of the solution."[12]

In a blog entitled "Money and the Spiritual Life," Richard J. Foster states:

> Martin Luther astutely observed, "There are three conversions necessary: the conversion of the heart, mind, and the purse." Perhaps today we find the conversion of the purse the hardest of the three![13]

We are confronted, again, with the intent of our hearts and the focus of our worship. Jesus said that we can only serve one Master. We cannot serve both God and money (Matthew 6:24). How we steward the financial resources God gives us is part of the "spiritual return on investment"[14] Jesus expects from those who follow Him (Matthew 25:14–30).

With the right perspective, such as promoted by Bishop Hannington and the God/neighbour-focused (Matthew 22:37–39) part of our Christ-follower experience, we find ourselves among those who when they

> see there is a need and they can make a difference, they will respond. Generosity [cheerful giver factors one, two, and three] is not lost; compassion is not discarded, because most of us realize that if you go back far enough, all of us benefited from someone who helped us in a way that was not required. Generosity pays dividends.[15]

Sometimes the dividend will include a charitable donation receipt, and sometimes it will not.

---

12 Toycen, *Power of Generosity*, 120.

13 Richard J. Foster, *Renovaré*, "Money and the Spiritual Life." February 16, 2007 (https://renovare.org/blog/money-and-the-spiritual-life).

14 I first heard the term "spiritual return on investment" (SROI) from Mark Petersen, President and CEO of Stronger Philanthropy, an organization that facilitates relationships between financial grant-makers and grant-seekers.

15 Toycen, *Power of Generosity*, 124.

CONCLUSION

National anthem (official bilingual version):
O Canada!
Our home and native land!
True patriot love in all thy sons command.
Car ton bras sait porter l'épée,
Il sait porter la croix!
Ton histoire est une épopée
Des plus brillants exploits.
God keep our land glorious and free!
O Canada, we stand on guard for thee.
O Canada, we stand on guard for thee.[16]

---

16 *Citizenship and Immigration Canada*, "O Canada." Date of access: January 10, 2017 (http://www.cic.gc.ca/english/celebrate/pdf/National_Anthem_e.pdf). Translation of the French lines: "Your arm knows how to wield the sword / And how to carry the cross! / Your history is an epic / Of brilliant accomplishments."

FEAR IS A (STRONG BUT) POOR MOTIVATOR

The Lord is my light and my salvation; whom shall I fear? The Lord is the stronghold of my life; of whom shall I be afraid? When evildoers assail me to eat up my flesh, my adversaries and foes, it is they who stumble and fall. Though an army encamp against me, my heart shall not fear; though war arise against me, yet I will be confident.

—Psalm 27:1–3

The Spirit of the Lord God is upon me, because the Lord has anointed me to bring good news to the poor; he has sent me to bind up the brokenhearted, to proclaim liberty to the captives, and the opening of the prison to those who are bound; to proclaim the year of the Lord's favor, and the day of vengeance of our God; to comfort all who mourn; to grant to those who mourn in Zion—to give them a beautiful headdress instead of ashes, the oil of gladness instead of mourning, the garment of praise instead of a faint spirit; that they may be called oaks of righteousness, the planting of the Lord, that he may be glorified. They shall build up the ancient ruins; they shall raise up the former devastations; they shall repair the ruined cities, the devastations of many generations.

—Isaiah 61:1–4

...for God gave us a spirit not of fear but of power and love and self-control.

—2 Timothy 1:7

As December 31, 2016 was rolling over to January 1, 2017, and official sesquicentennial celebrations began, overt hymns to God, prayers, and heaven-directed hallelujahs (Hebrew for "praise the Lord") may have been heard in the relatively few, by comparison to 1967, watchnight services seeing in the New Year at scattered church gatherings and private homes across the country.

Perhaps it was the snow, -10°C temperature (about 14°F), or widely advertised security measures—including barricades, expanded police presence, bag search, and patdown—but on Parliament Hill some counted the crowd in hundreds and others said a few thousand were gathered for an evening that started at 7:00 p.m. with a twenty-minute concert by Dominion Carilloneur Andrea McCrady on the Peace Tower carillon. Another carillon piece would play at midnight to welcome 2017. Was this reminiscent of church bells calling Canadians to worship and heralding a new year? Featured at 7:00 were Canadian composers celebrating Canada and freedom. The Centennial Hymn—better known as Bobby Gimby's "Ca–na–da" song—was familiar for those of us who remember Expo '67. Oscar Peterson's "Hymn to Freedom" preceded Leonard Cohen's "Hallelujah," both set in the context of breaking free from a heritage of spiritual faithfulness to seek hope in broken humanity. Another ode to freedom followed, K'naan's "Wavin' Flag."[1]

The Centennial Flame was extinguished and, following a smudging and blessing by Algonquin elder Albert Dumont (also known as South Wind), officially relit by Dumont, Governor General David and Mrs. Sharon Johnston, and Minister of Canadian Heritage Mélanie Joly. Joly was representing Prime Minister Justin Trudeau, who was in the Bahamas on vacation and appeared only by pre-recorded video, pointedly noting the accomplishments of his government. Originally intended to burn for the whole of 1967, the Centennial Flame, first lit by Prime Minister Lester Pearson, has remained a gathering place on Parliament Hill and a reminder of the continuing celebration of Confederation at the Flame's fiftieth anniversary.

A few minutes later, the Canada 150 celebration continued at precisely 8:17 p.m. (20:17 on the 24-hour clock, chosen to foreshadow the Canada 150 new year) with an early evening fireworks display set to music selected to "revisit different historical eras of our country over the past 150 years."[2] The memories evoked by familiar popular hits by Canadian artists—among them "Diana" by Paul Anka, "Taking Care of Business" by Bachman Turner Overdrive, "Sunglass-

---

1   *Parliament of Canada*, "The House of Commons Heritage Collection," Carillon, Daily Program. December 31, 2016 (http://www.parl.gc.ca/About/House/Collections/carillon/programme-e.htm?date=2016–12–31).

2   *Government of Canada*, "Unveiling the Lineup and Program for the Canada 150 Kick-Off Celebrations on Parliament Hill." November 28, 2016 (http://news.gc.ca/web/article-en.do?nid=1161249&tp=1&_ga=1.224945690.1443025109.1460946137).

es at Night" by Corey Hart, "Ahead by a Century" by the Tragically Hip, and "Pour que tu m'aimes encore" ("For you to love me again") by Céline Dion—has given those songs almost hymn-like status in the echoes of our minds, despite their lack of reverence for, or reflection upon, the Divine.

Headliners for the final hours of 2016 included Carly Rae Jepsen, Brett Kissel, and Radio Radio. For the benediction on 2016, the CBC's national coverage and mainstage screens cut to Toronto for a live broadcast of "Fire in My Soul" by Walk Off The Earth, a song expressing a sentiment not at all like John Wesley's experience of having his heart strangely warmed in a moment of deepening relationship with God (although the title is an interesting spin on Jeremiah 20:9).[3] As midnight approached, comedian Rick Mercer led the traditional countdown from ten. The crowd cheered, the second round of fireworks ignited, and the carillon played "Joyful Changes," a composition written by Milford Myhre who intended it to sound like the peal of church bells. Another mnemonic cue for a memory echo from our past? What of "Auld Lang Syne"? Is there an Old Acquaintance being "forgot, and never brought to mind"?

There were few references to God on the night. Those that were made were almost unnoticeable. Queen Elizabeth II's pre-recorded message to Canadians was perhaps the most direct. She said, in part,

> On this eve of national celebrations, my family and I are with you in spirit. We pray that God will bless Canada and that, over the next 150 years, Canadians will continue to build a better country and a better world.[4]

In his blessing, Albert Dumont invited the Good Spirit to bless the people of the country. Brett Kissel had the crowd dancing with his rendition of John Denver's "Thank God I'm a Country Boy." The other, following the relighting of the Centennial Flame, was the singing of "O Canada" by mezzo-soprano Julie Nesrallah, in which she and all singing called upon God to "keep our land glorious and free!"

From Parliament Hill to church pew, how well do Canadians know God whom we call upon to "keep our land glorious and free"? How well do we want to know God?

---

3   "If I say, 'I will not mention him, or speak any more in his name,' there is in my heart as it were a burning fire shut up in my bones, and I am weary with holding it in, and I cannot" (Jeremiah 20:9).

4   The Governor General of Canada, "Her Majesty the Queen's 2017 New Year's Message." December 31, 2016 (https://www.gg.ca/document.aspx?id=16669&lan=eng).

CONCLUSION

The start of 2017's sesquicentennial year was as distant from 1967's centennial celebrations as the state-of-the-art, kitchen-wall-mounted rotary-dial telephone in the home of my childhood is from the built-to-become-obsolete, pocket-size smartphone that accompanies me almost everywhere I go today. Media and social media reports focused on fun and fireworks, neither of which is bad and both of which are fleeting (#Canada150).

What will it look like when we welcome Canada's bicentennial fifty years from now? What will each of our roles have been in getting the nation, our neighbours—both Indigenous and non-indigenous peoples—and our families there? And if we envision beyond that date to the seven generations of Indigenous contemplation mentioned in Chapter Nineteen, what might we foresee for Church and nation beyond our lifetimes?

My mum turned ninety on October 31, 2016—a Hallowe'en baby. On October 30, the eve of All Hallowed Eve (Hallowe'en is preparation for the celebration of All Saints Day on November 1), we had five generations in one room for a great surprise party. The next morning, her birthday, I asked Mum what she had thought the world would look like before her oldest child, my sister, was born. Her thoughts then were very different from her ponderings about future generations a few years later when deciding to make the move from Barbados to Canada. Decades later, her perspective on a distant tomorrow is different again. Have you thought generations forward? Seven? Not as a predictor of the future, but as a gauge of our present-day responsibility?

I've heard that there are more "fear nots" in the Bible than there are days in the year. It's not something I've researched myself, but it did make me wonder: why so many fear nots? I've thought of a few reasons why God would inspire such a frequent reminder. They start with being sheep among wolves. Personal evangelism? Sheep to wolves (and the occasional sheep in hiding). Community service? Sheep caring for needy wolves (and other sheep). Speaking out on public policy? Sheep revealing themselves to wolves. Sometimes the exchanges with other sheep even make me wonder if perhaps I'm dealing with wolves in sheep's clothing! (Matthew 10:16)

It's a scary world out there. Knowing that, who wouldn't think, *It's easier to just close the door and worship God in private, in my stained-glass closet, where nobody will bother me.*

However, fear is a poor motivator. Decisions made based on fear tend to lack the wisdom and effectiveness of decisions founded in faith. When I think of the Russian hockey team from 1972, mentioned in Chapter One, their shared fear of

248

losing just one more game of the remaining three fed into a siege mentality that resulted in losing all three.

Christian faith is personal, intimately personal. And Christianity was always intended to be public, engaging, and sincere in its expression—not just private. Being a Christ-follower is a both/and experience, not an either/or one. We need to have the private devotion to follow and the public expression to convict us if we are ever on trial for being Christian.

Andrew Bennett, Canada's former Ambassador for the Office of Religious Freedom, has said:

> As faithful people living in 2016 in Canada and in this beautiful world of ours, we can feel so buffeted and unsteady when confronted by the deep changes in our society that run profoundly counter to the truth that we profess. Often our instinct is to shrink back or to feel that little can be done.
>
> This is not the posture of the faithful, regardless of which religious tradition we follow.
>
> We must recall and reaffirm the centrality of our faith in our lives and in the lives of the majority of Canadians both past and present who built this country and continue to labour in building communities founded upon truth, charity and justice...
>
> "Be not afraid!"
>
> Let us reject the post-Enlightenment myth that religious belief and practice is a purely private matter best kept out of the public realm. This is historically inaccurate. It is theologically wrong. And, above all, it robs from our fellow citizens the ability to actively participate in what can be tens of thousands of conversations, encounters, friendships and transformative actions that will strengthen and continue to build our country.[5]

The historic presence in Canada of Christian hospitals, homes for unwed mothers, orphanages, schools, soup kitchens, hostels, job centres, and universities have helped shape the social fabric and culture of the nation. Many of these social service endeavours have been absorbed by ever-expanding governments. But their existence should neither be relegated to history nor their absorption by

---

5   Andrew P. Bennett, "Acts of Faith in Canada," *Convivium Magazine*, June–July 2016, 42.

government constrain us from finding new expressions of biblically based community involvement, service that shares Jesus with a world in need of His presence.

When we consider the current situation in Canada, do we think it determinative of the future or just a marker in time? Think back to Chapter One. When absorbed in a hockey game, do we consider our favourite team to be losing at the end of the second period or just behind? Time only moves in one direction. Are we ready to get off the bench, out of the stained-glass closet, and into the game?

James asks, *"What good is it . . . if someone says he has faith but does not have works?"* (James 2:14) Let me paraphrase that: "What good is it if someone says they've got game but they don't get into the game?" Picture, if you will, Paul Henderson stepping onto the ice alone, without his teammates, in Moscow. Do you think he would have had three game-winning goals in the last three games of the series? What if Henderson hadn't responded to the prompting to call Peter Mahovlich off the ice? What if the Canadian team had decided they were the best hockey players in the world but they weren't up to the task of playing to win in the 1972 Summit Series—either because they were afraid of losing, unprepared, or unwilling—so they weren't going to bother playing at all? What if Henderson or the other players had refused to play cooperatively with those from other National Hockey League teams? With the reputation of the nation on the line (really, it was that serious to them and to us back home), the collection of Canadian ice hockey ambassadors embarked on a quest to work together to represent the nation well. And they did.

We know the rules of the game. Positioned with Christ, we have resources beyond our imagination. We have them for a reason: to conquer the fears we might imagine.

The Jesus factor in our personal relationship with Him and in our relationship with others who are part of His Body confirms the "we are better than me" environment in which we can overcome fears of our own inadequacy, temptations to seek our own relevance, popularity, or power, or just about anything else we might set up as a roadblock to living our Christianity outside of our private world.[6]

The resources at our disposal are easy to miss. They might surprise us in addressing what seem to me or you to be the most insurmountable obstacles. David Mainse recounts the following story, from *100 Huntley Street's* "Salute to Canada" tour, about the Centennial Flame on Parliament Hill. This took place while

---

6   The content of this paragraph was expressed by Kari Yli-Renko of LeaderImpact in a talk he gave on May 14, 2016 at a Souly Business men's conference. It fits nicely with Nouwen's advice in *In the Name of Jesus*.

setting up for filming in Ottawa. Remember, Prime Minister Pierre Trudeau and former Prime Minister Joe Clark were invited guests for the show.

> About fifteen minutes to air, a strange thing happened: the Eternal Flame [Centennial Flame] went out. Normally, it hovered over the centre of a circular fountain, but now there was just gas bubbling up through spilling water. I had never heard of it going out before, but it was certainly out now. Yet even as we were wondering what to do, Willis Eade, the driver who had raised his hand to receive the Holy Spirit in Sudbury, found a match somewhere, leaned way over, and re-lit it.[7]

One person's big stuff is another person's small stuff. Why? Because God is at work! And He's at work through the Body of Christ. No heroes. It's not about individuals. David Mainse would be the first to tell you that it takes more than a vision and a leader to make one television show, a regular program, or an entire network work.

We've heard it said, "Don't sweat the small stuff." Everything is small stuff to God! It's just a different way of saying "Fear not!"

Another way God communicated the fear not message was in His words to Joshua. Joshua was the successor to Moses. Moses had led millions out of Egypt and then for an additional four decades before arriving at the border of the Promised Land. But Joshua was to be the one to lead the nation into the land that had been promised by God. Here's how God framed it:

> *After the death of Moses the servant of the Lord, the Lord said to Joshua the son of Nun, Moses' assistant, "Moses my servant is dead. Now therefore arise, go over this Jordan, you and all this people, into the land that I am giving to them, to the people of Israel.*
>
> —Joshua 1:1–2

No pressure, eh? Next, we read about God calming Joshua down (at least that's how it reads to me) with a few reminders:

> *No man shall be able to stand before you all the days of your life. Just as I was with Moses, so I will be with you. I will not leave you or forsake you. Be strong*

---

7   David Mainse, *God Keep Our Land: A Salute to Canada* (Toronto, ON: Mainroads Productions Inc., 1981), 166.

and courageous, for you shall cause this people to inherit the land that I swore to their fathers to give them. Only be strong and very courageous… Have I not commanded you? Be strong and courageous. Do not be frightened, and do not be dismayed, for the Lord your God is with you wherever you go.

—Joshua 1:5–7, 9

"Be strong and courageous." Without fear, there is no need for courage. "I will be with you." That's the reason for courage. It sounds familiar:

And behold, I [Jesus] am with you always, to the end of the age.

—Matthew 28:20

It's scary out there, but He is with us. That's reason for courage. Without fear, there is no need for courage. Fear should not be our motivator, no matter how strong it is. The mission of Jesus is our motivation.

When Gloria and I first moved to Ottawa, high on our list of priorities was finding a home congregation for corporate worship. When we arrived at one with the motto "Growing People with Jesus and Others," that seemed worth exploring further. Nearly a decade later, we're still growing with Jesus and others in the same congregation. I mention this just in case the information encountered in *Under Siege* has left you thinking that you need to work on yourself some more before you open the door of your stained-glass closet and get in the game. Professional hockey players started as amateurs, most of them ankle-skaters as I was. Even those in the NHL continue to learn new skills, practising both alone and with teammates. It all happens in the context of being in the game. When it comes to the Church, some of us end up as professionals and some as enthusiasts. But we're all supposed to be in the game. We're all growing. In the Body of Christ, we get to grow with Jesus and others. We're not alone. He is with us. So are *they*. Or, should I say, so are *we*. The Body of Christ is us. He's the Head.

It's time for us—together—to get off the bench, through the gate, and in the game, even while we're growing in our capacity to be in the game. Canada needs us!

Christ has no body now but yours. No hands, no feet on earth but yours. Yours are the eyes through which he looks compassion on this world. Yours are the feet with which he walks to do good. Yours are the hands through which he blesses all the world. Yours are the hands, yours are the feet, yours are the eyes, you are his body. Christ has no body now on earth but yours.

—St. Teresa of Avila (1515–1582)

Bonhoeffer's two questions may help focus our minds on our own role before and after we have opened the gate. Who is Jesus Christ, for us, today? Who are we, for Jesus Christ, today? Our answers to these and other of life's questions are influenced daily by our personal, professional, social, and social media networks. The answers influence how we engage life.

As we step through the gate and into the game, the public sphere, Paul exhorts:

Only let your manner of life be worthy of the gospel of Christ, so that whether I come and see you or am absent, I may hear of you that you are standing firm in one spirit, with one mind striving side by side for the faith of the gospel, and not frightened in anything by your opponents. This is a clear sign to them of their destruction, but of your salvation, and that from God. For it has been granted to you that for the sake of Christ you should not only believe in him but also suffer for his sake, engaged in the same conflict that you saw I had and now hear that I still have.

—Philippians 1:27–30

The debate about what freedom of religion is in Canada will likely continue in public and in the courts for as long as there is a Canada and there are courts. The opportunity we are given to live our religion today mustn't be allowed to pass us by while that's taking place.

In November 2016, the British Columbia Court of Appeal issued its decision in *Trinity Western University v. The Law Society of British Columbia.*[8] The law society decided to appeal yet again, to the Supreme Court of Canada, but the penultimate paragraph of the B.C. court's 5–0 decision in favour of the university is an encouragement for all Christ-followers in our Canada, which is still guaranteed by the *Charter* to be a free and democratic society.

193. A society that does not admit of and accommodate differences cannot be a free and democratic society—one in which its citizens are free to think, to disagree, to debate and to challenge the accepted view without fear of reprisal. This case demonstrates that a well-intentioned

---

8 2016 BCCA 423.

majority acting in the name of tolerance and liberalism, can, if unchecked, impose its views on the minority in a manner that is in itself intolerant and illiberal.[9]

The public space outside our homes and church buildings beckons us to share our faith in Him. So does Jesus. As we engage, let's be wise as serpents and innocent as doves, ambassadors for Christ.

---

9   Ibid., Paragraph 193.

THE NICENE CREED

325 A.D., Council of Nicaea
Amended 381 A.D., Council of Constantinople

We believe in one God, the Father, the Almighty, maker of heaven and earth, of all that is seen and unseen. We believe in one Lord, Jesus Christ, the only Son of God, eternally begotten of the Father, God from God, light from light, true God from true God, begotten, not made, one in Being with the Father. For us and for our salvation he came down from heaven, by the power of the Holy Spirit he was born of the Virgin Mary and became truly human. For our sake he was crucified under Pontius Pilate; he suffered, died and was buried. On the third day he rose again in fulfillment of the Scriptures; he ascended into heaven and is seated at the right hand of the Father. He will come again in glory to judge the living and the dead, and his kingdom will have no end. We believe in the Holy Spirit, the Lord, the giver of life, who proceeds from the Father [and the Son]. Who with the Father and the Son is worshiped and glorified. Who has spoken through the prophets. We believe in one holy catholic and apostolic Church. We acknowledge one baptism for the forgiveness of sins. We look for the resurrection of the dead, and the life of the world to come. Amen.

THE APOSTLES' CREED

390 A.D., recorded in a letter from Ambrose, Bishop of Milan, to Pope Siricius, Bishop of Rome, following the Council in Milan

I believe in God, the Father, the Almighty,
Creator of heaven and earth,
I believe in Jesus Christ, His only Son, our Lord,
Who was conceived by the Holy Ghost, born of the Virgin Mary,
He suffered under Pontius Pilate, was crucified, died, and was buried,
He descended into hell; the third day He rose again from the dead,
He ascended into heaven, is seated at the right hand of God the Father
Almighty; thence He shall come to judge the living and the dead.
I believe in the Holy Spirit, the holy catholic Church, the communion
of saints, forgiveness of sins, the resurrection of the body and the life
everlasting.
Amen.

CANADIAN CHARTER OF RIGHTS AND FREEDOMS

Constitution Act, 1982

PART I
CANADIAN CHARTER OF RIGHTS AND FREEDOMS

Whereas Canada is founded upon principles that recognize the supremacy of God and the rule of law:

Guarantee of Rights and Freedoms

1. The *Canadian Charter of Rights and Freedoms* guarantees the rights and freedoms set out in it subject only to such reasonable limits prescribed by law as can be demonstrably justified in a free and democratic society.

Fundamental Freedoms

2. Everyone has the following fundamental freedoms:
(*a*) freedom of conscience and religion;
(*b*) freedom of thought, belief, opinion and expression, including freedom of the press and other media of communication;
(*c*) freedom of peaceful assembly; and
(*d*) freedom of association.

Democratic Rights

3. Every citizen of Canada has the right to vote in an election of members of the House of Commons or of a legislative assembly and to be qualified for membership therein.

4. (1) No House of Commons and no legislative assembly shall continue for longer than five years from the date fixed for the return of the writs at a general election of its members.

(2) In time of real or apprehended war, invasion or insurrection, a House of Commons may be continued by Parliament and a legislative assembly may be continued by the legislature beyond five years if such continuation is not opposed by the votes of more than one-third of the members of the House of Commons or the legislative assembly, as the case may be.

5. There shall be a sitting of Parliament and of each legislature at least once every twelve months.

Mobility Rights

6. (1) Every citizen of Canada has the right to enter, remain in and leave Canada.

(2) Every citizen of Canada and every person who has the status of a permanent resident of Canada has the right

(*a*) to move to and take up residence in any province; and

(*b*) to pursue the gaining of a livelihood in any province.

(3) The rights specified in subsection (2) are subject to

(*a*) any laws or practices of general application in force in a province other than those that discriminate among persons primarily on the basis of province of present or previous residence; and

(*b*) any laws providing for reasonable residency requirements as a qualification for the receipt of publicly provided social services.

(4) Subsections (2) and (3) do not preclude any law, program or activity that has as its object the amelioration in a province of conditions of individuals in that province who are socially or economically disadvantaged if the rate of employment in that province is below the rate of employment in Canada.

Legal Rights

7. Everyone has the right to life, liberty and security of the person and the right not to be deprived thereof except in accordance with the principles of fundamental justice.

8. Everyone has the right to be secure against unreasonable search or seizure.

9. Everyone has the right not to be arbitrarily detained or imprisoned.

10. Everyone has the right on arrest or detention

(*a*) to be informed promptly of the reasons therefor;

(*b*) to retain and instruct counsel without delay and to be informed of that right; and

(*c*) to have the validity of the detention determined by way of habeas corpus and to be released if the detention is not lawful.

11. Any person charged with an offence has the right

(*a*) to be informed without unreasonable delay of the specific offence;

(*b*) to be tried within a reasonable time;

(*c*) not to be compelled to be a witness in proceedings against that person in respect of the offence;

(*d*) to be presumed innocent until proven guilty according to law in a fair and public hearing by an independent and impartial tribunal;

(*e*) not to be denied reasonable bail without just cause;

(*f*) except in the case of an offence under military law tried before a military tribunal, to the benefit of trial by jury where the maximum punishment for the offence is imprisonment for five years or a more severe punishment;

(*g*) not to be found guilty on account of any act or omission unless, at the time of the act or omission, it constituted an offence under Canadian or international law or was criminal according to the general principles of law recognized by the community of nations;

(*h*) if finally acquitted of the offence, not to be tried for it again and, if finally found guilty and punished for the offence, not to be tried or punished for it again; and

(*i*) if found guilty of the offence and if the punishment for the offence has been varied between the time of commission and the time of sentencing, to the benefit of the lesser punishment.

12. Everyone has the right not to be subjected to any cruel and unusual treatment or punishment.

13. A witness who testifies in any proceedings has the right not to have any incriminating evidence so given used to incriminate that witness in any other proceedings, except in a prosecution for perjury or for the giving of contradictory evidence.

14. A party or witness in any proceedings who does not understand or speak the language in which the proceedings are conducted or who is deaf has the right to the assistance of an interpreter.

Equality Rights

15. (1) Every individual is equal before and under the law and has the right to the equal protection and equal benefit of the law without discrimination and, in particular, without discrimination based on race, national or ethnic origin, colour, religion, sex, age or mental or physical disability.

(2) Subsection (1) does not preclude any law, program or activity that has as its object the amelioration of conditions of disadvantaged individuals or groups including those that are disadvantaged because of race, national or ethnic origin, colour, religion, sex, age or mental or physical disability.

Official Languages of Canada

16. (1) English and French are the official languages of Canada and have equality of status and equal rights and privileges as to their use in all institutions of the Parliament and government of Canada.

(2) English and French are the official languages of New Brunswick and have equality of status and equal rights and privileges

as to their use in all institutions of the legislature and government of New Brunswick.

(3) Nothing in this Charter limits the authority of Parliament or a legislature to advance the equality of status or use of English and French.

16.1 (1) The English linguistic community and the French linguistic community in New Brunswick have equality of status and equal rights and privileges, including the right to distinct educational institutions and such distinct cultural institutions as are necessary for the preservation and promotion of those communities.

(2) The role of the legislature and government of New Brunswick to preserve and promote the status, rights and privileges referred to in subsection (1) is affirmed.

17. (1) Everyone has the right to use English or French in any debates and other proceedings of Parliament.

(2) Everyone has the right to use English or French in any debates and other proceedings of the legislature of New Brunswick.

18. (1) The statutes, records and journals of Parliament shall be printed and published in English and French and both language versions are equally authoritative.

(2) The statutes, records and journals of the legislature of New Brunswick shall be printed and published in English and French and both language versions are equally authoritative.

19. (1) Either English or French may be used by any person in, or in any pleading in or process issuing from, any court established by Parliament.

(2) Either English or French may be used by any person in, or in any pleading in or process issuing from, any court of New Brunswick.

20. (1) Any member of the public in Canada has the right to communicate with, and to receive available services from, any head or central office of an institution of the Parliament or government of Canada in English or French, and has the same right with respect to any other office of any such institution where

(*a*) there is a significant demand for communications with and services from that office in such language; or

(b) due to the nature of the office, it is reasonable that communications with and services from that office be available in both English and French.

(2) Any member of the public in New Brunswick has the right to communicate with, and to receive available services from, any office of an institution of the legislature or government of New Brunswick in English or French.

21. Nothing in sections 16 to 20 abrogates or derogates from any right, privilege or obligation with respect to the English and French languages, or either of them, that exists or is continued by virtue of any other provision of the Constitution of Canada.

22. Nothing in sections 16 to 20 abrogates or derogates from any legal or customary right or privilege acquired or enjoyed either before or after the coming into force of this Charter with respect to any language that is not English or French.

Minority Language Educational Rights

23. (1) Citizens of Canada
(a) whose first language learned and still understood is that of the English or French linguistic minority population of the province in which they reside, or
(b) who have received their primary school instruction in Canada in English or French and reside in a province where the language in which they received that instruction is the language of the English or French linguistic minority population of the province, have the right to have their children receive primary and secondary school instruction in that language in that province.

(2) Citizens of Canada of whom any child has received or is receiving primary or secondary school instruction in English or French in Canada, have the right to have all their children receive primary and secondary school instruction in the same language.

(3) The right of citizens of Canada under subsections (1) and (2) to have their children receive primary and secondary school instruction in the language of the English or French linguistic minority population of a province

(*a*) applies wherever in the province the number of children of citizens who have such a right is sufficient to warrant the provision to them out of public funds of minority language instruction; and

(*b*) includes, where the number of those children so warrants, the right to have them receive that instruction in minority language educational facilities provided out of public funds.

Enforcement

24. (1) Anyone whose rights or freedoms, as guaranteed by this Charter, have been infringed or denied may apply to a court of competent jurisdiction to obtain such remedy as the court considers appropriate and just in the circumstances.

(2) Where, in proceedings under subsection (1), a court concludes that evidence was obtained in a manner that infringed or denied any rights or freedoms guaranteed by this Charter, the evidence shall be excluded if it is established that, having regard to all the circumstances, the admission of it in the proceedings would bring the administration of justice into disrepute.

General

25. The guarantee in this Charter of certain rights and freedoms shall not be construed so as to abrogate or derogate from any aboriginal, treaty or other rights or freedoms that pertain to the aboriginal peoples of Canada including

(*a*) any rights or freedoms that have been recognized by the Royal Proclamation of October 7, 1763; and

(*b*) any rights or freedoms that now exist by way of land claims agreements or may be so acquired.

26. The guarantee in this Charter of certain rights and freedoms shall not be construed as denying the existence of any other rights or freedoms that exist in Canada.

27. This Charter shall be interpreted in a manner consistent with the preservation and enhancement of the multicultural heritage of Canadians.

28. Notwithstanding anything in this Charter, the rights and freedoms referred to in it are guaranteed equally to male and female persons.

29. Nothing in this Charter abrogates or derogates from any rights or privileges guaranteed by or under the Constitution of Canada in respect of denominational, separate or dissentient schools.

30. A reference in this Charter to a province or to the legislative assembly or legislature of a province shall be deemed to include a reference to the Yukon Territory and the Northwest Territories, or to the appropriate legislative authority thereof, as the case may be.

31. Nothing in this Charter extends the legislative powers of any body or authority.

Application of Charter

32. (1) This Charter applies

(*a*) to the Parliament and government of Canada in respect of all matters within the authority of Parliament including all matters relating to the Yukon Territory and Northwest Territories; and

(*b*) to the legislature and government of each province in respect of all matters within the authority of the legislature of each province.

(2) Notwithstanding subsection (1), section 15 shall not have effect until three years after this section comes into force.

33. (1) Parliament or the legislature of a province may expressly declare in an Act of Parliament or of the legislature, as the case may be, that the Act or a provision thereof shall operate notwithstanding a provision included in section 2 or sections 7 to 15 of this Charter.

(2) An Act or a provision of an Act in respect of which a declaration made under this section is in effect shall have such operation as it would have but for the provision of this Charter referred to in the declaration.

(3) A declaration made under subsection (1) shall cease to have effect five years after it comes into force or on such earlier date as may be specified in the declaration.

(4) Parliament or the legislature of a province may re-enact a declaration made under subsection (1).

(5) Subsection (3) applies in respect of a re-enactment made under subsection (4).

Citation

34. This Part may be cited as the *Canadian Charter of Rights and Freedoms*.

PIERRE TRUDEAU, 100 HUNTLEY STREET "SALUTE TO CANADA"

The full text of comments by Prime Minister Pierre Elliott Trudeau on *100 Huntley Street*, "Salute to Canada" (June 20, 1981)[1]

It's good for Canadians to celebrate the grandeur of our country's history and spiritual heritage. It's good to pause, occasionally, and give thanks for the privilege of living here together in this free and bountiful land. I therefore congratulate the Rev. David Mainse and the organizers of this Salute to Canada for inviting all of us to think about the debt we owe to the faith of our fathers, and to the spiritual heritage which finds expression in countless ways in our daily lives.

The golden thread of faith is woven throughout the history of Canada from its earliest beginnings up to the present time. Our native peoples lived a rich spiritual life long before the first white man set foot on our soil. Faith was more important than commerce in the minds of many of the European explorers and settlers, and over the centuries, as successive waves of people came to this country, many in search of religious liberty, they brought with them a great wealth and variety of religious traditions and values. Those values have shaped our laws and our lives, and have added enormous strength to the foundation of freedom and justice upon which this country was built.

It was in acknowledgement of that debt that the Canadian Government proposed that our new Constitution should begin with the words: "We, the people of Canada, proudly proclaim that we are and shall always be, with the help of God, a free and self-governing people."

---

1   Transcript accessed from the Public Service Christian Fellowship Newsletter, September 1981, 1–3.

It was in acknowledgement of that debt that the Parliament of Canada later gave its approval, during the Constitutional Debate, to the statement that Canada is founded upon principles that recognize the supremacy of God and the rule of law. Faith played a large part in the lives of so many men and women who have created in this land a society which places a high value on commitment, integrity, generosity and, above all, freedom. To pass on that heritage, strong and intact, is a challenge worthy of all of us who are privileged to call ourselves Canadians.

JOE CLARK, 100 HUNTLEY STREET "SALUTE TO CANADA"

The full text of comments by Leader of the Opposition Joe Clark on *100 Huntley Street*, "Salute to Canada" (June 20, 1981)[1]

I'm pleased to join in Salute to Canada from our nation's capital, and want to thank David Mainse and his Huntley Street team for bringing us together to think of our extraordinary country. Without any question, we are among the most fortunate nations of the earth, in our freedom, our physical wealth, our respect for the human individual. But there is more than that. In many ways, our Canada is a demonstration of the strength of faith, because, particularly in the early days, the people who reached out to build our country, had very little support except their faith. Their lives were lonely, but they found sustenance and support in their individual religious beliefs, in the sense that their lives were part of a whole, that their struggle would be remembered.

That support of faith is as important today, in modern times, as it ever was, and even more so because the forces of cynicism and doubt are so much more strong today. That's why it is so valuable for us to have occasions like this to remember together the immense good fortune that God has given Canadians, and to reflect on the way that our spiritual heritage has helped define and guide the nature and development of our nation. Not only did people of faith build and keep our Canada, but some of our most important laws reflect that spirit. Our Bill of Rights, written by the late John Diefenbaker, held that the Canadian nation is founded upon principles that acknowledge the supremacy of

---

1 Transcript accessed from the Public Service Christian Fellowship Newsletter, September 1981, 1–3.

God, the dignity and worth of the human person, and position of the family in a society of free men and free institutions. Now, we all have personal responsibilities to meet each day in ways that honour our own standards and our own beliefs. I want to take advantage of this opportunity to ask your prayers and your support for all of us who are active in public life in Canada. I ask that we never forget the faith and the vision of the people who originally brought this country together, the Fathers of Confederation, who from the depths of their own profound faith took as their guide a verse from the Psalms of David, the verse that has since become the motto for our nation:

He shall have dominion also from sea to sea, and from the river to the ends of the earth.

We pray today that God's sovereignty over Canada continues to guide us.

CHRISTIAN WITNESS IN A MULTI-RELIGIOUS WORLD

Christian Witness in a Multi-Religious World: Recommendations for Conduct as issued by World Council of Churches, Pontifical Council for Interreligious Dialogue and World Evangelical Alliance (2011)[1]

Preamble

Mission belongs to the very being of the church. Proclaiming the word of God and witnessing to the world is essential for every Christian. At the same time, it is necessary to do so according to gospel principles, with full respect and love for all human beings.

Aware of the tensions between people and communities of different religious convictions and the varied interpretations of Christian witness, the Pontifical Council for Interreligious Dialogue (PCID), the World Council of Churches (WCC) and, at the invitation of the WCC, the World Evangelical Alliance (WEA), met during a period of 5 years to reflect and produce this document to serve as a set of recommendations for conduct on Christian witness around the world. This document does not intend to be a theological statement on mission but to address practical issues associated with Christian witness in a multi-religious world.

The purpose of this document is to encourage churches, church councils and mission agencies to reflect on their current practices and to use the recommendations in this document to prepare, where appropriate, their own guidelines for their witness and mission among those of different religions and among those who do not profess any particular religion. It is hoped that Christians across the

---

1 *Christian Witness in a Multi-Religious World: Recommendations for Conduct*, World Council of Churches, Pontifical Council for Interreligious Dialogue, World Evangelical Alliance, June 28, 2011.

world will study this document in the light of their own practices in witnessing to their faith in Christ, both by word and deed.

A Basis for Christian Witness

1. For Christians it is a privilege and joy to give an accounting for the hope that is within them and to do so with gentleness and respect (cf. 1 Peter 3:15).

2. Jesus Christ is the supreme witness (cf. John 18:37). Christian witness is always a sharing in his witness, which takes the form of proclamation of the kingdom, service to neighbour and the total gift of self even if that act of giving leads to the cross. Just as the Father sent the Son in the power of the Holy Spirit, so believers are sent in mission to witness in word and action to the love of the triune God.

3. The example and teaching of Jesus Christ and of the early church must be the guides for Christian mission. For two millennia Christians have sought to follow Christ's way by sharing the good news of God's kingdom (cf. Luke 4:16–20).

4. Christian witness in a pluralistic world includes engaging in dialogue with people of different religions and cultures (cf. Acts 17:22–28).

5. In some contexts, living and proclaiming the gospel is difficult, hindered or even prohibited, yet Christians are commissioned by Christ to continue faithfully in solidarity with one another in their witness to him (cf. Matthew 28:19–20; Mark 16:14–18; Luke 24:44–48; John 20:21; Acts 1:8).

6. If Christians engage in inappropriate methods of exercising mission by resorting to deception and coercive means, they betray the gospel and may cause suffering to others. Such departures call for repentance and remind us of our need for God's continuing grace (cf. Romans 3:23).

7. Christians affirm that while it is their responsibility to witness to Christ, conversion is ultimately the work of the Holy Spirit (cf. John 16:7–9; Acts 10:44–47). They recognize that the Spirit blows where the Spirit wills in ways over which no human being has control (cf. John 3:8).

Principles

Christians are called to adhere to the following principles as they seek to fulfil Christ's commission in an appropriate manner, particularly within interreligious contexts.

1. *Acting in God's love.* Christians believe that God is the source of all love and, accordingly, in their witness they are called to live lives of love and to love their neighbour as themselves (cf. Matthew 22:34–40; John 14:15).

2. *Imitating Jesus Christ.* In all aspects of life, and especially in their witness, Christians are called to follow the example and teachings of Jesus Christ, sharing his love, giving glory and honour to God the Father in the power of the Holy Spirit (cf. John 20:21–23).

3. *Christian virtues.* Christians are called to conduct themselves with integrity, charity, compassion and humility, and to overcome all arrogance, condescension and disparagement (cf. Galatians 5:22).

4. *Acts of service and justice.* Christians are called to act justly and to love tenderly (cf. Micah 6:8). They are further called to serve others and in so doing to recognize Christ in the least of their sisters and brothers (cf. Matthew 25:45). Acts of service, such as providing education, health care, relief services and acts of justice and advocacy are an integral part of witnessing to the gospel. The exploitation of situations of poverty and need has no place in Christian outreach. Christians should denounce and refrain from offering all forms of allurements, including financial incentives and rewards, in their acts of service.

5. *Discernment in ministries of healing.* As an integral part of their witness to the gospel, Christians exercise ministries of healing. They are called to exercise discernment as they carry out these ministries, fully respecting human dignity and ensuring that the vulnerability of people and their need for healing are not exploited.

6. *Rejection of violence.* Christians are called to reject all forms of violence, even psychological or social, including the abuse of power in their witness. They also reject violence, unjust discrimination or repression by any religious or secular authority, including the violation or destruction of places of worship, sacred symbols or texts.

7. *Freedom of religion and belief.* Religious freedom including the right to publicly profess, practice, propagate and change one's religion flows from the very dignity of the human person which is grounded in the creation of all human beings in the image and likeness of God (cf. Genesis 1:26). Thus, all human beings have equal rights and responsibilities. Where any religion is instrumentalized for political ends, or where religious persecution occurs, Christians are called to engage in a prophetic witness denouncing such actions.

8. *Mutual respect and solidarity.* Christians are called to commit themselves to work with all people in mutual respect, promoting together justice, peace and the common good. Interreligious cooperation is an essential dimension of such commitment.

9. *Respect for all people.* Christians recognize that the gospel both challenges and enriches cultures. Even when the gospel challenges certain aspects of cultures, Christians are called to respect all people. Christians are also called to discern elements in their own cultures that are challenged by the gospel.

10. *Renouncing false witness.* Christians are to speak sincerely and respectfully; they are to listen in order to learn about and understand others' beliefs and practices, and are encouraged to acknowledge and appreciate what is true and good in them. Any comment or critical approach should be made in a spirit of mutual respect, making sure not to bear false witness concerning other religions.

11. *Ensuring personal discernment.* Christians are to acknowledge that changing one's religion is a decisive step that must be accompanied by sufficient time for adequate reflection and preparation, through a process ensuring full personal freedom.

12. *Building interreligious relationships.* Christians should continue to build relationships of respect and trust with people of different religions so as to facilitate deeper mutual understanding, reconciliation and cooperation for the common good.

Recommendations

The Third Consultation organized by the World Council of Churches and the PCID of the Holy See in collaboration with World Evangelical Alliance with participation from the largest Christian families of faith (Catholic, Orthodox,

Protestant, Evangelical and Pentecostal), having acted in a spirit of ecumenical cooperation to prepare this document for consideration by churches, national and regional confessional bodies and mission organizations, and especially those working in interreligious contexts, recommends that these bodies:

1. *study* the issues set out in this document and where appropriate formulate guidelines for conduct regarding Christian witness applicable to their particular contexts. Where possible this should be done ecumenically, and in consultation with representatives of other religions.

2. *build* relationships of respect and trust with people of all religions, in particular at institutional levels between churches and other religious communities, engaging in on-going interreligious dialogue as part of their Christian commitment. In certain contexts, where years of tension and conflict have created deep suspicions and breaches of trust between and among communities, interreligious dialogue can provide new opportunities for resolving conflicts, restoring justice, healing of memories, reconciliation and peace-building.

3. *encourage* Christians to strengthen their own religious identity and faith while deepening their knowledge and understanding of different religions, and to do so also taking into account the perspectives of the adherents of those religions. Christians should avoid misrepresenting the beliefs and practices of people of different religions.

4. *cooperate* with other religious communities engaging in interreligious advocacy towards justice and the common good and, wherever possible, standing together in solidarity with people who are in situations of conflict.

5. *call* on their governments to ensure that freedom of religion is properly and comprehensively respected, recognizing that in many countries religious institutions and persons are inhibited from exercising their mission.

6. *pray* for their neighbours and their well-being, recognizing that prayer is integral to who we are and what we do, as well as to Christ's mission.

Appendix: Background to the Document

1. In today's world there is increasing collaboration among Christians and between Christians and followers of different religions. The Pontifical Council for Interreligious Dialogue (PCID) of the Holy See and the World Council of Churches' Programme on Interreligious Dialogue and Co-operation (WCC-IRDC) have a history of such collaboration. Examples of themes on which the PCID/WCC-IRDC have collaborated in the past are: Interreligious Marriage (1994–1997), Interreligious Prayer (1997–1998) and African Religiosity (2000–2004). This document is a result of their work together.

2. There are increasing interreligious tensions in the world today, including violence and the loss of human life. Politics, economics and other factors play a role in these tensions. Christians too are sometimes involved in these conflicts, whether voluntarily or involuntarily, either as those who are persecuted or as those participating in violence. In response to this the PCID and WCC-IRDC decided to address the issues involved in a joint process towards producing shared recommendations for conduct on Christian witness. The WCC-IRDC invited the World Evangelical Alliance (WEA) to participate in this process, and they have gladly done so.

3. Initially two consultations were held: the first, in Lariano, Italy, in May 2006, was entitled "Assessing the Reality" where representatives of different religions shared their views and experiences on the question of conversion. A statement from the consultation reads in part: "We affirm that, while everyone has a right to invite others to an understanding of their faith, it should not be exercised by violating others' rights and religious sensibilities. Freedom of religion enjoins upon all of us the equally non-negotiable responsibility to respect faiths other than our own, and never to denigrate, vilify or misrepresent them for the purpose of affirming superiority of our faith."

4. The second, an inter-Christian consultation, was held in Toulouse, France, in August 2007, to reflect on these same issues. Questions on Family and Community, Respect for Others, Economy, Marketing and Competition, and Violence and Politics were thoroughly discussed. The pastoral and missionary issues around these topics became the background for theological reflection and for the

principles developed in this document. Each issue is important in its own right and deserves more attention that can be given in these recommendations.

5. The participants of the third (inter-Christian) consultation met in Bangkok, Thailand, from 25–28, January, 2011 and finalized this document.

ABOUT THE AUTHOR

Don Hutchinson, B.A., J.D., studied history and politics at Queen's University and law at the University of British Columbia. A lifelong learner and a student of the Bible since his conversion to Christianity at age twenty-one, Don studied theology with The Salvation Army and at Canada Christian College and School of Graduate Theological Studies.

Recognized by Christian leaders as a strategic thinker and planner, Don is a regular speaker and consultant on religious freedom, strategies for church engagement with culture, and preparing for communication in sensitive circumstances.

Following fifteen years in leadership with The Salvation Army, including eight as founding legal advisor for its Canadian legal department, Don consulted with World Vision Canada and others. He then joined The Evangelical Fellowship of Canada's leadership team, serving for seven and a half years in the roles of Vice-President, General Legal Counsel, and Director of the EFC's Centre for Faith and Public Life. He then filled the position of interim National Director/ CEO with the Canadian Bible Society while CBS was searching for a new CEO.

A member of the Law Society of Upper Canada since 1990, Don has appeared before the Supreme Court of Canada on several occasions as well as a number of parliamentary committees. In addition to being featured in print, as well as on television, radio, and online media, this avid motorcyclist has served on the boards of local and national charities.

Although a recipient of the Queen Elizabeth II Diamond Jubilee medal for contributions in promoting religious freedom and public policy development, as greater reward Don has been married with Gloria for over three decades. They are blessed with a daughter and a grandson.

Don currently serves as principal of *ansero*, a Christian ministry focused on facilitating partnerships for Christians engaged on issues of religious freedom in Canada and those working on behalf of the global persecuted Church.

Find more at:
www.donhutchinson.ca